Grandma's Letters from Africa

Grandma's Letters from Africa

Linda K. Thomas

iUniverse, Inc.
New York Bloomington

Copyright © 2010 by Linda K. Thomas

All rights reserved. No part of this book may be used or reproduced by any means, graphic, electronic, or mechanical, including photocopying, recording, taping or by any information storage retrieval system without the written permission of the publisher except in the case of brief quotations embodied in critical articles and reviews.

Unless otherwise noted, Scripture taken from the HOLY BIBLE, NEW INTERNATIONAL VERSION®. Copyright © 1973, 1978, 1984 by International Bible Society. Used by permission of Zondervan Publishing House. All rights reserved.

The "NIV" and "New International Version" trademarks are registered in the United States Patent and Trademark Office by International Bible Society. Use of either trademark requires the permission of International Bible Society.

Where noted, Scripture taken from the New King James Version. Copyright © 1979, 1980, 1982 by Thomas Nelson, Inc. Used by permission. All rights reserved.

iUniverse books may be ordered through booksellers or by contacting:

iUniverse
1663 Liberty Drive
Bloomington, IN 47403
www.iuniverse.com
1-800-Authors (1-800-288-4677)

Because of the dynamic nature of the Internet, any Web addresses or links contained in this book may have changed since publication and may no longer be valid. The views expressed in this work are solely those of the author and do not necessarily reflect the views of the publisher, and the publisher hereby disclaims any responsibility for them.

ISBN: 978-1-4401-9147-3 (sc)
ISBN: 978-1-4401-9145-9 (dj)
ISBN: 978-1-4401-9146-6 (ebook)

Printed in the United States of America

iUniverse rev. date: 1/28/10

Grandma's Letters from Africa is an engaging, memorable account of Linda's years in Africa. It was a privilege for me to read over the shoulders of her granddaughters as Linda tells her story through a series of letters. Through both laughter and tears, she learns to balance her roles as missionary, wife, mother, and grandmother. In the process, Linda falls in love with Africa, its people, and her work. Readers will be moved by this compelling story that reveals God's heart and extraordinary grace.

—Bob Creson, President/CEO, Wycliffe USA

No matter what age you are, *Grandma's Letters from Africa* transports you to that intriguing continent and gives you a glimpse of everyday life there. Make sure you have a box of tissues nearby because sometimes you'll cry and other times you'll laugh until tears roll down your cheeks. One caveat: Don't start reading this book late in the evening unless you want to stay up all night. It's a "can't-put-down" book.

—Aretta Loving, Author, *Together We Can! A Mosaic of Stories and Devotions Displaying the Impact of God's Word* and *Slices of Life, Stories and Devotions from a Bible Translator*

Grandparents and soon-to-be-grandparents, read this book and give a copy to all your grandchildren old enough to read. In it, you will discover how to leave a life-impacting legacy for the children of your children. You will laugh and cry your way through Linda's four incredible years in Africa … away from her children and grandchildren, but connecting with them in powerful ways as she skillfully weaves a tapestry of how her life made a difference.

—Don Parrott, President, Finishers Project, www.finishers.org

Linda tells it like it is—she and her husband actually lived and experienced what she writes about. TIS recruits teachers for the mission field, including those over fifty, and *Grandma's Letters from Africa* is a must-read for those potential teachers—even though many will never have the plethora of experiences Linda did.

—Thom Votaw, Ed.D., President, Teachers In Service, Inc.

"Great stories, great humor and real spiritual depth!"

—Susan Van Wynen, Director for Communication, Wycliffe International

For Maggie, Emma, Chase, Finn, Kade, and Claire

Always remember, and never forget, what you've seen God do for you, and be sure to tell your children and grandchildren!

—Deuteronomy 4:9 (paraphrased)

Table of Contents

PREFACE
xix

ACKNOWLEDGMENTS
xxiii

1
Quaint I Ain't
1

2
Streams in The Desert
13

3
The Perils of The Pearl
34

4
New Jobs, New Colleagues, New Places, New … Just About Everything!
49

5
Jambo, Mama! Buy Here! Goooood Price!
70

6
Margaret Laura Kathleen Thomas
85

7
Eet Eez A Loooong Sweem.
89

8
B'donk-b'donk Hips, The Apple Lady, Falling Sparrows, and Jitters in Jeddah
101

9
Empty Stomachs and God-shaped Holes in Hearts
108

10
Moving House
112

11
Family Matters
117

12
Merry Christmas and Happy New Year
125

13
Termites, Fresh Monkey, Gazelle, Zebra, Eland, Spiders, and Moving House—Again
129

14
Literacy
142

15
Monkey Business, Presidential Pageantry, and A Trip to The Emergency Room
145

16
Emma Elisabeth Anne Thomas
151

17
West Nairobi School
154

18
Job's Perspective
158

19
Hospitality
165

20
Zaire, and More Lessons on Hospitality
174

21
The Verge of The Unknown
181

22
Hurling Through The Valley of The Shadow of Death
188

23
Houseguests
193

24
Silly Foreigners!
197

25
More Accounts from The Heart of Africa
202

26
Am I A Real Missionary?
205

27
The Stuff of History Books, Recipe Books, Video Cameras, and Photo Albums
209

28
Of Elephants and Grass
214

29
Lord, Hear Our Prayers!
228

30
Of Porridge and Cornmeal
236

31
Utterly Amazed
241

EPILOGUE
243

POSTSCRIPT
246

About the Author
251

NOTES
253

RESOURCES
259

LIST OF ILLUSTRATIONS

Map of Africa

Map of Kenya

PREFACE

All I ever wanted was to live a quiet, secure life in a little white house with a picket fence and a rose garden, but my husband Dave—a free spirit who seldom limits himself to coloring within other people's lines—and our adventuresome God had other plans. Just when our youngest finished college, both Dave and God hollered, "Africa!"

Stunned, I asked myself, *How can we leave our kids and parents and live on the other side of the planet?* For months, I waited for God to convince me that He really wanted us to move to Africa. I gave Him every opportunity to either show us green lights and send us to Africa or red lights and keep us home—and He gave us only green. So I sighed, and turned, and took a radical, outrageous, blind leap of faith—!

A year after we moved to Africa with Wycliffe Bible Translators, our daughter-in-law Jill gave birth to our first grandchild and I discovered I was not the traditional, quaint little grandmother I always envisioned. No, I had stumbled into adventures most grandmas couldn't imagine—a hippo charged me, a baboon pooped in my breakfast, a Maasai elder spit at me, and I drank tea from a pot cleaned with cow's urine.

I decided to write down those stories, and more, in letters to my granddaughter, Maggie. I knew she was too young to understand them then, but I also knew that someday she, and my future grandchildren, would grow up and enjoy my tales. Recently the right time arrived. I gathered my old letters and compiled them for the grandchildren—six of them now—and for this memoir about my first four years in Africa.

Grandma's Letters from Africa is not merely an account of adventure. And, unlike many missionary stories, this is not a record of saving lost heathens. This is my story about balancing God's call with responsibilities toward my husband, children, grandchildren, and aging parents. It's my record of everyday life in a behind-the-scenes, yet important, role. It recounts hilarious incidents and frightful ones, joys and heartaches, answered prayers and those God seemed to leave unanswered. *Grandma's Letters from Africa* is my story about falling in love with Africa, its people, and the work—both official and unofficial—God gave me. Above all, it's a chronicle of God's heart, His delightful creativity, and His amazing power to help those in need.

A special note to mid-lifers, empty-nesters, and baby boomers:

A number of years ago my husband said, "At church they teach us to tithe—give 10 percent—of our money, so why not encourage people to also tithe their professional lives?" In other words, after people have worked, say, thirty years in their careers, how about working three years in a ministry? Great idea!

And, in fact, a number of mid-lifers, empty-nesters, and baby boomers—instead of retiring to a life of leisure—are transitioning into ministries, even overseas missions. Most people in this age group have good health, energy, and a wealth of experience and wisdom to share. Many organizations recognize this and actively recruit such people.

Maybe you, too, are ready to try something new, ready to make a difference that really counts, so I invite you to read over my granddaughter Maggie's shoulder and learn how a mid-life woman—I—moved to Africa and even lived to tell about it! And while you read, keep in mind that maybe you could do something like this, too.

First, though, consider this: change is inevitable. In the years since Dave and I returned home from Africa, Wycliffe Bible Translators has changed, as have other mission agencies. If you were to work with Wycliffe today, you would work with a different Wycliffe than we did. Field training (orientation) courses, such as Kenya Safari, have changed. Financial policies have changed, the U.S. headquarters has moved to Orlando, and furlough schedules are more flexible than they used to be.

Nairobi has changed, too. Kenya has changed. All of Africa has changed. If you were to travel today to Nairobi, you would find the city, suburbs, and life there different from the Nairobi I knew. People now shop in supermarkets with wide aisles, bright lights, and enormous selections. Cell phones and video conferencing have dramatically changed communication with loved ones back home. I hear that the police don't allow loiterers around City Market any more—that must make shopping there very different nowadays!—and that the city razed the blue stalls nearby. Friends tell me that even the potholes have changed for the better!

I'm sure, however, that some things in Africa have not changed: the flowers, animals, and birds; the vast open spaces, jungles, and deserts; and especially the African people—their laughter and their music, their spirit, soul, and faith.

Perhaps a second career in missions is just what you've been looking for—maybe for a few months, maybe for a few years. Working on the mission field is doable as long as people are willing, flexible, and strong in their faith. So while you read over Maggie's shoulder, I hope you'll say to yourself, "If that gal could do it, so can I! Where do I sign up?"

In many parts the world, not just Africa, the needs are enormous. The rewards are, too.

ACKNOWLEDGMENTS

The Maasai have a saying, *Meata nkerai lopeny* (a child is not owned by one person). In a similar way, a book manuscript is not owned by one author, so I send a huge *asante sana* to Esther, Aretta, Susan, David, Don, Karen, and Dave. And to Larry, *merci beaucoup*.

As another African proverb says, together, we're really stiff cooked cornmeal!

AFRICA

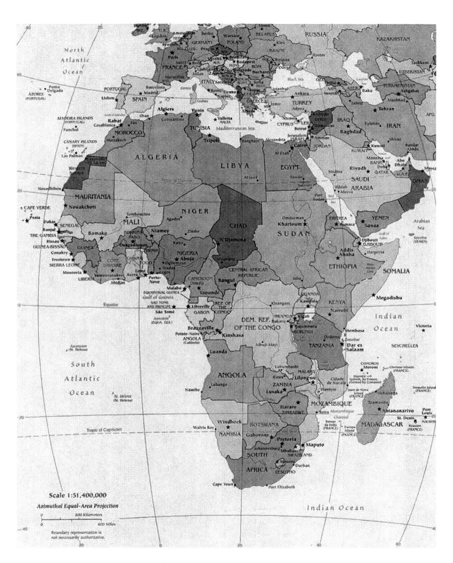

University of Texas Libraries

1

Quaint I Ain't

September 29, 1994
Nairobi, Kenya

Dear Maggie,
    I awoke at four this morning, unable to sleep any longer. *Ah,* I thought, surprised, *I'm still not over jet lag.* I had arrived back in Nairobi twenty-eight hours earlier and thought I should've recovered from jet lag but, to my dismay, I had not.
    I lay there in bed mentally drawing lines, tracing my journeys over the past fourteen months: the United States, England, Scotland, Kenya, Cameroon, Burkina Faso, Niger, back to Burkina Faso, Senegal, Ivory Coast, Togo, Ethiopia, Kenya, Canada, the United States, Holland, and back to Kenya. As of today, I have changed countries seventeen times in fourteen months.
    By tomorrow, Maggie, you'll have lived on this earth for two months and I'm scratching my head, trying to figure out how I can be your grandmother from way over here on the other side of the world. I always imagined I'd be a traditional, quaint grandma like my grandma, the kind that sits in a rocking chair and knits baby blankets—but quaint I ain't. How many grandmas have drunk tea made in a pot cleaned with cow's urine, or run from a charging hippo? How many grandmas have cooked breakfast over a fire, only to have a baboon poop into it? How many grandmas have

jumped out of the way when a Maasai elder spit at them? No, quaint I ain't!

What is your grandmother doing on this far-away continent of Africa?

All I ever wanted was to live a quiet, secure life in a little white house with a picket fence and a rose garden, but your grandfather saw God pointing us toward Wycliffe Bible Translators in Africa, and we agreed to go. Thus, last year, on August 21, our British Air 747 touched down at Jomo Kenyatta International Airport in Nairobi, Kenya.

Africa!

If someone had told me a few years ago that one day I'd stand on African soil, I never would've believed him.

Your grandpa and I ducked through the jumbo jet's little oval door, blinked in early morning sunshine, and clunked down a metal stairway. With carry-on bags and laptop computer tucked under our arms, we followed fellow passengers across the tarmac and up the stairs into the terminal—much smaller than the last three we'd seen, JFK and London's Heathrow and Gatwick.

Inside the dimly lit terminal, a man stepped out of the crowd and handed us forms. Bleary-eyed after traveling all night, we thumbed through our passports, searched for numbers and dates, and filled in the forms' blanks.

Next, we joined a line facing a row of narrow wooden booths that looked like something from my childhood back in the 1950s—hand-made and stained reddish-brown. When our turn came, we stepped forward and handed our passports to an official who spoke softly in a clipped Kenyan accent. He asked a few questions, stamped our passports, and waved us through.

We took a couple of steps forward and found ourselves on an escalator down to the baggage carousels—all two of them. Only one hummed around on its U-shaped journey, so that made it simple. Thank God for small airports. Our suitcases, boxes, and duffle bag showed up one by one and, after your grandpa lugged them onto our cart, we turned around and stood in line for an inspection. When our turn came, the official rummaged through a few bags and then pointed us toward large glass doors.

Your grandfather's cousin Paul stood on the other side of those glass doors, and by then we were mighty pleased to see a familiar face. He and his wife Barbara translate the Bible with people in Zaire, but they happened to be in Nairobi at the time. Paul loaded us into a borrowed van and we set out toward the city. He sat behind the wheel on the right side of the van and propelled it down the left side of the highway, a practice established in British colonial days. It seemed like we drove down the wrong side of the road, and I felt disoriented and dizzy. Add that to jet lag and sleep-deprivation—and I thanked God it was Paul's job to drive and not mine.

We drove through broad grassy spaces, punctuated by African thorn trees, with a clear view of escarpments in the hazy distance, wide and purple, and all of it spread under a vast dome of blue sky.

Before long, we passed a few shops and businesses, some shiny like new, others patched and rickety. The highway had no paved shoulders, only orange dirt littered with thousands of plastic shopping bags. Pedestrians and goats walked alongside speeding traffic. We passed piles of burning trash that filled the air with a foul odor. Enormous old trucks and buses spewed black exhaust, adding to the air's stench. The fumes burned my nose, and I could feel my chest tighten.

Within minutes, we entered the busy city of Nairobi, cloaked in blossom-covered trees, dense green shrubs, and tropical flowers—red, yellow, purple, and orange—lavish beauty in the midst of trash and polluted air.

Paul maneuvered the van through thick, aggressive traffic. I held my breath while he battled his way into a congested traffic circle, and around—clockwise.

Unruffled, Paul steered the van out of the traffic circle and onto a narrow, quiet lane lined with towering eucalyptus trees. Within seconds, he pulled up to a wrought iron gate with stone pillars on each side, and a blue-uniformed man stepped out of a narrow wooden guardhouse. He swung the gate open and Paul drove us into a small compound. We slid open the van doors, climbed down, and—stepped into springtime. Dappled sunshine filtered through tall old trees, and the temperature felt about seventy degrees. After wild city traffic, noise, and exhaust, this place was a hushed haven.

Paul explained that our offices would be there on the campus of Bible Translation and Literacy, or BTL, a Kenyan organization that partners with Wycliffe Bible Translators. I looked around at three charming stone buildings reminiscent of old British structures, three stories each, with quaint, small-paned windows and ginger-colored tile roofs.

Tropical gardens teemed with bright colors and textures—Bird of Paradise, lantana, begonias, rosemary, ferns, violets, marguerite daisies, banana trees, fig trees, hibiscus, and the grand centerpiece—lofty old palm trees in the center loop. I don't think the Garden of Eden could've looked any prettier.

A room in BTL's guesthouse was our first home in Africa while we awaited the start of our orientation. We didn't have to wait for the course, though, to begin our education—my head spun with all I'd taken in at the airport and on our drive to BTL. Little could I imagine how much more we would learn or how that learning would look, sound, taste, feel, or smell.

In the guesthouse, your grandpa and I slept in single beds in a room about nine feet square. Our hand-made beds, stained dark, had foam-pad mattresses four or five inches thick. We shared a kitchen and bathroom with several other people, most of them Africans who had traveled to Nairobi for a workshop.

On our first day, I made several trips to the laundry room. On my first trip, two Kenyan children played by the doorway. They looked up at me and whispered, "Hello." I smiled and said hello back. On my second trip, they smiled and said, "Hello," when I went in, but when I came out the children giggled and said, "Hi! Hi!" I giggled with them. On my next trip those charming little ones called out, *"Jambo!"* (Swahili for hello). I called back, *"Jambo!"* and we laughed together. Those bright eyes and quick smiles seemed like a serendipitous gift to me and, as a bonus, I even spoke Swahili on my first day in Africa.

On our second day, Sunday, a Wycliffe couple invited us to walk with them to a nearby Presbyterian church. The building showed its age, but God lived as surely in that Nairobi church as He'd ever lived in the United States. I felt strange as one of only a few white people, but no one stared or tried to avoid me, so I felt welcome.

When we sang old Scottish Presbyterian hymns, the Kenyans sang reverently, but when we sang Swahili songs, the congregation came alive. People sang out with great volume and rich harmony. They grinned, they clapped, they danced, and they lifted praise to God. I could see that their hearts and minds felt more in touch with God when they sang to Him in their own language. That first Sunday in Nairobi showed me how important it is for people to have worship songs in the language they know best—and that is one of Wycliffe Bible Translators' tasks and one of the reasons we had come to Africa.

Though everyone within the BTL compound spoke English, we heard accents from around the world: Kenya, Ireland, the United Kingdom, Holland, America, Switzerland, Germany, Russia, South Africa, and Scandinavia. And New Zealand. A dear young couple from New Zealand, Brian and Jenny Caston, served as directors of the three-month orientation course your grandpa and I would soon begin. When Jenny, a nurse, issued us our malaria prophylaxes, she explained that it was very good medicine but it gave some people "MEE-ooth-ool-suz." She sensed that I didn't understand so she smiled and said it again. I looked at your grandpa, and he looked back with a blank expression on his face. Within seconds, though, I saw him grin. "Mouth ulcers! Canker sores!"

September 9 through December 2, we participated in Kenya Safari, Wycliffe's field orientation course designed to teach basic skills for living in remote settings. We'd worked with Wycliffe in South America when your dad and aunt were youngsters but, because we'd made a short-term commitment then, only three years, we didn't take an orientation course. This time, though, we'd made a long-term commitment and had to take the course.

I could understand the rationale behind such training—Bible translator friends of ours in South America, for example, used such skills to set up their work in isolated areas within nearly Stone Age-type cultures. In addition, I knew two young women who fled from guerrilla soldiers and had to survive for several days in the jungle, awaiting their rescue.

Yes, I understood the importance of such rigorous training, but I dreaded it because I was not athletic, possessed no aspiration for adventure, and loathed roughing it. Moreover, I had already paid my membership dues and joined the over-the-hill society. Although I didn't know what to expect during the orientation, I knew I'd never experienced anything like it and that I'd need more strength and courage than I'd ever needed before. For two years I prayed, and prayed, and prayed, and psyched myself up for Kenya Safari but, by the day of our departure, I still didn't have a lot of confidence in myself. Nevertheless, somehow (well, not somehow, but by God's grace) my worries and doubts coexisted with faith that God would get me through if only I'd depend on Him and cooperate with Him. The Bible says, "In quietness and confidence shall be your strength" (Isaiah 30:15, New King James Version). I told God I'd keep my mouth shut and take care of the quietness part if He'd take care of the confidence part.

So, armed with a chocolate bar and my friend Esther's instructions on how to stare down a leopard, on September 9 your grandfather and I set out on our three-month orientation, Kenya Safari. With a clenched jaw, mixed emotions, and plenty of jitters, I gave God a stern reminder that I was counting on Him.

Our group of fifty trainees and staff drove out of the capital city in a northerly direction and eventually arrived at Fish Eagle Camp on the shores of Lake Naivasha. For thirteen days we lived in our tent under shade trees: eucalyptus—heavy-scented, with clouds of billowy dark leaves—and umbrella acacias, with horizontal layers of airy, delicate leaves and three-inch needle-sharp thorns. I'd seen acacias only in exotic African photos, and then at Lake Naivasha I found myself living in a tent under those trees.

Hippos lived at Lake Naivasha. On the day God created hippos, He must have run short on ingredients for beauty. When I see a hippo, the word bulbous comes to mind—blobs of steely gray-brown, bewhiskered fat. Hints of pink ring their dainty ears, noses, cold beady eyes, and the underside of their wide, boxy snouts. They can grow to fifteen feet long and weigh around three tons.

During the day, the hippos stayed underwater among the reeds, but at night, they grazed freely—even within two inches of our tent—and made monstrous grunting, munching, belching noises throughout our campground.

In the middle of our first night, the ground rumbled like an earthquake and your grandpa and I jolted awake. Within seconds I recognized hippo noises, and I knew what I heard—a stampede, right through our camp. Immediately I wondered if we had pitched our tent in their usual path because, if so, those spooked hippos would trample us to death. I asked myself, *Should we get up and run? If so, where? Which direction?* I couldn't think straight! But it didn't matter—I was so frightened I couldn't move. The hippos thundered through our camp in about twenty seconds—which seems like a long time when you're scared out of your wits—and then we heard colossal splashes in the lake as, one after another, they plunged in, their ghastly bellows and snorts echoing through the night.

One morning several of us unzipped our tents and headed for the outhouse, only to find that a couple of hippos still grazed among our tents. With sturdy, long, razor-sharp tusks in mouths that open four feet wide, hippos are deadly.

It seemed like we all stopped breathing and moved in slow motion. Some of us stood at a distance and watched to see what would happen. Fellow trainees Dick and Nancy Baggé and their two children stood near their tent, keeping an eye on a hippo about twenty-five feet away. I sensed Dick and Nancy weren't sure whether to stand still or run. After a few tense seconds, that hippo charged them—but in an instant of inspiration (divine, no doubt), they darted into their tent and zipped the flap.

When that hippo lost sight of them, it made a sharp left turn and kept charging—toward me. I stood about fifteen feet away but, like Dick and Nancy, I unzipped our tent flap and ducked inside, and that hippo ran on by, just inches away. Imagine! Only a filmy tent wall kept me safe. Thank God hippos quickly forget what they can't see. (Using the outhouse had to wait.)

Speaking of outhouses, a row of them lined the edge of camp—rough wood planks and black toilet seats. The place was dark, stinky, and full of flies. Ugh.

Actually, we had two rows of outhouses. The second sat equally close to our site, but I wondered why no one ever used them. One day I checked them out. (Maybe there was hope, after all, that I could become more adventuresome.) I pulled open the wooden door and—I'd never seen anything like it. I saw only a hole in a concrete floor.

Only a hole.

In the floor.

But how did people use it? I stood there trying to figure it out. I could envision how men could aim for that hole, but, but—what about women?

Hmmm. Little by little—okayyyyy—I pictured how a woman might use such a hole.

Suddenly, the scene solved a mystery. This explained the footprints I saw on the toilet seat in the guesthouse bathroom back in Nairobi. The other rooms had housed Africans from rural places, and it dawned on me, standing in that outhouse at Lake Naivasha, that some of them didn't know how to use our kind of toilets any more than I knew how to use theirs.

I shoved the door closed and hurried back to the other outhouses, the ones with black toilet seats. From that moment on, those black toilet seats were, in my opinion, things of beauty.

I myself, however, was not a thing of beauty. Without electricity, I couldn't use a blow dryer, curling iron, or iron, and my clothes stayed as wrinkled as when I wrung them out and pegged them on the line to dry. (They're not clothespins here. They're clothes pegs.) Women wore skirts because Kenyans believe trousers reveal too much of a woman's body. I wore safari boots with my skirts and, oh, if my friends back home could have seen me! Everybody—my friends, my relatives, and even I—had always expected I'd live a genteel life in a little white house with a picket fence and a rose garden. Instead, I was camping in Africa—with limp hair, wrinkled clothes, and no makeup. But, hey, little by little I realized that genteel and quaint were beyond my reach. No, quaint I ain't.

More than a thousand bird species live in Kenya and almost four hundred species make their homes at Lake Naivasha. Each kind has its unique song and, at first, I didn't like those songs because they weren't the ones I knew and enjoyed back home. Soon, however, those foreign birdsongs became familiar and sounded like a grand symphony, especially early in the morning.

Fish eagles' shrill, whistle-like cries reverberated throughout our camp. Raucous ibis calls—sounding like a crow's "caw!" broadcast over a loudspeaker—echoed among the treetops. Mourning doves' gentle, muffled warble enveloped us, "woo-OOO-ooh, woo-OOO-ooh." At Lake Naivasha, I heard the ring-necked dove's song for the first time and, above all Kenya's other birds, its song became the one that most signifies "Africa" to me. Its drawn-out warble, louder than the mourning dove's song, sounds like, "bup! POW-woe. bup! POW-woe. bup! POW-woe!" Cricket chirps and insect hums joined the birds' chorus and serenaded us all day long.

Superb starlings lived among us in large numbers and their striking beauty caught everyone's attention when we first arrived. Their black wings and back reflect a shimmery blue-green color. They have orange-colored bellies and black heads with bright white rings around their black little eyes. Before long, though, their arrogance and determination to steal our food soured our initial admiration.

The birds fascinated me, but they usually pooped on our laundry hanging on the line. Then I'd get out my little plastic basin, scrub the laundry clean, and hang it to dry—again under those birds!

We also shared our campground with fruit bats. At bedtime on our first night, our director, Brian Caston, warned us about their strange nocturnal noise. He said it sounded like someone striking a note on a xylophone, the same note over and over and over again. He forgot to mention that the note was flat.

Life at Lake Naivasha was so different from Nairobi. The capital city offers electricity, running water, and plumbing, but also the stench of burning trash. Cars, buses, and lorries (heavy motor trucks) spew out dark exhaust. Traffic churns through the city day and night. Pedestrians by the thousands flow river-like along streets. At Lake Naivasha, though, we breathed clean air and life was still. We relaxed. We could see blue skies. We heard only our own noises—laughter, children at play, and people talking together. And birdsong, too, of course.

Along the shores of Lake Naivasha, we began our studies in how to live in Africa. We studied hygiene, African anthropology, tropical diseases, and medicines to treat them. We also learned how to identify the currency—coins and bills—and how to calculate the Kenya Shilling's equivalent value in U.S. dollars.

We learned that in Kenya, everyone shakes hands when they say hello and goodbye. If we fail to do so, we offend them. When a person shakes your hand, if he also grips his arm with his left hand, he shows you special respect. What does it mean, though, when a person extends his wrist instead of his hand? It means he has dirt on his hand, so he extends his wrist, with his hand held away from you, and you simply grasp his wrist instead of his hand.

Africans are people-oriented. When they first greet one another, they take time to ask about each other's health, family, and extended family. Only after a lengthy discussion do they get to business. Many Americans struggle within a people-oriented culture because we are goal-oriented—we have work to do. Most of us believe that time is money and, in more ways than we realize, money is one of our gods. When we greet a person, we might say, "How are you?" but sometimes we don't really want to know his answer and we don't wait for it. If he tries to answer, we don't pay attention. Instead, we get right to business—"Would you please make fifty copies of this," we ask with thin smiles, "and have them on my desk by ten o'clock? Thanks." And then we hurry off to our next duty.

We learned that Kenyans will not look you in the eye, and they wish you wouldn't look them in the eye either—it affronts them. I'm not sure why it's offensive, but perhaps it's too personal. Instead, they look at your shoulder while they talk to you, or off in the distance. This is hard to remember because we Americans usually look people directly in the eye. I suspect it helps us discern their words' deeper meaning.

We discovered that what is polite in one culture could be rude in another. Here we should never to use the left hand to give a person something because people use their left hands for "dirty" work—for example, without toilet tissue, people use other things, such as leaves, and they use their left hand to do that. As a result, over time people have come to think of the left hand as dirty in general so, out of courtesy, they offer things to others with only their right hands. I struggle to remember that, especially since I'm left-handed.

Throughout our Kenya Safari orientation, we learned to listen, observe, stretch our thinking, and scrutinize our assumptions. We had frequent opportunities to stand back and examine our ways, and many times the African way seemed better than ours. Your grandpa and I often said to one another, "We Americans have much to learn from the Africans."

We also had to learn to get along with fellow trainees who came from all over the world—Finland, Holland, South Africa, Germany, New Zealand, England, and the United States. And oh, yes, one feisty Scottish lass lived among us, too. A couple of our British colleagues told us first thing that they don't like Americans—arrogant know-it-alls with take-charge tendencies. Their perceptions surprised many of us, and hurt a little, but mostly I appreciated their candor. It taught me, in a new way, the importance of my talk with God earlier about that Bible verse, "In quietness and confidence shall be your strength" (Isaiah 30:15, New King James Version). Back at the beginning of orientation, I told God I'd keep my mouth shut and take care of the quietness part if He'd take care of the confidence part, but it took only a few days to realize I'd need His help with both the quietness and the confidence.

Shel Arensen, a missionary with AIM (Africa Inland Mission), invited us to a rural Kenyan church one Sunday among the Dorobo people. Along the way, off in the distance, Shel spotted old Sarababi walking toward us on the track. "Oh-oh," he said, "I forgot to bring him a blanket."

He explained that Sarababi needed a blanket to complete the bride price for his second wife. Wife number one, old and crippled, told him to find an additional wife, a younger one, to help with work. He had found one. She'd given birth to three children by a man who never came up with the bride price, so the woman's father had taken her back, along with her children. The father agreed that Sarababi could take his daughter if he came up with the bride price, and he still lacked one blanket, which he hoped Shel would give him.

Shel pulled our vehicle over and visited with him. Sarababi had gray hair and a beard and wore tattered, dusty clothes. He limped and walked with a stick because, Shel told us later, a Cape buffalo had gored his hip. I couldn't understand anything Sarababi and Shel said—I don't know which language they spoke—but I suppose Shel explained he'd forgotten the blanket, and we set out again.

While Shel maneuvered his sturdy four-wheel-drive over the lumpy, dusty track, he told us a story about old Sarababi. During Africa's hunting safari days, he worked as a gun-bearer and guide. On one such trek, Sarababi was stalking an elephant through high grass when it turned to face him. Sarababi dropped to the ground, played dead, and hoped the elephant would leave. Instead, it lifted him up with its tusks and carried him some distance away. When the elephant put Sarababi down, he still played dead. The elephant, believing he had died, buried him the way elephants bury their own—it piled four feet of branches and grass on top of him. Only later did Sarababi's hunting party find him and uncover him.

By the time Shel finished his story, we had arrived at the remote Dorobo village. A dozen people hurried over to greet us with handshakes and broad grins. Shy children looked up at us and then turned toward each other and giggled. The adults spoke back and forth with Shel. We didn't understand their language, but their smiles sent the message that they were pleased we had come.

Our new Dorobo friends led us up a dirt path toward their church. Along the way, children grabbed our hands, and when they did, I heard the echo of Brian's brief comment before we left camp: some among the Dorobo have a reputation for poor personal hygiene. Now, I'm a germ freak so I wanted to drop their hands, but something—probably God—stopped me. Instead, I silently prayed the prayer my sister-in-law, Nancy, taught me, *Oh, God, please cause my immune system to work well.*

Shel told us the Dorobo Christians built their church with pride and excitement. He led us into a dim room about ten feet square, made of sticks and mud, with a dirt floor. Under the corrugated tin roof, they had strung wires from corner to corner and had hung things on them—dried flowers, ferns, moss, squares of colored toilet tissue, and lined notebook paper on which someone had practiced penmanship. On the walls, they had tacked pages out of European and American magazines—ads for coffee, panty hose, and nail polish.

They'd built hand-hewn benches around the walls and when our group joined them, we packed that little room. The Dorobo worshiped God with their songs, sometimes in Swahili, sometimes in Maa. They listened to Shel's Bible stories and studied his pictures. He talked with them at length to be sure they understood the lessons and knew how to apply them to their lives.

Looking back on it now, I never imagined I'd visit a rural village or worship in a church like the Dorobo church, but I'm so glad I did. On our drive back to Lake Naivasha, it occurred to me that despite the remote setting and my germophobic tendencies, the Dorobo people blessed us. They welcomed us and invited us to worship God with them. Nothing could be finer than that. Maybe the stuff on those children's hands was angel dust.

Well, Maggie, I want to tell you about more adventures but jet lag is pulling tricks on me, so I'll close for now. I promise to write again soon and tell you about camping among baboons and leopards, hiking across the desert to visit a Maasai family, and pushing a Toyota Land Cruiser uphill backward near Mt. Kilimanjaro. Even though you're too young to understand my stories now, I hope you'll enjoy reading them when you're a big girl.

Love,
Grandma Thomas

KENYA

2

Streams in The Desert

October 1, 1994
Nairobi, Kenya

Dear Maggie,
    I want to tell you more about our orientation course in Kenya. While we camped at Lake Naivasha, a couple of times someone brought mail from Nairobi. We treasured letters from home, especially from your daddy and your Aunt Karen. We couldn't wait to rip open those red, white, and blue airmail envelopes!
    Maggie, I must confess that moving to Africa and leaving your dad and Karen hurt more than anything I'd ever experienced.
    A couple of years before we moved to Africa, your grandpa asked me each day, "Have you filled it out yet?"
    "It" was my application for Wycliffe Bible Translators. I knew your grandpa wanted a different job. Maybe his current one lacked purpose. Or perhaps he suffered from a mid-life crisis. All his life, he has yearned to avoid mediocrity, to break out of the status quo. Probably all those factors led to his urgent need to serve God in Wycliffe Bible Translators.
    For some reason, though, I couldn't fill out the application. I tried several times. I placed my pen on the application, but I couldn't fill in the blanks.
    Finally, I figured out my problem. I didn't want to apply to Wycliffe. I didn't want to get rid of our furniture, our treasures, or our possessions.

I didn't want to dismantle our home. The house I could leave—it needed repairs—but I didn't want to tear apart what it symbolized—"home." We had raised our children in it, we had made memories in it. I didn't want to live far away from my mother or your grandpa's parents. I didn't want to say goodbye to friends. I didn't want to leave Port Angeles, with its forests, mountains, and sea. I didn't want to give up the security of your grandpa's job, his income, and good health insurance.

But mostly I didn't want to leave my children.

Everything within me cried out that my children still needed their parents. I recognized they didn't need us the way they did when they were little, but I believed they needed our behind-the-scenes support to transition out of the world of college and into the world of professionals. However, your grandpa didn't understand my thinking. He pointed out that by the time we'd leave, your dad and Karen would have graduated from college, and that your dad didn't need us because he had already married your mom. Yes, your mom and dad had each other, their own support system, but your Aunt Karen was alone.

So, your grandpa and I were stalled at an impasse.

We found it easier to talk about our parents—your Great-grandma Kay and Great-grandparents Thomas. We agreed that we should help them if real needs arose, whether physical, emotional, or financial. With that in mind, we assessed their current situations. They lived in their own homes, drove cars, and traveled the world. They led busy social lives and enjoyed many church activities. Because they were still energetic and healthy, we had an opportune time to set out on this African adventure. One additional factor further freed us: we were not their only children. Your grandpa's four brothers and my two brothers lived nearby. All those reasons gave us peace about leaving our parents.

But, our children! How could we live half a world away from your dad and Karen for four long years?—and then another four years? Silently I cried out, *When I became a mother, I did not plan to walk away from my children after only twenty-one years!* I always dreamed our children and grandchildren would live nearby and that we'd get together often—but now, this! This felt like a tragic surprise ending to the motherhood I always envisioned.

At the same time, I knew how much your grandpa wanted to join Wycliffe. We had worked with Wycliffe before—in South America, when your dad and Aunt Karen were little—and I believed wholeheartedly in their work. When I thought rationally about working with them again, part of me felt okay, but I could find no peace about leaving my children. I feared I might die of a broken heart if I had to live so far away from them.

What should I do? For months, I asked God to show me how to balance my responsibility to my husband, our children, and my Lord.

I sensed God asking me to do what He had asked Abraham—to place his son Isaac on an altar as a sacrifice to Him. God's request would reveal to Him, and perhaps just as important, it would reveal to Abraham, whether God was Number One in his life. God told us in the Ten Commandments, "You shall have no other gods before me" (Exodus 20:3). Jesus called that the first and greatest commandment, saying, "Love the Lord your God with all your heart and with all your soul and with all your mind and with all your strength" (Mark 12:30). I knew that God wanted, and deserved, my highest loyalty, and that He didn't want me to let anything or anybody—not even my children—take priority over Him. However, I knew those things in only an academic way.

The time had come to move beyond mere head knowledge and to apply those principles to my real life. I thought of the times I had felt God's tug, and the accompanying pain in my heart, while I sang the words—sincerely, I thought—"Love so amazing, so divine, demands my soul, my life, my all."[1] My all. Had I really meant those words? My *all*? Even my children?

God seemed to stand there and ask if I would give highest priority to Him and His plans for me rather than to my plans to live near my children. But I had questions. First, when Abraham obeyed God and put Isaac on the altar, He let Abraham untie his son and take him home. If I, figuratively, placed my children on the altar, would God "untie" them and give them back to me? Or did He want me to sever my relationship with them? Or, could there be something in between?

Eventually I knew what I had to do.

One by one, I placed each person on an altar I had pictured in my mind. I began with Karen. I had to let go, offer her up to God, walk away, and grieve for a few days. I repeated the process with Matt and our parents. I did the same with our possessions, our life in Port Angeles, our home, your grandfather's job, and its security. This month-long process left me emotionally spent but, afterward, I could fill out the application.

I filled it out because I knew that if joining Wycliffe was not God's plan for us, He had power enough to prevent it. I gave Him every opportunity to show us green lights and send us to Africa or red lights and keep us home. In the meantime, I kept taking the next step, and the next, all the while watching for God's answer.

He gave us only green lights.

I had my answer.

I could almost hear God whisper, "It's okay to dismantle your home. Give family heirlooms to your children or put them in storage, and throw out the junk. You worry about your parents, but your brothers and I will care for them. You feel bad about leaving your friends, but true friendships will endure, and I will introduce you to new friends in Africa. You don't want to leave the beauty of Port Angeles, but wait until you see Africa's splendor. Let go of your tight grip on your husband's income and health insurance. Find a better security in Me."

Then God seemed to say, "Now, about your children—don't you know I love them even more than you do? You can trust Me with them."

Knowing God's answer didn't take away the pain, but my heart melted when He asked me to believe He loved your dad and Aunt Karen even more than I did. I could do only two things: trust Him to manage their consequences because of our move to Africa, and then turn and take an extreme, and blind, leap of faith.

On July 3, 1993, we moved out of our home of fourteen years. We could call no other place "home" as much as that one. Your Aunt Karen and I shed tears when we pulled the door closed for the last time on our empty house. Grandpa and I were on our way to Nairobi, Kenya. Little did we know we wouldn't have a place to call home for another nine months.

July 11, 1993, at seven minutes after five in the morning, we drove out of Port Angeles. My mother stood beside our car with her arm around Karen, only twenty-one years of age, and together they waved goodbye. Tears streaked down their faces. I choked on my own sobs. How could I survive four years without seeing them?

I then entered into another type of grief. Before, I only imagined walking away from the altars. The time had come to live out the reality of it. I felt almost dead inside but, at the same time, something in me whispered to God, *I lift up this offering to You. Please find it an acceptable sacrifice. Find in it a sweet aroma.* (See Philippians 4:18 and Exodus 29:18.)

We were heading toward Dallas for pre-field meetings, stopping first at your parents' home in California to say goodbye. That first morning in the car, after the sun rose, I opened my favorite devotional book. To my surprise, your Aunt Karen had lettered several Bible verses and slipped them into the book on special dates. For August 11, the date of our flight out of the States, she wrote in her graceful script, "Anyone who loves his father or mother more than me is not worthy of me; anyone who loves his son or daughter more than me is not worthy of me; and anyone who does not take up his cross and follow me is not worthy of me. Whoever finds his life will lose it, and whoever loses his life for my sake will find it" (Matthew 10:37–39).

On the date of her birthday, she had written, "And everyone who has left houses or brothers or sisters or father or mother or children or fields for my sake will receive a hundred times as much and will inherit eternal life" (Matthew 19:29).

Inserted at your dad's birthday, she'd written, "If anyone would come after me, he must deny himself and take up his cross and follow me. For whoever wants to save his life will lose it, but whoever loses his life for me will find it. What good will it be for a man if he gains the whole world but forfeits his soul?" (Matthew 16:24–26).

When I read those words in Karen's handwriting, I sensed that she had placed her parents upon the altar, lifted us up before God, had gone through her own grieving, and in the process had come to some understanding of those verses' meanings.

On another day of our trip toward Dallas, in another book, I read about Abraham when he placed his son Isaac on the altar, and about those who, like Abraham, surrender to God what is most precious to them. In the past I'd made sacrifices to serve God, but this time I surrendered up to Him your daddy and your Aunt Karen—the two things most dear to my heart. I felt like God had required me to pay a terribly high cost.

Countless times I'd heard in sermons and read in books—and had even taught people in Bible classes—that if we're not willing to make an Abraham-like sacrifice, we'll miss out on God's best for us. I sat on that car seat beside your grandpa and asked myself, *What would I have forfeited if I'd refused to go to Africa?* I wondered what Jesus meant when He said those who leave houses and families for His sake would receive a hundred times as much. *What, specifically, is that "hundred times as much"?* I couldn't envision the answers. I sensed only that I'd have regrets if I missed that elusive "best" and that mysterious "hundred times as much."

Over the years, I'd also heard that Abraham was not an exception to the rule. No, those people who commit their lives—their all—to God must, at times, make enormous sacrifices. I sat for a long time and pondered those words. I stepped back mentally to look at myself. I had an "Ah-ha" moment: my heartache was not an exception to the rule, not an uncommon experience. No, many people who walked this earth ahead of me, and even beside me, paid far higher costs. The time had come for me to stop feeling sorry for myself, place my children in God's hands, and focus instead on the work in Africa—and on the work He wanted to do within me in the process.

I had mixed emotions. I felt excited to see Africa, a place of wonder and mystery. I pictured the continent's unending savannahs and wild animals. I thought of Teddy Roosevelt's grand safari—even the word *safari* sounded romantic and thrilling. Soon I would experience it all—and more—but on the other hand, leaving my children still hurt. Letting go of them, and my heartache, was not like turning a switch—it was an ongoing process.

One day on the car radio, Chuck Swindoll said that God does not waste our suffering. Those words reached out and touched my raw heart, and I grabbed hold of them and held on—*God does not waste our suffering.* Those words gave me a glimmer of hope, hope that God had more for me than I could see or imagine right then.

A few minutes after our Boeing 747 lifted off U.S. soil, I wrote in my journal in capital letters, "God does not waste our suffering. I'm counting on that to be true for Karen, Matt, my mother, Dave's parents, and me." I sat there and mentally shook my finger at God and told Him He had a lot of work to do and that He'd better not let me down.

And so, at Lake Naivasha when we received mail from our children or parents, we could hardly wait to rip open those airmail envelopes. Your grandpa and I read those letters over and over again. The Maasai have a saying, *Meata nkerai lopeny* (a child is not owned by one person), and when I read letters from home, I thanked God that other people filled in some of the gaps your Aunt Karen felt with her parents far away. She wrote,

> It has been very nice to get letters from both Grandma Kay and Grandma Thomas. And it was wonderful to talk with Matt. It always makes me feel reassured to talk to MT. He was a very good big brother and lectured me on taking care of myself and going to the doctor. And I was a good and obedient little sister and went promptly.

Toward the end of our stay at Lake Naivasha, your grandpa got sick with an ailment common in Africa: vomiting, diarrhea, fever, and weakness. God answered our prayers through our nurse, Jenny Caston, and her trunk of medicines, but my response to your grandpa's illness surprised me. For all those days, I'd kept my bravery intact despite living among strangers from countries around the world. I'd been a good sport about roughing it, about the birds pooping on my laundry, the hippo charge, using an outhouse, holding the Dorobo children's dusty hands—but when your grandpa got sick, I had to fight discouragement. The time had come to rip open my chocolate bar! I let myself eat just a half-inch square, though, because that one little chocolate bar had to last a long time.

I didn't have long to mope because on the thirteenth day we left the shade and lush vegetation of Lake Naivasha and set out across the desert for our next phase of Kenya Safari. Much of our route took us through The Great Rift Valley where, for three thousand miles, the surface of the earth is pulling apart, leaving a gaping scar across the earth's face. The valley runs all the way from Mozambique to Syria, from southern Africa to southwestern Asia. Heat waves shimmered over that vast low gap and the deeper we descended, the higher the temperatures in our Toyota Land Cruiser.

Zebras and giraffes grazed beside us, along with Thomson gazelles and dikdiks—tiny antelopes. We could see zebras only when they foraged close to the road. If they roamed a short distance away, their white and black stripes blended into one color, the tawny gray-golden color of the desert.

The road surface soon deteriorated until it resembled an old-fashioned washboard. Without a paved shoulder, we had limited options. We could slow down to about five kilometers an hour and crawl and lurch our way through and around the holes, but instead, Brian did what most drivers do—he pulled off the pavement and drove on the dirt where we might have expected the shoulder to be.

That worked okay sometimes, but soon those would-be shoulders sloped down dangerously on the far side, and they habitually developed huge holes. Because of that, Brian taught us another way to drive on potholed roads: if you drive fast enough, you can skim right over the low spots.

Eventually we stopped alongside the road to empty our bladders. Squatting down in a skirt was not the hardest part. The hardest part was the knowledge that wild creatures lived out there in the bush. A woman on our orientation staff had told me about sitting in her outhouse in Zaire when she felt a sharp pain on her behind. She found two wounds, side by side, and nearly passed out wondering what kind of snake made those fang marks. In her panic, she radioed to request evacuation, only to discover later that those were not fang marks. No, she found a chicken down inside that outhouse.

Well, I said to myself, wandering deeper into the bush to find a private place, *just because her bite turned out to be harmless, that doesn't guarantee I'll be as lucky*. Many a time your dad and aunt heard me warn, "It doesn't always happen to the other guy, you know."

All I ever wanted was to live in a little white house with a picket fence and a rose garden! And a toilet!

We climbed back into our vehicles—no one suffered any mishaps—and continued our dusty drive across the Great Rift Valley. The drive took several hours but eventually, in the gray-golden distance, we looked down into a broad valley, Maasai territory. Brian pointed out a thin line of green trees that ribboned through an enormous parched land. That, he said, was our next home.

When the pavement ended, we followed a track in the sand. When that faded, we made our own way. Before long, we found ourselves driving alongside that meandering line of trees. We had arrived in Eleng'ata Enterit, a place you can't find on the map, in southwestern Kenya. It wasn't a village; we saw no dwellings. I felt filthy, sweaty, sticky, and dehydrated. Thank God, we'd finally arrived.

I don't know why I didn't figure it out before, but when we arrived at Eleng'ata Enterit, I realized that those trees grew there because of a stream, a stream in the desert. One of my favorite devotionals, Mrs. Charles E. Cowman's *Streams in the Desert*,[2] is based on God's words in Isaiah 43:20, "I provide water in the desert and streams in the wasteland." Over the years, I've cherished the way God provides streams in the desert places of our hearts and lives, but I never dreamed I'd one day live by a stream in a real desert.

For the next six weeks, we lived in the shade of massive, spreading fig trees, the same as sycamore trees in the Bible. Oh, blessed, blessed shade. In Seattle, where I grew up, we never got enough sunshine, but in Eleng'ata Enterit—oh, yes, this Seattle girl bowed down and thanked God for shade.

The first afternoon, we cleared spaces in the undergrowth and pitched our tents beside the stream. We soon learned that those fig trees offered us only a mixed blessing because they housed dozens of baboons, which, upset at our invasion, pelted us with figs. Baboons make a variety of grotesque noises. The worst, a blood-curdling shriek, sounds like a baby's scream.

A couple of young ladies struggled to clear their underbrush so your grandpa, still sick and weak, helped them, too. Bless his heart, he worked hard.

Those gals seemed comforted by our presence and before long, they called me "Mom." They named our part of camp the Thomas Estates and, since it happened to be on the opposite side of camp from families with children, our young ladies enjoyed calling the Thomas Estates an adults-only community.

While we scurried to set up on that first afternoon, Brian assigned several men to dig holes and set up two outhouses. They consisted of nothing more than a yellow tarp around a hole in the ground—pit latrines like those I discovered in the "other" outhouses at Lake Naivasha.

How could I ever use such a toilet? At my age! Day by day I grew closer to—er, day by day my husband grew closer to carrying an AARP card in his wallet. Someone my age should not have to squat down over a pit latrine and fumble with a bulky skirt and a roll of toilet tissue (and sometimes even a torch—a flashlight), all the while watching for scorpions. I longed for the Naivasha outhouses with black toilet seats. I hurried back to our tent and rifled through my backpack until I found my chocolate bar. This situation required a chocolate fix!

Jesus said that even before we ask, God knows our need (Matthew 6:8). In this case, He answered on the spot through one of our Thomas Estate gals, Joy. She cut a circle out of the bottom of a red plastic basin and turned it upside down over the hole. It was only about six inches high, but it helped! God bless her!

That first afternoon we also set up water-filter systems to get rid of microorganisms that cause diarrhea, vomiting, typhoid, and other illnesses. Back at Lake Naivasha Brian had water barrels trucked up, but at Eleng'ata Enterit our water came from our stream, a few inches deep and maybe fifteen feet wide. Maasai bathed in it, washed their laundry in it, and herded cattle through it. Other wild animals splashed around in it, too, and baboons up in the trees pooped into it.

We set up our gravity-fed filter system with half a dozen red plastic barrels, rubber tubing, and ceramic filters. Those filters, called candles, looked like rolling pins without handles. We immersed them into a barrel of dirty water that, in a few minutes, passed through the slightly porous ceramic. In the process, that murky water turned clear and pure, and it came out through rubber tubing. A crew of people cleaned the candles on a regular basis because slime from the brook built up on them.

A day or so after our arrival, your grandfather lashed sticks together with twine and made shelves for our tent. He also built a shower stall for the Thomas Estates—the envy of the other campers. He used fig trees, ropes, and a yellow tarp to improvise an enclosure, and he placed smooth, flat stones on the ground so we didn't have to stand in mud.

We used a solar shower—a pillow-like vinyl bag—which your grandpa filled each morning with water from the brook and placed in a sunny spot to warm. In the afternoon, he hoisted that heavy bag high on a stick hook he'd rigged up, and then we took turns taking a warm, though brief, shower.

We controlled the water flow with a lever on a plastic tube at the base of the water pouch. First, we did a quick hose-down and then stopped the water's flow. We lathered up our bodies, shampooed our hair, and then turned on the water to rinse off. We kept our mouths closed, though, because the water came straight from that filthy brook. If we got water on our lips, we dried them and prayed for the best. A shower felt so good—a highlight of each day.

Tourists flock to Africa to see wildlife in its natural habitat, but most of them stay in tourist lodges protected by walls and fences and guards. We, however, experienced Africa's wildlife for real at Eleng'ata Enterit. The

Maasai say that the day is for people but the night is for wild animals. Leopards, hyenas, and cheetahs roamed through our camp at night so we didn't leave our tent between bedtime and daybreak. In the morning, we unzipped our tent flap and examined the ground for animal footprints. On several mornings, your grandpa told me that during the night, he had heard a big cat outside our tent making a purring growl. I'm so glad I slept through each incident!

One morning when we got up, forty baboons sat across the stream from us, grooming each other and scolding their young. Another day, Brian told us the Maasai spotted *chui*—a leopard—near our camp during daylight hours. We knew they wandered around at night, but they posed a different threat during the day when people, especially children, roamed freely—a tasty meal for a leopard. Brian's spare, monotone words, his tight throat, and taut face showed us his degree of concern. He asked everyone to pray for safety, and I rehearsed my friend Esther's instructions on how to stare down a leopard.

We had a choice of two routes from our tent to the central gathering place. We could walk in the desert under blazing sun or we could walk in shade under fig trees. One day while I walked in the trees' blessed shade, the sun's rays filtered through the leaves and highlighted a fine sprinkle of raindrops. Rain! What a blessing there in the desert. God had said, "I will send down showers in season; there will be showers of blessing. The trees of the field will yield their fruit and the ground will yield its crops…" (Ezekiel 34:26–27). *Thank you, Lord, for rain!*

Then I realized rain wasn't falling anywhere else. I stopped. I looked up. I saw a Colobus monkey high in the trees—emptying its bladder. It occurred to me once again: quaint I ain't. Suddenly the hot walk in the desert seemed the better choice.

Walking in the desert posed its own challenges, though. Scorpions favored a path close to our tent and whenever I spotted one, I stomped on it because I remembered how much your daddy suffered from a scorpion sting when he was a boy. After one stomp, the scorpion usually skittered around on the sand to get away—or maybe to position itself to sting me—but by then the scorpion and I had engaged in a fight to the death, and I made sure I won.

One morning on my way to breakfast, I passed an elderly Maasai dressed in his typical red cloths (not clothes), squatting on the ground. I said "*Sopa*," the Maasai greeting. He replied, "*Sopa*," and spit a big wad of saliva at me. I had just received a Maasai blessing, but I leapt out of the way anyway and hurried on, outraged—though I tried hard not to show it.

Shortly after we arrived in Maasai-land, one of the young ladies in the

Thomas Estates, Sue, had a birthday—within a day or two of your Aunt Karen's birthday. I felt heartsick—I wanted to see my Karen on her special day. Then I thought of Sue's mother. No doubt she longed to be with her daughter. That's when it occurred to me that, in a small way, I could stand in for Sue's mom, so I gave Sue a birthday hug and told her it was from her mother. I prayed that someone would do the same for my Karen Anne. As the Maasai say, a child is not owned by one person.

While we camped at Eleng'ata Enterit, if our staff drove to Nairobi for supplies they also brought back mail. Everything halted when mail arrived. One day we received a letter from your daddy, Matt. He wrote it back on May 17, almost three months before we left the States. He didn't mail it, though, until we got here. He wrote on the back of daily pages of a *Far Side* calendar:

> I can honestly say now that I am very excited that you are going to Africa. Knowing that my parents are passionately doing God's work not only gives me tremendous peace of mind, but it also provides an inestimable amount of motivation, courage, and drive to do so, myself, in whatever God has planned. I just can't tell you how excited I am about it now. I will surely miss seeing you, but now I feel like our relationship supersedes life as most people on earth know it. If I never see you again on this earth, it matters very little to me, and I sense that it means little to you, too. Of course, that sounds worse than it is. I love being with you and I eagerly anticipate many more earthly adventures together with you. But on the scope of eternity, if for some reason we never are together again, big deal, because we're just passing through this place, dedicated to a common holy purpose, heading for the same destination where we can spend eternity. Does that make any sense? Well, whether it does or not, it has given me a lot of peace and real excitement to see you on your way.

He set that letter aside for more than three months and resumed writing on August 31:

> All of that courageous rhetoric is the way I feel when I'm feeling brave. Sometimes though, I feel like screaming as loudly as I can, *"I want my mommy and my daddy!"* I

> really miss knowing where you are and what you're doing each day. That will take some getting used to.

Those words cut me to the heart. I'll never forget them.

We also got a letter from your Aunt Karen, busy in Port Angeles as a middle school English teacher and Young Life Leader. She wrote:

> Oh, my sweet parents, my friends, I got another postcard from you yesterday. It made me cry. I love you so much. I think of and pray for you every day. I worry about you. I do little things and think, "Oh! That sounds just like Mom," or "That's exactly what Dad would've said or done."

My heart ached for my son and daughter. Sometimes the pain seemed almost more than I could bear. When that happened, I took a mini-break and spent time alone with God. I hoped and prayed that my children's struggles would make them stronger and better, not break them. I wanted to ask God to prevent their difficulties, but instead I asked Him to help them succeed within their difficulties. In Psalm 138:8, David said he knew the Lord would fulfill His purposes for him, and those words gave me hope that God would fulfill His purposes for my children. I reminded myself that Christ, at the right hand of God, intercedes for each of us. Trusting God for that was the only way I could cope sometimes. I chose to believe that God was working out good things for my children and growing them in their faith.

And so, life went on. In ways I'll never fully know, God helped me, moment by moment, step by step.

❖ ❖ ❖

October 4, 1994
Nairobi, Kenya

Dear Maggie,

Tonight I sit at home in Nairobi, but my thoughts take me back to Maasai-land where, one year ago, your grandpa and I were living in our tent. Let me tell you more about that six-week segment of Kenya Safari, our orientation course.

We cooked meals for our group over an open fire. Our crew set up the kitchen tent and cooking fire under the fig trees, to take advantage of their shade, but the baboons overhead threw figs at us. Our Kenyan staff hollered to drive them away, but they sat there with defiance in their eyes and kept pelting us. One morning while I crouched beside the fire, cooking breakfast for our group of fifty, a baboon up in a tree pooped into the pot of food. I threw the whole thing out and began again. No, quaint I ain't.

"Can God spread a table in the desert?" the Israelites grumbled against God (Psalm 78:19). Yes, He gave them manna in their desert, and He gave us *chapatis* in ours—round, flat, bread-like, and fried in lard. Unleavened, and with a dense, rubbery consistency, *chapatis* are a staple throughout Kenya.

God also gave us *ugali*, a thick, stiff porridge of white cornmeal. We Americans found it flavorless because Kenyans don't put salt or sugar in it, but they love it and eat large mounds a couple of times a day. We also sampled dikdik, ostrich eggs—one equals ten chicken eggs—and warthog, a gift from our Maasai friends who shot it with bows and arrows. It tasted delicious. In fact, your grandpa called it succulent. We enjoyed fresh fruit and vegetables, pasta dishes, stews, sandwiches, salads, and soups.

Our menu also included Marmite (sometimes called Vegemite, depending on the continent), a dark brown sticky substance the Brits and New Zealanders spread on their bread and butter. They're wild about it, but we Americans found it nasty.

Maggie, I wonder if you think that when a hen lays eggs, they look just like they do when your mother buys them at the supermarket. No way! On Kenya Safari, before we cracked our eggs, we washed off straw, poop, and an occasional feather, and—since people don't refrigerate eggs here and there's no such thing as a "use by" date—we tested them for freshness. We poured water into a container and dropped an egg in; a fresh egg sinks to the bottom but a spoiled egg floats.

Our dining room, which adjoined the kitchen tent area under the trees, consisted of wooden folding tables and canvas safari chairs. I used both hands to eat. One hand navigated a fork, the other waved above my plate to protect it from flies, figs, and baboon droppings from above.

Those chairs and tables also served as our classroom where we continued studies in Swahili and African anthropology. We learned to recognize our ethnocentrism—the assumption that we do things the right way and they do them the wrong way, or that ours is superior while theirs is inferior. We re-examined our notions of a tribal mentality compared to a democracy. The Kalenjin people of Kenya have a proverb, "A hyena cannot smell its own stench." (And believe me, hyenas have a foul stench.) Similarly, sometimes we Westerners don't recognize our "own stench"—

ethnocentrism and arrogance. Our goal was to learn to honor Africans, humble ourselves, and live in Africa without causing offense.

We learned that Africans consider greed a grievous sin. They believe that if we have money and they need money, we should buy what they're selling (cut flowers, wooden spoons, or mangos, for example) whether we need them or not. They believe that if we don't, we commit the sin of greed.

We could sort of wrap our minds around that, but then our anthro instructor, Jon, presented us with this scenario. On the way to the bank to deposit money from Sunday morning's service, a church pastor ran into a friend with an urgent need. He asked the pastor for money, and the pastor gave him the church offering. Jon finished his story and paused for our reaction.

We voiced unanimous disapproval of the pastor's conduct—the congregation had given their money to the church and trusted their pastor to use it for the church. Someone even suggested the congregation should fire him because he had violated their trust.

Jon smiled and let us talk, and when we finished he explained the way Africans think. They believe the pastor would have committed the sin of greed if he had not given the man the money. We realized we had a lot to learn.

The Bible says we're to help the poor, but our instructors warned that sometimes missionaries receive so many requests that they don't know where to draw the line, especially since conmen target missionaries. They said we'd have to decide for ourselves how to handle such situations, though some told us they helped only those they knew personally as well as beggars on the street that truly needed help.

Our instructors taught us that when we help the needy, we must also let them keep their dignity intact. They don't want handouts—they want jobs. They want and need the satisfaction of hard work, responsibility, and achievement. The staff also encouraged us to help our Kenyan friends or employees to get additional training and move into better-paying jobs.

We learned the reason Kenyan men often wear suits, or sport coats and slacks, even if sometimes they're well used and ill fitting. In the colonial years, the British wouldn't allow Kenyans to wear suits. However, after Kenya's independence in 1963, Kenyan men could wear anything they wished, and now many wear suits to show their freedom and, I suppose, their self-esteem. Some Kenyan men, though, wear traditional African clothes to show pride in their heritage.

The orientation staff taught us that Africans don't think of time the way Westerners do. If we receive a wedding invitation for one o'clock, for example, we shouldn't arrive at that time because the ceremony might not begin until four o'clock. The process of getting ready for an event is more enjoyable and important than what time it starts.

And then we learned about African humor. A Kenyan man told us a joke: Why don't *wazungu* (white people) fill their coffee cups to the top? Because they have such big noses. (Don't worry; I don't get it either.)

In the shade of those giant fig trees, we studied Swahili. A toilet or outhouse is a *choo* (which rhymes with go). *Asante* means thank you, and *asante sana* means thank you very much. When you arrive at someone's home, you say *hodi*. To welcome a person to your home, you say *karibu* or *karibu sana* (you are very welcome). When you meet a friend, an informal greeting is *habari* or *jambo*. A title for a man is *bwana*. Africans esteem old men and call them *mzee* (pronounced mm-ZAY). Your grandpa is an *mzee*. People address women as the mother of their oldest child, so they call me *Mama Matt*.

Most Kenyans speak at least three languages: their mother tongue (their tribe or clan language, the one mothers speak when they tell stories and sing their children to sleep); English, the official language, used in government and education; and Swahili, the national language, spoken in most other situations. Kenyans have their own unique accent and often use British words, some of which puzzled us until we figured them out. For example, here are a few words that are different in American and British English:

    gasoline = petrol
    kerosene = paraffin
    paraffin = jelly wax
    Jello = jelly
    jelly = jam
    flashlight = torch
    car trunk = boot
    car hood = bonnet
    flat tire = punctured tyre
    burlap = Hessian cloth
    Thermos = flask
    rubbing alcohol = surgical spirits
    trucks = lorries
    hamburger = mince
    stove or kitchen range = cooker
    French fries = chips
    potato chips = crisps

zucchini = corgettes
Q-tips = ear buds
green onions = spring onions
diapers = nappies
napkins = serviettes
vacation = holiday
laundry detergent = washing up powder
green peppers = capsicum
corn = maize

Our anthropology studies included lessons on the Maasai, the warlike and sometimes most feared tribe in Africa. They live on cow's blood and milk, consider agricultural work a disgrace, and measure their wealth by the number of cattle, wives, and children they have. The Maasai consider your grandfather the poorest of the poor because he has only one wife, only two children, and no cattle. Our poverty shocked them.

Maasai men pierce their ears and insert ever-larger plugs until their earlobes dangle against their necks. Some men tuck that loop of earlobe over the top of their ears.

Foreigners recognize Maasai men for two things: first, their appearance—tall, lean, and wrapped in bright red cloths. They carry a long spear and stand with their weight on one leg while they herd their wealth. Second, in their traditional dances, they're famous for jumping high into the air from flat-footed positions, repeatedly, with little effort—an amazing sight.

Maasai women wear large, colorful jewelry, especially necklaces and headdresses, which they make from beads and metal disks. To show their worthiness of marriage, women must give birth to one or more babies. This puzzled us until we remembered they consider children a form of wealth.

One day several Maasai women walked to our camp and performed their traditional rhythmic song and dance for us. To my ears, their voices sounded shrill and off-key. While they sang, they danced, thrusting their shoulders and neck forward.

We don't have a concept of time the way the Maasai do. They see only "today." Maasai don't survive in jail because they can't see into the future or understand they'll one day get out. Instead, they comprehend only the present day and, in their despair, they usually die within a few months.

Brian had hired several Maasai to guard our campsites, especially at night, but despite our guards' grace and friendliness, we couldn't communicate well with them. Their first language is Maa, not Swahili, and most don't understand English. Our head guard, John ole Maloy, knew some English and served as our official host in Maasai territory. He wore a suit instead of red Maasai cloths, maybe as a statement of independence from the British, but also perhaps in recognition of his responsibility as head guard.

John invited some of us to tea in his home and, after a fifteen-minute walk across the desert, we spotted his *manyatta*, a cluster of seven or eight huts enclosed within a thick wall of thorn bushes that kept wild animals out at night. The Maasai kept their goats and cattle inside the wall at night so manure littered their yard. Children played in the yard, too, their faces dotted with tenacious flies. When we stepped inside their compound, the youngsters walked up to us with the traditional greeting for Maasai children—they bowed their heads and waited for us to touch them.

Maasai women build their homes—squat, rectangular, dome-shaped huts about six and a half feet tall. They make both walls and roofs out of sticks covered with sun-dried cow dung and mud. John led our group of twelve *wazungu* through a narrow door about four feet tall.

Your grandpa bent down and followed a couple of people inside, and I stooped inside behind him. Suddenly blackness enveloped me, and I caught my breath. Outside, we had stood in intense equatorial sunshine, but I when I ducked through that little door, the sheer darkness shocked me.

Immediately I received another surprise: in front of me, within about two feet of the doorway, I came face to face with a wall. I must have gasped because your grandpa took my hand and led me to the right. We felt our way down a short hallway and entered a room, also dark except for a tiny hole in the roof—about four inches across—to let smoke escape.

Little sunlight entered through that hole. Everything appeared dark—mud-colored dung walls, dirt floor, and smoke-covered ceiling. (I realized then that's why the Maasai, their possessions, and artifacts always smell of smoke). Gradually my eyes adjusted to the dark and I could see that the room measured about nine feet square. Some of us sat on a low, rough-hewn bench attached to one wall, while others sat on beds—wooden frames attached to two walls, with loosely woven strips of cowhide for mattresses.

A small pile of coals burned on the floor in a fire pit made of three stones. In the shadows, I noticed a couple of children and one of John's three wives. He had children by all of his wives, and each family unit lived in its own hut within the compound. Apparently, John took turns living in each hut.

Our Maasai hosts had invited us for *chai* (tea, milk, and sugar boiled together), and the wife tended to it in a large metal pot over the coals. Two things worried me about their *chai*, though, because they made it with water from that dirty little brook, and because I heard that Maasai clean their pots with cow urine and charcoal. This germ-phobic old woman found the situation stressful.

When the *chai* was ready, John prayed in English and, to my surprise, he prayed only for us. On and on he prayed, asking God to shower His blessings upon us. Only a man well acquainted with God could pray the way John did. His prayer brought tears to my eyes.

John's wife poured the *chai* through a strainer into a metal teapot, and then John took over. First, he poured the *chai* into a metal cup and then

Our Maasai guards in Eleng'ata Enterit.
John, our head guard, stands in the middle.
"Only a man well acquainted with God could pray the way
John did. His prayer brought tears to my eyes."

into other metal cups—the kind with a rolled rim. Brian had warned us about those cups. Washed in water from the stream, the rolled rims could trap that dirty water. Since we couldn't know how clean the cups were, Brian coached us ahead of time to pour, as inconspicuously as possible, some *chai* over the rim and hope it was hot enough to kill germs where we put our lips.

So, there in the dark, each of us reached down and dumped *chai* on the ground. I wonder if our hosts noticed—they probably did—and I wonder what they must have thought about us.

The room had no cross-ventilation, and sweat ran down my back and neck. We visited for about an hour—John and Brian apparently conducted introductions and made speeches in Swahili—and then we hiked back to camp. Along the way, I pondered how John and his family lived in what Westerners might consider poverty, and yet they were rich in hospitality, dignity, and the love of God. I had worried about manure, soot, cow urine, and contaminated water, but in reality, I had stood on holy ground. God lived in that place.

While we lived among the Maasai, we saw that contaminated water often left them sick. Denny Grindall, your Great-grandma Thomas's cousin, vacationed in Kenya a number of years ago and he, too, saw how much they need clean water. He returned to Kenya many times to develop wells and water systems for them, but he left them responsible to keep the systems running. They either couldn't or wouldn't, though, and someone speculated that they found sickness from bad water more tolerable than maintaining Denny's water systems. (The Maasai erected a monument in Denny's honor, and a book entitled *Accidental Missionary* tells of his work among them.)

One of my favorite experiences during Kenya Safari was singing in Swahili with Jacinta, a gentle young Kenyan woman hired to help with childcare while parents attended classes. Jacinta led us in the traditional way of singing—she sang a line, then the rest of us sang an answering line. We sang back and forth until we finished the song. We didn't need musical instruments. Someone tapped on a kettle, someone else kept rhythm with a stick on a chunk of wood, and the rest of us clapped our hands. I'll never tire of those African rhythms and harmonies.

In Eleng'ata Enterit, we learned hands-on things like how to soak vegetables and fruit in bleach-water to kill amoebas and other critters. We also learned to drive The Pearl. Ah, The Pearl. I haven't told you yet about The Pearl of Africa, a 1974 Toyota Land Cruiser, perfect for travel in Africa. Brian taught us to drive it across deserts and through streams and showed us how to change punctured tyres. He trained us to note our surroundings when we traveled and to remember key markers, such as a tree or dwelling, to help us find our way back to camp.

Brian also taught us to develop coping mechanisms—things that ease frustrations and make life manageable. For example, the twig shelves your grandpa made for our tent were coping mechanisms—they allowed us to unpack our luggage for six weeks and stay organized. Do you remember how our friend Joy turned an upside-down basin into a makeshift toilet seat? That was also a coping mechanism. Developing coping mechanisms can make the difference between staying on the mission field or giving up and going home.

We also learned practical things such as how to sanitize the *choo* (outhouse) with ashes from our cooking fire and how to cut hair. One day I helped Nancy Baggé cut her psychiatrist-husband's hair. Never in my wildest dreams could I have guessed I'd one day run my fingers through a psychiatrist's hair. Quaint I ain't.

One day Brian loaded us into The Pearl and another vehicle and we drove around the vast Maasai territory. We stopped in a remote, dusty, parched town, but it seemed like a lively city compared to Eleng'ata Enterit. I spotted a man there who wore a tattered, faded T-shirt advertising Spokane's famous Bloomsday Race—Spokane, my birthplace. We just never know where our thrift shop donations might end up.

We motored on and came to a stream and, since the temperature felt like a hundred degrees, people begged Brian to let them go swimming. He said they could but warned that the water might have microorganisms that make people sick. A few people wanted to swim anyway and they scouted around for a private place to change clothes—except for the Dutch family. They walked a short distance away and changed where anyone could see. And oh, yes, critters lived in that stream and they made those swimmers sick, sick, sick for several days.

Our nurse, Jenny Caston, and her trunk of medicine blessed us richly at such times. I know first-hand because while we camped at Eleng'ata Enterit, I got a urinary tract infection. I knew how serious those infections could become, so I shot prayers heavenward and God answered through Jenny and her antibiotics. The meds kicked in immediately, yet I knew, too, that I had to avoid dehydration under that equatorial sun. On one such afternoon, I knew I had to lie down.

There on my back, I watched a tiny insect crawl up our tent wall. It climbed higher and higher, but when it got to within a foot of the top, it flew off the wall and screamed in wild little circles. After ten seconds of this, it landed back on the wall, several feet lower than before. Again, it climbed higher but, within sight of the top, it tore into its screaming fits and landed low on the tent wall. For fifteen minutes, I watched that little critter repeat its self-defeating behavior. I cheered him on and urged him not to have a meltdown and give up. He had climbed so close to the top! I wanted to tell him the hardest part was behind him and if he could just hold on for a few more seconds, he'd reach his destination. But no, he always gave up just before he reached his goal.

Sometimes we humans do the same thing. Impatient and weary, we don't realize how close we are to success so we give up and indulge in wild fits, and by the time we get back in focus, we've lost ground.

Cape buffalo—massive, dense, and dark as ebony wood—occupied the same land we did in Eleng'ata Enterit. Fierce and bad-tempered beasts, they usually rip open a person's groin with their thick, steely horns—an especially gruesome wound that most people don't survive. One day a group of Maasai arrived at camp and said a buffalo had gored a man. They asked Brian to arrange a flight to a hospital, which he did, and that little plane landed in the desert near our camp. We never found out, though, if the man survived.

I'll write again soon, Maggie, with more stories from Africa.

Love and hugs,
Grandma

3

The Perils of The Pearl

October 6, 1994
Nairobi, Kenya

Dear Maggie,

 I remember our stay in Eleng'ata Enterit as a mellow time, a serene time, a gentle time—for the most part, anyway. I enjoyed the quiet, the clean air, and the slow, simple lifestyle. God had indeed provided streams in the desert, both literally and figuratively.

 After six weeks in Maasai-land, we moved again, this time to the Taita Hills in southeastern Kenya, close to Mt. Kilimanjaro. We left the desert and entered a lush, verdant region.

 We knew that our directors, Brian and Jenny, would leave us trainees to fend for ourselves during our final stage of orientation. However, someone among us needed to be in charge so Brian called for a vote. The group chose your grandpa to serve as the Chairman of the Executive Committee, the *samaki kubwa*—the big fish. In order to carry out his duties, he had the use of The Pearl of Africa.

 Before his tasks began, our entire group congregated in the small town of Dembwa, at the base of the mountains, where local people welcomed us with lunch and speeches. We gathered in the yard of a new elementary school with six or eight classrooms, and your grandfather, a life-long educator, wanted to see a classroom. Since the children didn't have school that day, we stepped inside. The room's concrete floors and walls kept the temperature nice and cool, but the school had no electricity; teachers and students depended on sunlight through the windows. The room was furnished with a slate blackboard and rough-hewn desks and stools. A world map hung on the wall—the classroom's only educational material. The room had no textbooks, dictionaries, or anything else. In place of textbooks, we noticed pencils and thin tablets in which children had written lecture notes from the teacher. We found it hard to grasp the poverty displayed in that school—it seemed unthinkable—but we also knew the teachers and students did the best they could with their meager resources.

Well after dark on Saturday, November 6, after Brian dropped off the other families in their respective villages, he pulled The Pearl to a stop high in the Taita Hills. Trees and darkness surrounded us, but The Pearl's headlights shone on a little mud-plaster house. Brian walked to the door and spoke to the people inside. Then he turned and ambled back to us.

"They didn't get word you'd be living with them," he said. "It'll take them a few minutes to get ready." Only later did I realize that they had already gone to bed.

A few minutes later, Brian introduced us to our hosts, an older couple, Rafael Mwakodi, whom we called Bwana, and his wife, whom we called Mama. Looking back on it, I suspect this "older" couple was younger than we were. In the dim glow of a kerosene lamp, we visited with Bwana and Mama, all smiles. Bless the Mwakodis' hearts—I would not have smiled if foreigners awakened me at night and announced their three-week stay. After a few minutes, they led us to our room and we settled in for the night. Our "village living" stage of Kenya Safari had begun.

The next day we measured our bedroom: seven feet square. Rustic wood shutters covered a glassless window opening. Our bed, three feet wide and five feet, seven inches long, had both a headboard and footboard. Grandpa stands over six feet tall so that bed posed a problem, but he did what Brian taught us—he developed a coping mechanism. He put a suitcase along his side of the bed and put one foot on it, and he spread-eagled the other foot across the bed. That left me one corner in which to curl up. That room also housed two large storage barrels, a suitcase that belonged to Bwana and Mama, a chair with another of their suitcases, and our belongings—suitcases, backpacks, plastic basins, and canteens.

I didn't know at the time—only much later did your grandpa tell me—that the Mwakodis had moved out of their own bedroom to let us have it and that they slept on the floor in another room. That makes me want to cry. In Bwana and Mama, I beheld the sacrificial heart of God Himself.

The Mwakodis didn't live in a village. Their house seemed to be the only one around and it measured about twenty feet wide and twelve feet deep. Inside, they had painted their mud-plaster walls aqua blue. Over time, however, large patches of mildew had stained the walls. The Mwakodis' main room reminded me of the Dorobo church we visited near Lake Naivasha—they had strung wires from corner to corner under a corrugated tin roof, where a ceiling might have been, and from the wires, they had hung papers and greeting cards. Their cement floor crumbled in places. The room had one small window opening—no glass—with a shutter of unpainted planks. The Mwakodis kept it closed so the house remained dark except for sunlight that came in the wood-plank front door.

Since the Mwakodis' home had no electricity, they used a paraffin (kerosene) lamp after dark. They had no running water or toilet, only a pit latrine in a clean, stick-and-mud enclosure some distance from their house. I recalled the red plastic basin-turned-toilet-seat that our friend Joy had made back in Maasai-land and wished I'd thought to make one of my own for this phase of our orientation. Even better would've been those outhouses with black toilet seats back at Naivasha. I should have appreciated them much more back then.

Bwana could speak Swahili and a little English, but Mama didn't know English and didn't speak Swahili much either. Apparently, she and Bwana talked to each other in the Taita language.

On our first full day with Mwakodis, a Sunday, Bwana and Mama put on their one set of fine clothes to go to church. When the four of us walked out the door, Bwana said, "We will take the vehicle." Your grandpa was supposed to drive The Pearl for only Executive Committee duties, not for our convenience, so he said, "No, we can walk." Bwana, who didn't understand why we had The Pearl, said, "We will take the vehicle," so we did.

We meandered among the hills for three miles on a narrow dirt track. The Taita Hills reminded me of the Olympic Mountains' foothills near Port Angeles, about the same elevation and covered with green. Tropical plants grew in the Taita Hills—papaya, citrus, and banana trees—but I also spotted plants that grew back home in the Pacific Northwest: bracken ferns, purple lobelia, berry vines, pine trees, and cedar.

When we stepped into the Anglican Church, a stick-and-plaster building painted white inside, we interrupted the children's class. I don't suppose white people had stepped foot in their church before, and we *wazungu* caused a stir. Each little face turned our direction. Their song leader scurried to regain the children's attention. Eventually, she convinced them to sing a couple more songs, though they turned and watched us while they sang. I loved hearing the children sing. Their voices filled the room—a sharp contrast to so many Sunday school children back home who rarely sing louder than a whimper.

In the break between Sunday school and the church service, people welcomed us with courtesy, but we knew they found us curious—and very white—beings. For the first time in my life, I found myself a member of the minority race.

For the three-hour worship service, we sat on hand-hewn plank benches. The congregation spoke Swahili in their prayers, songs, and Scripture readings, but I suspect they spoke the Taita language in conversations and the sermon. I had no idea what people said. For all I knew, the pastor might have preached in Chinese. Your grandfather and I had lived in Kenya only a few weeks and—wham! God gave us a first-hand experience like that of millions of people around the world, week after week, year after year. Without a Bible in a language they understand, they walk out of their churches with little or no understanding of Scripture readings or their pastor's sermon. I had known this in theory, but that day I experienced why people need Bibles in their own languages—and why we came to Africa.

The congregation took up two offerings. Some people had no money so they brought produce, eggs, milk, or dried beans. Only then did it start to dawn on me how poor those people were. For forty-five minutes, they auctioned off those items. Everyone bantered and laughed while they converted the food into cash for the church's expenses. Eventually people had paid for four eggs and two bunches of Swiss chard. Your grandpa calculated they'd raised the equivalent of thirty-eight cents.

Then the auctioneer walked into the congregation and stopped in front of us. I could not believe what I saw him do next. He handed us the eggs and chard. Stunned, I wanted to cry because, as Americans, we were rich—and I mean shamefully rich—compared to them. Every day of our lives, we've had more than enough to eat and yet those dear people, who had so little, gave us the food donated to the church. In them, we beheld God's grace—they gave us what we did not deserve. I will never forget that as long as I live.

Around four o'clock that afternoon, Mama served soup made of beans and the chard from church. At six o'clock, she served us boiled potatoes. Bwana said that she and a neighbor worked for hours to peel them and that they prepared them especially for your grandpa and me.

At the end of our first day with the Mwakodis, I walked outside at dusk. I leaned against The Pearl, listened to bush babies call from the trees, and surprised myself. I cried. I don't know what triggered my tears, but probably a combination of things. For a long time, I had dreaded this part of orientation. I knew it would be the hardest part. I felt nervous about living with strangers. I had lived among strangers for a couple of months already, but each family lived in its own tent. Now we lived with strangers in their home, not our tent.

Then, too, I had lived almost two and a half months in the bush and felt weary. Physically speaking, I had left the desert and entered a land cloaked in luxuriant vegetation, but emotionally I had left a lush spot and entered a desert place. I didn't know all the reasons for my unexpected tears, but I knew I didn't want to have a meltdown like that insect in my tent back in Maasai-land. I had successfully completed most of Kenya Safari and shouldn't give up now, not with the end in sight.

I didn't bawl out loud so I don't think the Mwakodis knew, but your grandpa knew. Part of me felt wimpy, but I reminded myself that even Jesus wept. Tears are not bad. They can bring release and healing. The Bible tells us that God sees our tears and hears our weeping. Sometimes we can't put our woes into words, but He knows our hearts, and I knew that Christ stood at the right hand of God the Father, interceding for me.

I thought back to August when, on our way to Africa, we spent a few days in England and Scotland, thanks to a money gift for our twenty-fifth wedding anniversary. At the Wycliffe Centre in Horsleys Green, England, we lived in an old World War II barracks. A poster in our dorm room displayed Psalm 126:5–6, "Those who sow in tears will reap with songs of joy. He who goes out weeping … will return with songs of joy."

I pondered those words at length because I didn't know what they meant for me specifically, but I did understand about tears. I shed tears on my way to Africa because I couldn't see our children or parents for four long years and because I wondered if I could endure the orientation course. But, what about those verses about tears turned to joy? Could I believe it? Would I believe it? Would I believe that God could turn my tears into joy?

I thought about it for a couple of days and then, there in our dark little barracks room in England, I stood before that poster and told God I'd give Him time to show me songs of joy in Africa. Since that day, I had often wondered what, precisely, could lead to that gladness.

So there I stood in the lovely, yet terribly foreign, Taita Hills, leaning against The Pearl and shedding tears. Good old Habakkuk came to mind, my friend from the Old Testament, a man troubled over things that didn't seem right. God told him, "Look … and watch—and be utterly amazed. For I am going to do something in your days that you would not believe, even if you were told" (Habakkuk 1:5). Habakkuk, still upset, laid out his complaints to God and then said, "I'll stand at my watch.... I will look to see what he will say to me" (Habakkuk 2:1). Okay, then, I would do what Habakkuk did. I would watch to see what God would do about both tears and joy.

Now, looking back, I think my tears flowed because of the Mwakodis' kindness, their church's food gift, the neighbor who helped Mama peel potatoes, and Mama's thoughtfulness in preparing them for us. Only now do I see that Mama probably thought we Americans always peel our potatoes. Truly, God lived in the Taita Hills. The people's generosity in the midst of their poverty melted my heart and, on that Sunday evening, my gratitude oozed out in the shape of teardrops.

I understand that now, but that night I didn't understand my tears. I took a deep breath, walked back inside, closed the door to our room, and indulged in a half-inch square of my chocolate bar. I slept well, and things looked better in the morning.

Someone—we didn't know who—had scheduled Monday morning appointments for your grandpa, as our group's leader, to meet with the local District Commissioner, the Bishop, and the police. Brian had explained that relating with those officials would assure them our group had no suspicious motives.

We had a problem, though. We didn't know how to find their villages or offices. We didn't even know where we were. We had arrived at the Mwakodis' home after dark and, along the way, we lost our sense of direction. No electricity or streetlights lit our surroundings over twisting one-lane dirt tracks—with no street signs—cloaked in tropical forests, uphill and downhill and around corners. Before Brian left us, he told us all we knew—that the closest trainee family lived nine and a half kilometers away. The nearest phone was miles away, and we had no idea what to do. Just when we felt ourselves slipping into a panic, God provided a helper with a willing heart. Bwana offered to come along and direct us to the various villages. I find it hard to explain the enormity of our relief.

The three of us climbed up into The Pearl and your grandpa turned the key, but The Pearl did not start. He tried several times but—nothing.

We decided to push The Pearl to start it by compression, but we had to be careful because only thirty feet away we would come to a drop-off of nearly five hundred feet. Bwana and I pushed The Pearl a few times, but it still wouldn't start. The nearest mechanic was probably dozens of kilometers away. I looked at your grandpa. He looked as sick as I felt.

We had only one option: turn The Pearl around and face it downhill. However, whether we turned to the right or to the left, we had to push The

Pearl uphill. If and when we got the back wheels up on the hill, we had to avoid yet another drop-off. We tried, and tried, but didn't have enough muscle to push The Pearl uphill.

Eventually several of Bwana's neighbors materialized out of the forest. For an hour, we pushed and maneuvered and turned The Pearl around, faced downhill. We pushed once again and that time it chugged, and sputtered, and came to life. Oh, what a sublime sound! Our new friends cheered and laughed along with us.

How could we ever thank them enough? I wanted to hug and kiss each one, but I suspected a public display of affection wasn't appropriate in their culture. Then Bwana Mwakodi told us the men were on their way to another village for market day, so, to thank them, we loaded them into The Pearl and gave them a ride. We had witnessed, again, God's love for us through dear Kenyan people.

After that, we always parked The Pearl facing downhill because we never knew when we'd have to push to get it started.

In addition to relating to the District Commissioner, the Bishop, and police, your grandpa's duty was to keep in touch with the families in our orientation group, each living in a different village. I thoroughly enjoyed climbing into The Pearl and riding around the beautiful hills with him.

When we visited trainee families in their hosts' homes, we tried to set aside American customs and do things the Kenyan way. Kenyans consider it an honor to entertain guests, serve them *chai* (tea, milk, and sugar boiled together), and have a long visit. In America, if we stop at a friend's house, usually we say, "I can stay for only a minute," but since that would offend Kenyans, we accepted their *chai* and stayed to visit. Each family welcomed us and, without realizing it, they taught us a new way to relate to others. Your grandpa and I suspected that their way pleased God more than our usual American way.

On our way to visit a trainee one day, the narrow track turned into a dry riverbed full of boulders. The Pearl lunged over and around them, and your grandpa wondered aloud how much longer he should keep driving. When we spotted the home in the distance, up on a high spot, we stopped and hiked the rest of the way.

That host family had electricity! And, even more amazing, they owned a little television. When we arrived, the man of the house plugged it in and left it on the duration of our stay. They had no reception, though, so we sat and watched the black and white speckles on the screen and listened to its scratchy hiss.

Another day we stopped in a more remote place to visit trainees. That house didn't have electricity, but the owners had tied a light bulb to the end of a shoestring and suspended it from a rafter in the middle of the room.

On a different day, a host family killed a chicken and cooked it for us even though they could rarely afford to eat meat themselves. Their generosity nearly broke my heart—we didn't need the nutrition! They did! The Taita people owned next to nothing, but they shared it with us. I could only ask God to bless them abundantly in return for their sacrifices on our behalf.

In visiting our trainees, we discovered that not only did the Mwakodis live in the most remote place of all the host families, they also lived in the most primitive of the homes. They lived at six thousand feet, but our other trainees lived lower in the hills closer to villages. Up where Mwakodis lived, I'm sure we were the first white people locals had seen in their territory for decades.

The Mwakodis' cookhouse, a stick-and-mud building separate from the main house, measured about eight feet square. Its lack of windows kept it dark except for the fire. Smoke filled the room and soot coated the walls and ceiling. A small dome-shaped clay cook-stove, in the center of the dirt floor, had an opening in the bottom for firewood and two holes on top to hold *suferias*, aluminum pots. Mama sat on a low, hand-hewn bench while she cooked. She seemed apologetic about her cookhouse, and Bwana told me, gently, that Mama didn't want me to help her cook. *Hakuna matata* (no worries!) because the smoke made me choke. One day, though, I offered to make pancakes for the four of us. Mama and Bwana giggled and whispered to each other while I cooked over the fire, and they were good sports about eating strange-tasting American food.

Breakfast at Mwakodis' usually consisted of black tea boiled with milk. They and your grandpa put sugar in theirs, but I liked my tea without sugar—which puzzled Bwana and Mama. Each morning after our first cup, Bwana offered me more, but I put my hand over the top, smiled, and said *bas* (enough). It tickled him when I spoke Swahili. Sometimes while your grandpa and I drove about visiting trainees, we bought bread and jam for the next morning's breakfast.

Mama always served tasty soup for the evening meal—cabbage, tomatoes, onions, kidney beans, a lot of water, and occasionally some tough meat. She spent several hours each afternoon simmering this soup over the fire.

Mama also spent a long time making *chapatis*, those flat, round breads that we'd eaten since the first days of Kenya Safari. One day I watched Mama make them and learned there's an art to it. She mixed the flour dough and rolled it out like a round piecrust, layering lard into it. Next, she cut slits around the dough so that it resembled a flower with petals. Mama folded each petal-like piece at an angle over the one beside it and toward the middle of the circle, and then rolled out the dough again. She did this several times before frying them in lard over the fire. It took a long time to make them properly.

When we sat down to eat on the first evening, I noticed Mama forgot to put spoons on the table. I thought back to the start of Kenya Safari when I told God I'd be quiet, and I decided this would be a good time to say nothing. Surely, in a few seconds Mama would realize her oversight.

While I waited and watched, Bwana and Mama tore their *chapatis* into pieces, dropped them into their soup, and then used their fingers to pick up one bite after another. I could hardly believe my eyes. I had no choice but to do likewise. Apparently, white people need a lot of practice to perfect that skill. By the third evening, I asked Bwana and Mama if I could use a spoon. They didn't seem offended so your grandpa asked for one, too, and from then on both of us took great pleasure in the luxury of a spoon.

On the equator, the sun rises around six o'clock year round and sets around six in the evening, and since Mwakodis had no electricity, they went to bed shortly after their evening meal. Mama placed the dirty dishes in a basin and covered them with a cloth to await washing outside the next morning, probably because animals roamed freely at night. However, since we Americans like to brush our teeth before bed, each night I said, *kupiga mswaki* (I'm going to brush my teeth). Bwana always laughed when I said that. I'm not sure if he laughed at my Swahili or because I wanted to brush my teeth, but I took my toothbrush and canteen outside in the yard and scrubbed.

After we lived there a few days, I offered to wash dishes. I'd been looking for a way to help, but I also had another motive. I noticed that Mama used only water to wash the dishes; I suspect they couldn't afford soap. I often prayed sister-in-law Nancy's prayer, *Oh, Lord, please help our immune systems to kick in,* but I still worried about your grandpa's health. He had fallen ill at both Lake Naivasha and Maasai-land with vomiting, diarrhea, and fever—caused by the water. After he'd suffered a few days in Maasai-land, by God's grace someone had to drive back to Nairobi for supplies so our dear nurse, Jenny, sent your grandpa's stool specimen along. When our friend returned the next day, he brought back powerful antibiotics. I didn't want your grandpa to get sick again in remote Taita, so I hoped that if I washed the dishes, perhaps I could keep him healthy.

Outside in the yard, I squatted down on the ground in front of a basin and sprinkled in my powdered laundry detergent. After I washed the dishes, I rinsed them in bleach-water, all the while shooing away cantankerous chickens. I dried the dishes and stepped inside to put them away in Mama's dark, small storage room. I looked around. She owned a couple of rough plank shelves but most things sat on the concrete floor. I spotted a couple of aluminum pots, one tin bowl, and four glass bowls that we used for our dinner soup. She owned three teaspoons, four tablespoons, one fork, one knife, three cups and saucers, one mug, and one tin mug. Mama also had a small supply of food: dried beans, salt, a small brick of lard, a tiny plastic sack of flour, and another of gray-brown sugar.

Our adventures with The Pearl continued. One morning we climbed in and expected it to chug to life by compression as it wobbled down the hill—but it did not. My heart nearly stopped. I looked over at your grandpa. He looked pale. Had The Pearl gasped its last breath?

Grandpa looked around for a way to avoid pushing The Pearl uphill backward to try again. He scouted out a steep, forested trail beyond the Mwakodis' house, one we'd never driven before. It took travelers away from civilization, but it was a downhill slope, so the two of us pushed The Pearl that direction. Your grandpa jumped in at the last moment and worked the clutch—but it didn't start. We were stuck worse than ever before.

What should we do? We could push it further down into that unpopulated mountain valley and hope it would start, but if we had already tried twice without success, why should we expect The Pearl to come to life the third time? If it still didn't start, towing it out would be all the harder, if not impossible.

Your grandpa decided to push once more before he gave up, and The Pearl sputtered to life. Hooray! At that point, your grandpa faced another challenge: he had to back The Pearl up that narrow steep trail, up and up and up, until he got to the dirt road at the Mwakodis' place. "Ah," your grandpa sighed, "the perils of The Pearl."

One of the local people told us they seldom have problems with crime in the Taita Hills. That puzzled us because crime is a problem elsewhere. When we questioned him, he pointed to a bare shoulder of rock, an almost-vertical side of a mountain hundreds of feet high. "If someone commits a crime here, we push him off that mountain. That discourages crime." Apparently it did. We always felt safe in the Taita Hills, and when we drove around, we offered rides to people along the roads. That seemed to be the African way, the Golden Rule. Kenyans pack in a dozen people where we might squeeze in only six, and they always looked delighted when we picked them up. I don't suppose they rode very often with a white person at the wheel. As we drove throughout the Taita Hills, our white skin always made us a curiosity.

We visited trainee families and local officials on the first several days, but then, for two reasons, we took a day off. First, we were exhausted, and second, we needed to wash our laundry. Bwana said he'd show us the nearest water source. We followed him down a steep, meandering path through the forest, descending about five hundred feet. At the bottom, he led us through dense undergrowth to a spring. Clear, fresh water! What a treat after that stream in Maasai-land.

Bwana hiked back up the hill while we washed, rinsed, and wrung out our laundry. Your grandpa's participation no doubt caused gossip to echo back and forth among the hills. I could almost imagine the voices, "A man doing women's work!"

Afterward, we began the arduous hike back up the hill with our heavy wet laundry and a couple of water jugs. Your grandpa held one side of the basin and I held the other but, to our surprise, we really struggled. I suppose the elevation had something to do with our difficulty.

An elderly man and a couple of women hiked up behind us. They greeted us and visited like Africans always do, and then they reached for our laundry basin and water jugs. We objected, but they kindly insisted. One of them, a petite woman, lifted the basin to the top of her head, balanced it perfectly, and, without effort, scurried up the hill. Your grandpa and I huffed and puffed up the path behind them. When we arrived back at the Mwakodis' place, we gave our new friends a few shillings. They no doubt appreciated the money and we were grateful for their help—but even more, in them I glimpsed God Himself. In Psalm 68:19, David said that God bears our burdens, and those dear people came alongside us that day and, like God, helped us bear our heavy loads.

We strung a clothesline between The Pearl and a tree and soon we had clean, dry clothes. Sweet! Only later did we learn that hanging one's underwear where everyone can see it is a no-no in Kenyan culture. Ah, well, quaint I ain't.

About every third day, we took a sponge bath. At first we couldn't figure out where the Mwakodis' water came from, but eventually we learned that Bwana paid a young woman ten Kenya Shillings—a few pennies—to carry it from the bottom of the hill in a five-gallon bucket on her head. When I think how much a gallon of milk weighs and then multiply that five times, well—just think how much that water bucket must have weighed! How could that frail little woman lift that bucket? How could she place it on her head? And climb up a steep hillside with it?

For our sponge baths, Mama heated a little of that precious water over the fire and I took it into a room attached to the cookhouse. I poured an inch of hot water into a plastic basin and lathered up, starting at the top of my head. I used an even smaller amount of water to rinse. It felt so good to get clean. When I finished, your grandpa used the other half of the water.

In that same room, we stored a water filter system made of a plastic bucket and a jerry can. Everywhere we went, we each carried a canteen filled with filtered water.

The Taita people grew fruit and vegetables on steep terraced hillsides, but the previous year's scanty rainfall caused crops to fail and the people suffered terribly. We were deeply touched because the Mwakodis, despite their poverty, were so generous with us. We sensed, though, that they thought we didn't like their food, despite our assurances that we found Mama's meals tasty. Looking back now, perhaps they thought we didn't like their food because each time your grandpa and I went out, we brought back food or supplies: papayas, bananas, dried beans, cabbage, lard, paraffin (kerosene) for their lamp, and sometimes meat. We brought it back not because we didn't like theirs, but because we wanted to help feed two extra people during a year of crop failure.

One day Bwana asked what people eat in America. We thought he simply wanted to learn about America so we named some foods, only to discover later that he and Mama thought they needed to buy those foods for us. Those dear folks nearly broke our hearts. They had almost no money, yet they bought food for us that they would never—could never—buy for themselves.

While we lived with the Mwakodis, rain fell in the Taita Hills—a big blessing—but maneuvering roads afterward resembled driving through greased peanut butter. Grandpa endured more than one anxious moment slipping and sliding up a steep hill through deep gunk. One day he wondered aloud, "Will we ever get to the top of this?" Another day we got a punctured tyre and The Pearl broke down twice. The roads were so bad that at the end of a long day, holding on for dear life, our bodies felt bruised.

If a Taita Hills family didn't own a car, they had no need for a road so, in that case, your grandpa just pointed The Pearl in the right direction. One day, with The Pearl chock full of people on our way to a trainee's home, we had to drive across the steep rock face of a hillside. To my amazement, even though The Pearl tipped at a steep angle, it clung to the rock. The Pearl's stability and agility astounded me.

Eventually we reached the house, perched on a boulder-strewn peak. We dropped off our friend and then, there on that rocky little point, your grandpa began to turn The Pearl around. I knew it wouldn't be easy because I couldn't see any flat ground and the land dropped off in every direction. I had turned to speak to a fellow passenger when suddenly Grandpa hollered, "Everyone sit perfectly still!"

I had never heard him yell like that. Something was wrong. The Pearl faced downhill at a steep angle, toward a deep ravine, and he whispered to me, "The Pearl's about to fall off the mountainside." I could hardly breathe, much less speak, but eventually I pulled myself together enough to ask him if we passengers should get out.

"No!" he yelled. "Everybody sit perfectly still!"

He told me he would put The Pearl in four-wheel drive. I didn't know what that required, and maybe he didn't either, but again he warned us not to move. In fact, he himself sat perfectly still. His face and neck glistened with sweat.

When I saw your grandfather petrified at the wheel, I envisioned newspaper headlines in Kenya and across the United States, "Missionaries die when vehicle plunges off mountain."

I felt faint. I couldn't watch. I had to look down.

After a tense few moments, your grandfather composed himself, planned what to do, no doubt rehearsed in his mind how to work the clutch, and then he took action. Seconds later he backed The Pearl up and away from the drop-off in front of us, stopping before it backed too far toward the drop-off behind us. He inched The Pearl back and forth, and *kidogo, kidogo*—little by little—he turned it around. No one said much for the rest of the trip, and it took a long time for my heartbeat to return to normal.

Brian had asked your grandpa to line up a bus to transport our group out of the Taita Hills on November 29, so about a week in advance we set out for Mombasa, a large seaport on the Indian Ocean. The highway, the major link between the coast and the capital city, was scarred with the usual thousands of potholes so your grandpa drove just fast enough to skim over the high points, the way Brian taught him. The highway was busy with enormous lorries (trucks) that belched out black exhaust while hauling their loads to or from the seaport.

At one point, your grandpa pulled out around one of those lorries and accelerated to pass it—or "overtake" it, as they say in Kenya—when before our eyes, hidden just beyond the crest of a slight rise, we spotted something much larger than a pothole. At sixty miles an hour, we sped alongside that truck toward a gap where an entire section of pavement had gone missing from the centerline to the far side of the highway—four feet across and more than a foot deep. Instinctively we knew we'd hit that hole within three or four seconds. We both screamed and braced ourselves, but to our utter amazement, The Pearl soared right over that massive gap and sped on down the highway. (I didn't even have time to envision a newspaper headline to announce our deaths.)

When we arrived in Mombasa and found the bus company, your grandpa stepped inside to make arrangements, but I stayed in the car park (parking lot) adjoining a junkyard full of wrecked buses. When your grandpa finished inside, he walked back to The Pearl with a puzzled look on his face.

"I took care of the paperwork, but where are the buses?"

We looked around, but we could see only the wrecked ones in the junkyard. The man who helped your grandpa must have overheard us because he stepped outside and told us that indeed those were the buses. After he moved out of earshot, we sighed and shook our heads. Your grandpa said, "That guy promises someone will show up with a bus for us." We wondered if he would.

Our final days of village living wound down and I thought of the ways Bwana Mwakodi and his wife had shown us generosity, patience, and grace. Nevertheless, living in their home felt awkward because of cultural and language differences. From the outset, I had counted the days until we could leave. The final few days I even counted hours. November 29 arrived and I celebrated—I ate the last ragged square of my chocolate bar.

We shook hands with Bwana and Mama. *"Asante sana!"* (thank you very much) we said, and we really meant it. We climbed up into The Pearl, waved goodbye, and then your grandpa motored down through the lovely Taita Hills for the last time. We gathered with our fellow trainees at Dembwa, the little village at the foot of the hills where that segment of our odyssey had started. The day we drove out of the Taita Hills was a happy, happy day for me, though I have only the best memories of our stay there. The Taita people had shown us what it looked like to live as people after God's own heart.

And, just as he promised, the bus driver showed up.

For the final three days of our orientation, we debriefed with Brian and Jenny at Tsavo Safari Tent Camp in southeastern Kenya. To get there, we drove as far as we could on a dirt road. When that ended, we crossed the Athi River in an inflated raft, dodging crocodiles along the shore.

Our accommodations at Tsavo couldn't have been more different from those in Taita Hills. Running water! A shower! A toilet! Electricity! And your grandpa could stretch out on the bed. In the candle-lit dining room—rustic yet luxurious with thatched roof and walls—we dined leisurely at tables set with white linens, goblets, and six or seven implements around each china dinner plate. Soft-spoken, ever-gracious Kenyan waiters wore crisp white shirts, black bow ties, and sharp black trousers.

The dining room had only three walls; the fourth side opened to gardens, wildlife, and the heavy fragrance of a tropical night. One evening we watched a porcupine waddle by and disappear into the bush. With his quills, he must have stood about three feet tall. In the evening around a crackling campfire, we listened to then-familiar and beloved African night sounds.

Speaking of night sounds, one evening your grandpa and I had zipped the tent flap, turned off the light, and crawled under the mosquito net—when we heard a scream. A couple of seconds later, we heard the thump-thump-thump of someone's feet pounding the ground past our tent. By that time we had heard another scream, followed by another thump-thump-thump; and another scream and thump-thump-thump; and yet another scream and thump-thump-thump. Then everything grew silent. The next morning we learned that the shouts had come from the mouths of the four Baggés—Dick, Nancy, six-year-old Sarah, and four-year old Nathan—sprinting to their tent beyond ours. After dinner, they had run into a hippo in the dark.

In Tsavo, we wondered if we would hear lions outside our tent at night. At the turn of the last century during the railroad's construction from Mombasa to Nairobi, lions killed dozens of people in their tents at night in the Tsavo area. With that in mind, we wondered if we could sleep well. Would we hear lions roaring in the distance? Or, even scarier, would we hear the soft *pad, pad, pad* of their enormous paws outside our tent? However, each morning we awoke, intact and alive.

When our Kenya Safari course ended December 3, we returned to Nairobi. God had made possible what I had feared might be impossible—my survival of the orientation course—and throughout those three months, He showed me the goodness of both His people and Kenya.

The work for which we had come to Africa was about to begin. Your grandpa and I were eager to get started.

Lots of love,
Grandma Thomas

4

New Jobs, New Colleagues, New Places, New ... Just About Everything!

You have never been this way before.
Joshua 3:4

October 8, 1994
Nairobi, Kenya

Dear Maggie,

  After Kenya Safari, our boss gave us time to set up our offices and celebrate Christmas. A couple thousand years ago when a man told Jesus he'd follow Him, He cautioned the man, "Foxes have holes and birds of the air have nests, but the Son of Man has no place to lay his head" (Luke 9:58). We told God we'd follow Him to Africa but we wondered if, like that man, we would have no place to lay our heads. For the past three months, the "place to lay our heads" had been in our tent, but after Kenya Safari, we lived temporarily in an apartment owned by a colleague on furlough.

  In the city, I could again use my blow dryer and curling iron. I even got a haircut and perm. But best of all, we had a toilet. May God forever bless the inventor of toilets. I felt guilty, though, showering and flushing. They seemed downright sinful after the past three months when water had been so scarce.

With toilets, running water, and electricity, our lives seemed close to sublime, but we made trade-offs living in the city. No longer did we live in a quiet place, live a slow-paced lifestyle, or breathe clean air.

Our handsome apartment building, white stucco and red brick, stood three stories tall, and guards and gardeners kept the grounds tidy. The moment we walked in, I knew we'd like it. Our small unit consisted of a living and dining area, a kitchen, two bedrooms, one bathroom, and a small balcony. The kitchen looked functional with tile countertops and handmade cabinets painted antique white. The appliances, however, surprised me. Both the stove, called a cooker here, and the refrigerator were miniature compared to those in the States, but I had lived three months in the bush without either one so, despite their size, they looked delightful to me.

I was eager to make that apartment into our home. Since we didn't own a car, we walked the mile to and from the store, Nakumatt, and hand-carried groceries and supplies. To get there, we walked down a rocky (and sometimes muddy) hill and turned onto a red dirt path through a maize crop and across a railroad track. There we joined a sidewalk and from that point on, thick, wild traffic surrounded us and we inhaled billows of black exhaust. We walked around trash, spittle, and people grilling maize on wheel rims and charcoal.

Eventually we spotted Nakumatt, school-bus yellow, on the other side of Uhuru Highway, a six-lane road between the airport and downtown. Cars, lorries, and buses thundered by. In Kenya, pedestrians have no rights, but we needed to cross that highway. Your grandpa led the way, sprinting across the first three lanes of traffic. After a brief stop in the median, we scurried across the next three lanes.

I felt a thrill when I stepped into that store and—oh, such bliss!—I spotted a glass baking dish, the traditional nine-by-thirteen-inch, just like the one I'd used back home. I wanted that dish so badly, but I wondered if we should spend money on it. I told myself we should buy only things we absolutely needed, and besides, that dish would be heavy to carry home. I talked to your grandpa, though, and he urged me to buy it. In utter joy, I placed it in our cart and walked around that store picking out ingredients for one of our favorite recipes. I could hardly wait to get home and put that casserole together.

I heated up the oven, layered the ingredients in just the right order, pulled open the oven door, and slid the casserole in—but the door wouldn't close. I tried again, but it still wouldn't close. That oven was too small for a thirteen-inch baking dish.

Kenya Safari taught people how to live in the bush, which was helpful if they planned to do Bible translation in remote settings, but it didn't teach us how to live in the city. We had to figure out for ourselves—sometimes with help from coworkers, bless them—how to drive in city traffic, use a pay phone, shop downtown, buy produce, take care of bank business, go to the doctor, get a car repaired, and stay safe in the city.

We also needed to learn new terms. Signs warn car drivers, "No hooting allowed." On gates across driveways, metal signs warned *Mbwa Kali*—beware of the dog. Local people pronounce the word battery as "BAT-tree," and camera film as "FILL-um," and if you're all dressed up and look fabulous, they say you look "smott" (smart).

Just like on our orientation course, here in Nairobi we can't drink the water. We either filter or boil it. At this elevation, around 6,000 feet, we must boil water for twenty-three minutes before it is safe. Instead, your grandpa made us a filtering system using two ceramic filters, two plastic buckets (one for dirty tap water and the other for purified water), and a spigot. We could've bought a ready-made one, but they're expensive and smaller than the one your grandfather built.

I wash dishes with soapy water and rinse them in a bleach solution, and I soak fresh produce in potassium permanganate to kill amoebas and parasites. I sift bugs and larvae out of flour, and I wash rice before I cook it to get rid of insect parts, grass, and other unidentifiable foreign substances. For the first few months in Kenya, most food tasted unusual. Certain things tasted almost like they did back home, but not quite. Eventually, though, I got accustomed to the new flavors and now I can't remember which foods used to taste different.

Shortly after we finished our orientation course, we reported to the U.S. Embassy to fill out paperwork. While we waited our turn, I walked over to the restroom and pushed open the door. To my surprise, I found myself in an American-style public restroom. Up to that point, I hadn't noticed how different Kenyan restrooms are from American ones. That restroom had shiny white American-style toilets and pink tiled walls and floors. Each metal stall had a roll of American toilet tissue—soft and white, not coarse and bright blue or pink or yellow—and a flat stainless steel container attached to the wall that dispensed tissue toilet seat covers. Oh, what a delightful surprise!

During our first Christmas season in Nairobi, daytime temperatures reached the low eighties. We had no family nearby. Your grandpa and I hadn't bought gifts for each other or for relatives back home. We owned neither Christmas music nor decorations—I'd left them with your Aunt

Karen. Nakumatt sold a meager selection of decorations but not in my style. I left them at Nakumatt.

We received a Christmas card from our Karen Anne that read:

> It was so fun to look through and put up all your decorations and ornaments. They are so pretty and so special to me. But, it all has made me quite homesick. Somehow, it just doesn't look right. It doesn't feel quite right. I miss you very much. It isn't complete without you. I would cherish just one hug from you each right now, and a smile. All is going really well—I just miss you.

We knew that others around us missed their loved ones, too, and from our years in South America, we knew that at times like Christmas, missionaries get together and stand in for those loved ones. With that in mind, we prepared Christmas dinner for the young ladies who'd lived in the Thomas Estates in Maasai-land, the ones who almost felt like children of our own. They couldn't spend Christmas with their families so we served as a substitute Mom and Pop for them.

On the day after Christmas, people in Great Britain celebrate Boxing Day, and here in this former British colony, white Kenyans—people of British or European background who settled here during the colonial period—observe Boxing Day, too, with horse races, ostrich races, and dog shows. They also set up booths and sell food, art, and jewelry.

A couple of our colleagues invited us to the Boxing Day celebration. There, nibbling on strawberries and cream, we found ourselves no longer in the minority—throngs of white people surrounded us. White Kenyans have their own culture here, separate from that of native Kenyans. A cavalier, timelessly tweedy group, they make up the privileged class. They stick together, smoking and laughing, drinking and partying. Descendants of aristocratic early settlers, they own enormous tracts of land. White Kenyans have their suburban communities, country clubs, doctors, and favorite restaurant hangouts. As far as I can tell, they don't exclude Africans, but those places tend to be white places. White Kenyans speak in their clipped, crisp British way—no sloppy enunciations for them! We lazy-mouthed Americans drink "boddled wadder," but they drink "boTT-l'd WOE-Tah." We pronounce the word duty as "doody," but they say "deuty." We park our cars in a parking lot, but their drivers pull their motor vehicles into a "cah pahk." I couldn't help but notice their customs, speech patterns, and interactions with each other—a study of their unique culture within this culture.

The missionary community makes up another culture within this Kenyan culture. If we wish, we, too, can separate ourselves from everyday Kenyan situations and people. We can avoid downtown and the usual places Kenyans work and shop, and instead we can shop at the huge mall geared toward white Kenyans, foreign diplomats, tourists, and missionaries. Kenyans call whites *wazungu*, "people who build fences around themselves," and for good reason—we tend to separate ourselves into cliques. Sometimes it's okay to escape to that separate world if cross-cultural stresses get too great, but usually I avoid setting myself apart. I prefer to shop where Kenyans shop and live where Kenyans live.

Day by day, Maggie, I try to picture your daddy and Aunt Karen back home. What are they wearing? What are they doing and where are they going? Do they eat well? Do they get enough sleep? Mostly I hope their hearts, minds, and spiritual lives are strong. I pray that they're at peace. However, I don't know—really know—how well they're coping with their parents living on the far side of the planet. Usually I'm sure they're okay. Sometimes, though, I worry, and must pause and tell God I will trust Him to care for them every moment.

One day shortly after we moved into our borrowed apartment, we received a letter from your daddy, written on November 21, 1993, while we lived in the Taita Hills. Your Aunt Karen had flown to Los Angeles to visit your parents. At the end of her visit, your daddy wrote,

> We sent Karen off on her way. Poor girl. I love her so much, but things are hard for her now. She hugged us and started to cry. It is all starting to take a toll on her with mom and dad in Africa. It is no wonder in the world to me that she cried. All that at just twenty-two years old. It just makes me very sad. I feel like crying myself sometimes. I do not know what stops me, but something always does. I guess that I just cry on the inside. I felt very spiritually uneasy today. I went for a walk and talked with God and I know that He will bring the indescribable peace back, but I did not feel it today. When I recognize all of the sorrow in life, I feel heavy in my heart. I sometimes wish that God would hurry up and make all things right again: no more sorrow, no more pain, no

> more darkness. But I still can't figure out how He will make up for all of the pain that has already occurred. I will have to leave that one up to Him. It still haunts me though, on days like this.

When I read such words, I reel. What am I doing here? How can this be God's plan for me and my kids?

My thoughts returned to our first Sunday in Nairobi when a Kenyan man reported to the congregation about his ministry. The church had sent him as a missionary to Philadelphia—in America! I nearly fell off my chair. Something seemed terribly backward. My church in America sent me to Africa, and this African church sent him to America. Both he and I wrenched ourselves from our families and cultures and spent all that money on plane tickets—but wait! Why couldn't I stay in the States and he stay in Kenya? It didn't make sense.

True, from a human perspective it didn't make sense. However, God's thoughts and ways are much higher than ours. I reminded myself that I gave God time and opportunity to keep us home if working in Africa was not His will for us. He could have kept us home in a number of ways—Wycliffe could have spotted something they didn't like in our applications, or God could have kept us home, at least temporarily, if we hadn't raised financial support. Instead, He removed every potential obstacle. He assured me He saw no reason for me to stay home. He sent us to Africa with His blessing. Only He knew all the good reasons He sent us here.

A few days later, we received another letter from your daddy—written while we lived with the Mwakodis in Taita Hills—a group letter written to family members and friends. He said,

> We received two great letters from my parents today with those fancy stamps from Kenya! It was fascinating to read. It gave me so many mental pictures of their daily lives. Up until now, I have slowly been piecing together a strange idea of how they live. I suppose it was sketchy to me because it was very dynamic and unstable to them. They were in such a training mode. But this time, it sounds like they have real adventures and challenges that they are tackling and I feel like I have a much better idea of what they are up to now. My dad seems to have a lot of responsibility and is doing all sorts of amazing things like four-wheeling people all over the African wilderness in a

Toyota Land Cruiser with no clutch. I know God is giving them the adventure of their lives and they are hanging on like rodeo clowns: giving it their best and loving nearly every minute of it.

I'd never thought of myself as a rodeo clown. A rodeo clown! Quaint I ain't! But, then! Then, the most important part of his letter came next:

> Jill and I are on track to bring to life the old saying "MT and the 'Tree for Three!" That's right folks, Jill is pretty sure that she is pregnant. She took a little home test two days ago. We even started a video. "What?" I keep saying subconsciously to myself, but this was no accident. We were trying, and hey, it works. The end of July, 1994, is the guess. I threw in the year in case the poor person who reads this is ever confused between the gestation period of humans as compared to say, elephants.

A baby! We would soon have a grandchild! Our joy knew no bounds! Your dad also wrote,

> It is true that only three things are eternal: (1) God; (2) God's Word; and (3) the souls of men, and that to the extent that we invest in these three things we are investing in eternity. Everything else fades away into meaninglessness. I hope and pray that I can teach this truth to my children, that they may always live wisely.

October 10, 1994
Nairobi, Kenya

Dear Maggie,
We can walk from our apartment to the office in just five minutes, through a quiet neighborhood, but I'm afraid to walk alone because of Nairobi's crime rate. A friend told me that if she suspects someone might mug her, she looks him in the eye and acts confident. Looking Africans in the eye goes against their culture but because of that, I suppose it gets their attention and serves as a warning. Despite her advice, I'm still

uncomfortable—though I'll probably get over it—so I plan my schedule around your grandpa's and we walk to work together.

The downhill road to our office is a narrow dirt track with sharp boulders poking through the soil. I don't know whether God placed those outcroppings on that hill when He formed the crust of the earth, or if mankind dumped them there, but man has left them here in the capital city of this advanced and stable African nation. During rainy season, the road turns into an oozing, slippery, eroding mess with deep furrows. In the dry season, those muddy ruts turn into solid formations that, along with jagged stones, make driving a car a longer process than walking.

You might remember that our offices are part of the BTL compound—Bible Translation and Literacy—the Kenyan organization that partners with Wycliffe. (We stayed in their guesthouse our first couple of weeks in Kenya before our orientation.) Japheth, a gentle, shy soul, grooms BTL's gardens and sweeps the grounds. He fashions a broomstick from a tree branch and, to make broom straw, he attaches leafy branches of herbs. He uses that to sweep the grounds and those branches give off a spicy, herbal fragrance. When we arrive each morning, Japheth's quick smile lights his face, he pauses from his gardening, and greets us in almost a whisper, "Gooood mawning to you."

At the beginning of January, your grandpa and I jumped into our new jobs. In Wycliffe lingo, we fill support roles. Your grandpa and I are too old to start the years of training that Bible translators need but, like lots of other people, we aren't too old to fill behind-the-scenes roles that help Bible translators carry out their specialized jobs.

Your grandpa explains support work this way: In the Army, for every soldier on the front line, ten soldiers fill support roles—for example, doctors, janitors, mail carriers, and mechanics. It takes a whole team of people to enable one soldier to do his job on the front line. In Wycliffe, translators are like soldiers on the front line, and support personnel keep them there—teachers, secretaries, pilots, airplane mechanics, administrators, doctors, nurses, computer specialists, librarians, and many more. We form a team committed to the Great Commission—going into all the world. Whatever our role, we are privileged to help feed the hungry, comfort the sorrowing, clothe the needy, empower the weak, and care for the sick.

As a support worker, your grandpa makes sure that, across the continent, children of both front-liners and support workers receive an adequate education, one that prepares them to return to schools in their home countries (mostly European and North American countries) when their parents return home on furlough and when the youngsters are old enough for college.

I work in Communications. My responsibility, as a journalist, covers the same broad swath of Africa that your grandpa's job does, some twenty-three nations. I help generate materials for publications such as Wycliffe-USA's *In Other Words* magazine and similar publications produced in Canada, Australia, the United Kingdom, and several European countries.

We had much to learn about working with our staff and within BTL, but our colleagues helped us transition into our jobs and routines. After Kenya Safari, we received dinner invitations from many people on our staff. Since we'd learned the importance of visiting at length with others and asking about their families, we practiced that in each home we visited. At one such dinner party, after we answered and asked questions about hometowns and families, I asked a Swiss colleague about her family, but she looked down and didn't say a word. She appeared flustered, and her long pause left all of us uncomfortable. Eventually she lifted her head and told us briefly about her family in Switzerland. A few months later, someone told us that in Swiss culture it's rude to ask about a person's family until you've known him or her for a long time. (So much for our training. Quaint I ain't.)

Your grandpa and I talked often about your Aunt Karen, and by then he understood my worry about leaving her. One evening, it seemed like God walked in, sat down with us in our living room, and pulled a sweet surprise out of His sleeve. It was as if He asked, "Why don't you invite Karen to visit you during her school's summer vacation?" Great idea! Why hadn't we thought of that earlier? We splurged—we called her long-distance—and asked her to think about it. Before long, we received an e-mail from her:

> I just talked to you a few hours ago. Thanks so much for calling. I am sorry if I have worried you by not writing more. I have wanted and tried to write a bunch lately and I have failed most times because I haven't been able to read through my tears. But don't get me wrong, I am not miserable in the least. In fact, everything is going quite well overall. I just do miss you very much and I get frustrated when I have to try to explain everything in letters. I wanted to say much more on the phone this morning. I was so thrilled that you called but I didn't want to cry. I really, really want to come see you this summer. Can I stay for a long time? I know I won't want

to leave.

Karen seemed to feel better over the next couple of months, mostly, I suspect, because she knew she could visit us.

We enjoyed living in that borrowed apartment but after two months, we hit the road again—well, actually, the skies—to carry out duties in several African countries. Your grandpa, though, had fallen sick again with digestive problems. The lab hadn't diagnosed his problem but the doctor gave him strong antibiotics, hoping they'd work. On February 9, we set out. We wouldn't return until March 19, five and a half weeks later.

In much of Africa, airlines don't put checked baggage on the plane. Instead, for security reasons I suppose, they place luggage on the ground near the plane and when they open the gates, passengers swarm across the tarmac to identify their bags. Only then will airline employees load bags onto the plane.

Considering that, and considering that airlines don't issue seat assignments, your grandpa and I developed a procedure: I put my carry-on bag under one arm, put his under the other arm, elbowed my way across the tarmac, climbed the stairs, and scurried to find two seats together. In the meantime, your grandpa identified our suitcases on the tarmac, waited until the man put them on the plane, and then climbed up the stairs to find me. It worked.

I recall a few highlights—or lowlights—of that trip. Along the way, we flew low over the Congo River. I read Conrad's *Heart of Darkness* decades ago but never dreamed I'd one day see the Congo River! We experienced *harmattan* all over West Africa. The air appears smoggy but actually, fine sand fills the air, blown from the Sahara Desert, so thick it sometimes blots out the sun. In each airport on that journey across Africa, we stood in long lines while officials gave us body pat-downs, checked our immunization records, stamped forms in our passports, signed those forms, sold us postage-like stamps, pasted them into our passports, charged us for visas, stamped visas into our passports, and thoroughly inspected our luggage, once we found it.

We had only one problem on our long trip. At the visa checkpoint in one airport, a man ushered us into a back room. A uniformed official closed the door behind us, fixed his dark, defiant eyes on grandpa, and told him how much money he had to pay—the cost of three visas instead of the two we needed. We recognized our precarious vulnerability. So did the official. Your grandpa handed him our money. He took it, reached into his back pocket, took out his wallet, and put our money in—looking grandpa in the eye the whole time. Then he told us we could leave.

We had heard stories about the Douala airport in Cameroon, through which we traveled on the way to the capital city, Yaoundé. Our colleagues warned us about lines, fees, conmen, frequent confusion, and the need to carry out each step in order—all in French. Our soon-to-be director for Cameroon, Paul, had written out detailed procedures for us. Bless his heart! We followed them one by one and made it through each procedure in that sweltering airport.

Sweat ran down our faces and our bodies so, while we awaited our connecting flight, we stepped into the only air-conditioned place, a little café. My heart sank when I looked at the menu and read that a soft drink cost the equivalent of $2.50 U.S. It seemed a shame to spend that much money on a drink so, instead of buying two, we shared one there in the blessed cool.

For breakfast in Cameroon, and in most of West Africa, people eat freshly baked baguettes (skinny loaves of French bread) with jam. Vendors sold them on the streets, carrying them on their heads and under their arms. I prayed Nancy's prayer, *Oh, God, help our immune systems to work well!* We learned a helpful hint in Cameroon that served us well throughout West Africa. To kill germs on a baguette, we turned on the burner of the guestroom's gas cooker, rotated the surface of the loaf over the flame, and—*voilà*—we had a sanitized breakfast. Here are a few other memories from Cameroon: we listened to mourners drum all night, watched "Good Morning America" live at three in the afternoon, and received word to cancel our trip to Ghana due to ethnic clashes.

After a heavily scheduled week in Yaoundé, we flew out at daybreak and returned to the Douala airport. We stood in line after line in the terminal, sealed up and oppressive with heat. Dehydration set in and I needed a drink, but we didn't want to lose our place in line outside the luggage-examination office. After a long wait, we figured out it wouldn't open until eleven o'clock, even though staff worked inside and throngs of passengers waited outside its door. Once we realized we had plenty of time, we grabbed our bags and returned to that air-conditioned café. During our week in Yaoundé, Cameroon devalued its money. That meant soft drinks cost half as much as the week before, so we ordered two. I'll long remember the relief and refreshment we found in that little café.

We didn't know it then, but it would be a long time before we'd reach our final destination that day, Burkina Faso. After our first stop in Douala, we stopped in Nigeria, Togo, and then Ivory Coast. There we disembarked so a cleaning crew and new flight crew could board. We stood in long lines, waiting and sweating and dripping, to process through checkpoints. Then we stood in long lines, waiting and sweating and dripping, to re-board.

Well after dark on Valentine's Day, 1994, after we had traveled through five steamy airports, we disembarked and stepped into a sultry little airport in Ouagadougou (pronounced WAH-gah-DOO-goo), Burkina Faso, West Africa. Weary, sticky, and impatient, your grandpa and I hovered over the luggage conveyor belt. So far, our bags had not appeared.

While we waited, I stretched up on tiptoe and searched beyond the partitions to look for a white face—a colleague from SIL (*Société Internationale de Linguistique*, Wycliffe's sister organization in much of West Africa). In each country an SIL person met us, someone who knew that country's customs procedures, someone who would help us push through throngs of porters, bring us currency for that country, and drive us to the SIL center. We'd had a long day, and I searched the crowd for that special person so we could have a much-needed glass of water, take a cool shower, and fall into bed. We'd left the guesthouse in Cameroon fifteen hours earlier. Surely, one of our colleagues would arrive soon to care for us, like a substitute mom or dad. That was the SIL way.

When our bags showed up, we endured the familiar routine: officials jostled, poked, patted, inspected, pushed, questioned, and laughed at us—all in French. Then a smiling, uniformed African waved us through the final gate. Free at last!

But, where was the SIL person?

I looked through the glass doors and into the night. No lights lit the walkway or parking lot.

Your grandpa and I took a deep breath and braced ourselves—we knew what awaited us. We pushed through the doors and out into the night. A mob of porters pressed against us. They shouted. They waved their arms. They tugged at our bags, desperate to earn money. We almost staggered from the crush, the heat, and the weight of our luggage. Both of us scanned the crowd. No white faces.

Then we heard one shout above the others. "Seal? Seal?"

In French-speaking West Africa, "seal" is the way locals pronounce SIL. In a flash, both Grandpa and I assumed SIL sent this man. After all, SIL employs many Africans.

"Seal?" the man called again.

"*Oui!*" Grandpa called back over the shouts of the others. The man nodded.

We pried ourselves out of the grasping hands of other porters and pushed through the crowd. When we reached the man, he snatched two of our bags and swept across the parking lot, enveloped in blackness. Grandpa followed close behind with his laptop computer and carry-on bag. I ran to keep up, lugging my carry-ons.

But this didn't feel right. I stopped and turned around. I examined the crowd for an SIL person—a white person—but no one stepped forward.

I jogged across the unlit pavement to catch up.

"Dave," I called in a whisper. "How do you know SIL sent this guy for us?"

Preoccupied, he talked with the man in part French, part English, and part hand gestures.

With a knot in my stomach, I was following the two through the dark parking lot when abruptly the porter stopped and, in the shadows, I saw a car, the only car in sight, a rusty, dented car—our taxi. It looked like a demolition derby car. A man inside jumped out and joined the conversation.

"Seal," Grandpa said. "You know Seal?"

"*Oui, monsieur,*" the taxi driver nodded. I heard eagerness in his voice.

"Dave," I tried again. "How do you know they sent this guy to pick us up? Dozens of SIL people come through the airport—maybe he made a lucky guess."

"It'll be fine, it'll be fine," he brushed me off and shuffled through his papers to find SIL's address.

I persisted, "We could wait a while for an SIL person. Maybe we got through customs faster than he expected, and maybe he'll be here in a minute. Or, we could telephone to see if they really sent this guy. We have the phone number."

He showed the driver his scrap of paper with SIL's address. "You know Seal? You know how to find Seal?"

The taxi driver refused to look at the paper, and that worried me. "*Oui, monsieur, je comprend le Seal.*" He claimed to know SIL.

"But I don't have any CFA," Grandpa spoke slowly in English, "no money." The men looked at him, uncomprehending.

I sighed, more apprehensive with every moment. And I was disappointed. An SIL person should have brought us local currency. I turned again and searched the crowd.

"I have no money!" The men still didn't understand.

The porter paused and then asked in halting English, "How many francs you have?"

"None," we both waved our hands back and forth. "No francs."

The porter sighed. He realized he'd get no money for carrying our bags.

"But," Grandpa turned to the taxi driver, "if you take us to Seal, someone there will pay you."

"Okay." The driver bent down and opened the taxi's trunk. The porter spoke in rapid French to the driver while he tossed in our bags. They whisked us into the back seat and slammed the door. The porter turned and disappeared into the night.

I gulped hard. *Oh, Lord,* I prayed, *take good care of us.*

The driver hopped in, yanked his door closed, and turned the key. My heart nearly stopped at the noise—a grinding, scraping, shuddering, clanging noise. Surely, such a car would never start. However, after three tries it gasped, sputtered, and coughed to life. It jerked and chugged across the vacant parking lot, then crawled onto the road.

The taxi lurched and rattled through the night. Cars, motorbikes, pedestrians, and bicycles clogged the road. I gasped when only a few feet away, a bicycle with no headlight came straight at us, driving down the middle of our lane. Our driver jerked to a stop, the bicycle turned in front of us, and we once again clattered down the road.

After about ten minutes, it seemed we had left the most populated part of town. I began to keep track of our surroundings. Sure enough, I counted fewer pedestrians, fewer cars, and fewer streetlights. Where was the driver taking us?

Suddenly I remembered stories about con men who victimized naïve foreigners, took them to out-of-the-way places, robbed them, or sometimes killed them. Our U.S. passports alone could sell for $12,000 on the black market. We wore watches. And gold wedding bands. We carried a laptop computer. I hadn't thought of us in those terms before but, with a jolt, I realized we were worth thousands of dollars and surrounded by masses of people who earned only a few hundred dollars in an entire year. My heart sank—we were so vulnerable! And we were at the mercy of that driver. My stomach churned.

The car wheezed and belched and took us ever deeper into the night. I could keep quiet no longer. I leaned over and whispered my fears to your grandfather. He nodded. "Yeah, I thought of that, too."

I had hoped he'd say it was just my imagination. I wanted him to say something to put my worries to rest, but no—he felt uneasy, too! I fought off a temptation to panic.

"Let's wait a while longer," he whispered. "We'll see what happens."

I stared at the back of the driver's head and prayed, *Lord, if this man has evil plans, please change his mind.* On and on I prayed.

Not long before we started our trek across Africa, I read Joshua 3:4, "You have never been this way before." I had a keen awareness that, immersed in cultures altogether new to us, potential difficulties awaited us. And now, in Ouagadougou, I found myself in the midst of a scary situation. I thought of Exodus 33:14 in which God said, "My Presence will go with you." *Oh,*

Lord, thank You. I sensed His presence, but I worried nevertheless because I didn't know that driver's plans.

The street grew darker. I could hardly breathe as I thought about what might await us. I prayed harder. I thought of friends and relatives back home who prayed for us. At that moment, they could not know our specific needs, but in the midst of my panic it occurred to me that God knew.

A few minutes passed and then a heavy, putrid odor filled the air. I covered my nose and choked out, "What a sickening smell!"

About two seconds later, we turned to each other and grinned. "The tannery!"

A lady named Anita, who lived and worked in Ouagadougou, had attended meetings with us a few weeks earlier in Nairobi. She told us about a tannery in Ouagadougou and said that breezes carried its bad odor toward the nearby SIL center.

So, we were driving toward the SIL center after all!

The taxi driver turned down a lumpy, bumpy dirt road and soon, in the headlights, I spotted the familiar SIL logo on a gate. *Thank You, Lord, thank You!*

Psalm 146:9 says that God watches over aliens and frustrates the plans of the wicked. Your grandpa and I were aliens in Ouagadougou, and God had watched over us. I don't know if that taxi driver had evil plans, but if so, God frustrated them.

On the other hand, maybe God gave us that taxi driver to protect us. The day before we left on our trip, I read Luke 22:43, in Amy Carmichael's *Edges of His Ways*, about an angel who came from heaven and strengthened Jesus. She wrote, "His love understands and He sends an angel to strengthen us."[1] Perhaps God sent us that specific taxi driver—like an angel—to keep us safe from other drivers who might have had evil intentions.

Only God knows the heart and plans of that taxi driver, whether good or evil, but I had just experienced first-hand that God had watched over us and brought us safely to the SIL center.

Inside the gate, the guard on duty phoned an SIL lady named Sarah who lived with her family within the walls of the compound. Despite the late hour, Sarah came to our rescue and paid the taxi driver. He charged more than a reasonable price so she questioned him. He replied, "But they have white skin."

Sarah told us she didn't know why the center host hadn't met us and asked us to wait while she asked him which guestroom he had assigned us.

She hurried back with a key. "He's not home, but you're in Room Two."

She led us across the darkened center to the guesthouse. At Room Two, she rattled the key in the lock, then again, and again, but the lock wouldn't open.

"I don't know what's going on here, but why don't you go in the guesthouse kitchen, right over there. In the refrigerator you'll find cold filtered water." She hurried away.

A drink of cold water sounded heavenly. We were so hot and so tired. When the plane landed in Ouagadougou, the flight attendant announced the temperature: eighty-nine degrees. That kitchen felt a good ten degrees hotter than outside. I downed my second glass of cold water and felt almost giddy at the thought of taking a cool shower.

Sarah hurried back and rattled the keys at Room Two again. From inside came a sleepy voice. "I'm in here. What do you want?"

Surprised, Sarah called out, "What are you doing in there? This room is signed out to Dave and Linda Thomas."

"When I arrived, someone else was in my room so the center host put me in this room."

Sarah's forehead wrinkled. She sighed, turned, and hurried away, promising to find us a room. We considered her another angel God sent to care for us—the second angel in one evening!

We returned to the kitchen and waited a long time. When Sarah came back, she sighed again. "The host is gone, and I have no idea when he'll be back. I've checked and rechecked and, you're not going to believe this, but we don't have a room for you. There's a conference going on and all our rooms are occupied."

I glanced at my watch: ten-thirty. Our journey had started eighteen sweltering hours earlier and I felt ready to drop. I looked at the kitchen floor. I thought I could sleep even there.

Then your grandpa spoke up. "Maybe we can wait a while longer for the host to return."

"I don't know what good that will do," Sarah said. "We have no more rooms."

We decided to wait anyway. That dear Sarah walked us to her apartment and served us ice-cold lemonade.

At eleven o'clock, she said we had waited long enough. She had a plan. We followed her to an office that housed a stack of mattresses. Grandpa picked one up. "Follow me," Sarah said. "You're going to sleep in my husband's office."

We moved a couple of chairs and plopped the mattress on the concrete floor. Sarah hurried off and returned with sheets and towels. "We have no showers here because this is an office building, but if you go down the hall and around the corner, you'll find a toilet and sink." The shower I longed for would not happen, but I did get the blessed drink of cold water I craved, and we had a "place to lay our heads."

The next day the temperature climbed to nearly 110 degrees in the shade—and people said hot season had not yet arrived. Mid-afternoon, we moved into our own room and took a cool shower. It felt so good!

I have two other lasting memories of Ouagadougou, or Ouaga for short. First, after a short while, everything turned the orange-tan color of the sand, from clothes to cats to car interiors. And, second, Grandpa and I watched a crew of Muslim men erect a building, laboring all day without food or water in observance of their holy month of Ramadan. We agonized for them, amazed that they could endure that cruel sub-Saharan sun until after sunset when they could eat and drink.

From Ouaga we flew to Niger, most of which is located in the Sahara Desert. Much of the remaining land is located in the semi-arid Sahel, a band along the Sahara's southern edge where the Sahara encroaches more and more. Drought frequently poses problems for Niger's subsistence farmers and leaves it one of the poorest and least developed countries in the world. The official language is French, but many people speak Arabic or one of several indigenous languages. Muslims make up 80 percent of the population and most of the remaining 20 percent practice traditional religions. Only a few Christians live in the cities.

Our work kept us busy in Niger's capital, Niamey—where camels ambled alongside the city's cars and trucks—but we also squeezed in a little regional culture. We attended a local Sunday evening church service, shopped briefly in one of the city's open-air markets, and enjoyed Niamey's cuisine. We tasted our first camel-milk cheese in Niamey, and one evening we dined on goat-meat kebabs on the banks of the Niger River at sunset—the sun blood-red through the sand-filled *harmattan* air.

We were surprised—and somewhat amused, but mostly dismayed—that the airline cancelled our flight from Niamey back to Ouaga; instead, they filled the plane with pilgrims and flew them to Mecca for the Haj. We *needed* to get back to Ouagadougou so we could catch our flight to Togo—sometimes people wait a week if they miss a flight!—so, instead, we drove to Ouaga, seven hours through the grim Sahel, in a small four-wheel-drive vehicle with three children (ages three to seven), five adults (one in her eighth month of pregnancy), plus luggage.

From there we flew to Togo, a narrow, tropical, sub-Saharan nation on the Atlantic Ocean. With daytime temperatures around 110 degrees in the shade, a shower sure felt good at 10:00 PM when the water came on! We worked in both the capital city, Lome, and about 250 miles upcountry in Kara where we met with coworkers from Great Britain, Germany, Switzerland, America, Sweden, France, Singapore, Canada, Australia, and Holland.

After Togo, we flew to Dakar, Senegal. I still remember stepping out of the plane when we arrived—moist ocean breezes enveloped us and reminded us of home. Fresh, cool air felt especially nice after several weeks in sub-Saharan desert. Dakar sits on the Cape Verde Peninsula that juts out into the Atlantic, the westernmost point of the African continent. Dakar's unique music, food, and culture have developed over time, a result of influences from North Africa, Arab countries, and French colonization. Ninety-five percent of the Senegalese practice the Muslim faith, 4 percent practice Christianity, and the remaining 1 percent practice animism.

At the end of our trip, we calculated that we'd waited thirty-four hours in airports prior to departures. We didn't even try to count the hours we spent in customs or waiting for luggage. When we returned to Nairobi, we didn't have a place to call home. First we stayed in the apartment of our colleagues Marvin and Joyce Hyde for ten days while they traveled across Africa on business. When they returned, we spent three nights at a friend's apartment while she attended a retreat in Mombasa. On April 4, the day before she returned, our Kiambere apartment came available. We hadn't lived in a home of our own for nine months and five days, and we'd found forty-eight different "places to lay our heads." But hey, quaint I ain't.

Our home in Kiambere Estates—a two-story red brick townhouse with three bedrooms and two bathrooms—includes a miniature yard, front and back, and a tall fence for security. With the exception of the slums, sturdy iron bars cover doors and windows in Nairobi, including ours, to discourage crime. Businesses, apartment compounds, and private residents put up tall walls or fences and hire security companies and guards day and night. At Kiambere, for example, several guards stand duty, and they open the gate only for residents or people with legitimate business. (The name of one of our Kiambere guards is Wycliffe. What a coincidence.)

An abundance of tropical plants grow in our yard—cannas, bamboo, honeysuckle, plumbago, hibiscus, jasmine, split-leaf philodendron (which we babied as a houseplant back home), and geraniums, ten feet tall or more.

With palms, ferns, flowering vines, banana trees, and lush undergrowth, the Kiambere grounds resemble a tropical arboretum. Towering jacaranda trees burst into purple blooms in October even before their leaves open. Their blossoms drift to the ground like a layer of purple snow. The bushy moonflower, one of my favorites, has large trumpet-like flowers that release heavy perfume at dusk. Mimosa trees also grow here, with lacy, fern-like leaves and red-pink blossoms that resemble silky pom-poms.

Various bird species live in our neighborhood. I haven't learned their names yet, but I often see a tiny red one, and sometimes I see a brown-orange bird with a small body and a sweeping tail about twelve inches long. I love to wake up in the morning to the birdsongs.

One bird's song I don't enjoy, though. A couple of peacocks live within Kiambere and they make a shrill honking sound. One day my brother called from the States and the peacocks made such a racket that he could hear them over the phone.

When we moved into our townhouse, I heard the echo of Brian and Jenny's voices from Kenya Safari encouraging us to have something personal to make a house a home. Missionaries often live in someone else's home for a while, like we did, but families feel more settled if they have a photo, a tablecloth, a blanket—that special something that signifies "home."

With that in mind, I made a bedspread and curtains, but first I bought an old-fashioned treadle sewing machine like my Grandma MacDermid's. When I was a girl and she taught me to use her old treadle machine, little did she or I know that I'd use those skills to set up an apartment in Kenya.

Our home has a fireplace! Here on the equator, I never expected to find—or need—a home with a fireplace. However, because of Nairobi's elevation, around 6,000 feet, during winter months, May through September, neither our home nor office gets above sixty-six degrees because we have no heating systems. Walls, floors, and ceilings, all made of cement and stone, hold in the coolness. One evening I built a fire in our fireplace, pulled my chair up to it, stretched out my cold feet, and delved into a good book—only to discover later that the fire melted the bottom of my slippers.

The apartment we borrowed briefly after Kenya Safari came with a househelper, Elizabeth, who cleaned our place two days a week. In Kenya, a large segment of the population lives in poorer conditions than most Americans can imagine, and those desperate throngs yearn to find employment. In the Kenyans' eyes, all white people are wealthy (and we are, compared to them, though living on a missionary's income makes us look poor compared to our friends and family back home), and they believe that if we have money but don't hire them, we're greedy—one of the worst sins a person can commit.

We Americans believe that our money belongs to us and that we can spend it as we wish, and we're offended when people ask us for money. However, 1 John 3:17–18 says, "If anyone has material possessions and sees his brother in need but has no pity on him, how can the love of God be in him? ... Let us not love with words or tongue but with actions and in truth." We Americans nod in agreement with the philosophy of those words and perhaps we give money to causes we deem worthy, but we don't look at those verses the way Africans do. They observe them in a more literal way than we do, and I suspect God intended for us Westerners to do so, too.

With that in mind, when we moved into our Kiambere townhouse, we hired Elizabeth to work here two days a week. I'm pleased to employ her because, as a widow with two young girls, she needs a job. One day I brought home a flimsy bag of rice and it sprang a leak just as I walked into the kitchen. About a quarter of a cup spilled on the floor, but I figured that amount wasn't worth the hassle of cleaning so I swept it into the dustpan. When Elizabeth saw my intentions, she hurried over and politely intercepted my journey to the trash. "Here, let me clean that for you," she offered. "We mustn't waste any of it." While she sorted through the grains, I replayed her gentle words in my mind. Even a quarter of a cup of rice mattered to her.

We Americans have a saying, "Every little bit helps," and in Kenya people say, *Haba na haba, hujaza kibaba*, which translates something like "Little by little, fills the measure." Even a small bit of food helps feed a hungry person.

I'm thankful for Elizabeth's help because she frees me to carry out my ministry. If I had to scrub laundry by hand in the bathtub, hang it on the line to dry, do the ironing, mop dusty floors two or three times a week, soak vegetables, make meals from scratch, and keep the apartment clean, my hours at the office would be reduced significantly. Employing Elizabeth, then, is a win-win situation for both of us. We provide her lunch, pay her the standard wage—about two dollars a day—and help with medical bills.

Elizabeth belongs to the Kikuyu tribe, a group known for motivation and hard work, and I can trust her not to steal anything. Sometimes she takes medicine, which she pronounces MED-sen, but she always tells us when she does. She has a sunny disposition and a bright smile. While she works, she sings worship songs in Swahili or Kikuyu. Even though I don't recognize most of the words, I know she's singing praises to God and they always bless my heart.

We get dirty every day from dust, smoke, and exhaust, so we always have a pile of laundry. At first I scrubbed it by hand in the bathtub (usually with Elizabeth's help), but one day a colleague advertised an old-fashioned wringer washer for sale at a reasonable price. I snatched it up. In my childhood, our family couldn't afford a new-fangled spin washer so we used a second-hand wringer washer. Since I'd been responsible to wash laundry on Saturdays, I knew how to use such a machine in Kenya. Just think! God prepared me all those years ago.

Our Swahili teacher during Kenya Safari, a young Kenyan named Enoch, recently stopped by to visit your grandpa. He wants to earn money to pay for university courses so your grandpa thought up some jobs for him. Now Enoch works in our yard half of each Saturday and teaches your grandpa Swahili a couple of hours a week.

Well, Maggie, I'd better go to bed because the neighbor's roosters will crow early tomorrow morning.

Love,
Grandma

5

Jambo, Mama! Buy Here! Goooood Price!

October 12, 1994
Nairobi, Kenya

Dear Maggie,

    We finally own a car! It's little, and it's old, but it's red! For a long time I knew it reminded me of something—but what? One day it dawned on me. Our car's side mirrors are not mounted where we'd expect—they sit toward the front of the car, almost over the headlights, like tusks at the end of a warthog's snout! Our squat little car looks like a warthog! I call it The Little Red Warthog.

    Yes, we have a car! However, I refuse to drive. For one thing, car accidents kill more missionaries here than anything else. Secondly, compared to what I'm accustomed to, people drive in aggressive, non-traditional ways. If you need to drive over the kerb (curb) to reach your destination, why not? And in Kenya, the biggest vehicles, like buses and lorries, have the right of way and they bully their way through traffic. Driving includes honking, and sometimes hollering, and every time I approach one of Nairobi's many roundabouts—traffic circles—I get confused. The entire scene discombobulates this small-town gal's sense of driving etiquette.

    Right here in the heart of this nation's capital, wooden carts transport produce on city streets and highways. Donkeys sometimes pull those carts, but people who can't afford a donkey must pull the cart themselves. Pulling a cart on a busy highway must be scary for them, and I applaud them for working hard in the best way they can. Nevertheless, carts travel slowly and cause traffic backups.

And have I told you about Nairobi's potholes? Some roads have more potholes than pavement. I suspect that if your grandpa had to choose one word to describe Nairobi, he'd say "potholes." Counting the city's potholes resembles God's way of counting when He told Abraham how many children he'd have. In Nairobi's case, God might say, "Look up at the heavens and count the stars. So shall your potholes be." People in America or Europe would never believe us if we tried to describe these roads.

We drive on the left side of the road here—like the British—and that's another reason I don't drive here. The driver sits on the right side of the car and uses his left hand to shift gears. Oh, yes, that's another reason I won't drive in Nairobi—most cars are stick shift. I never got comfortable driving stick shift in the States and can't imagine doing it left-handed in hectic traffic here in Nairobi.

When I travel beside your grandpa, sometimes I pretend I'm the driver—I rehearse in case I ever do drive. This imaginary driving has shown me that even as a passenger, by instinct I react opposite to the way I should. For example, if I see a car coming toward me in my lane, my instinct is to swerve to the right. In the States that would be the correct thing to do, but it's the worst thing in Kenya. Here I should swerve to the left. I simply don't trust my instincts, but your grandpa, bless his heart, drives me in the Little Red Warthog when I need to go places.

A white Kenyan named Diane owns a beauty salon that's almost identical to beauty shops in the States. She charges more than most shops, but some of my friends and I have Diane cut our hair because she's careful about hygiene and understands our hair texture and the styles we like. In Kenya, or at least in Diane's shop, one employee gives a customer a shampoo and another cuts and styles. So, let me tell you about Rosie, a short little gal, maybe five feet tall and almost that wide. Her ready smile lights up her face and, like so many Kenyans, she speaks in almost a whisper. Rosie gives a shampoo like nothing I've experienced before—she gives me a thorough head massage. Barely taller than the sink, she stands there and performs wonders. I always give her an extra big tip, and that makes her smile even more. She's a bright spot in my life.

Grandpa also drives me to the grocery store—small, dark, and dusty. Here we have no supermarkets with bright lights, wide aisles, and abundant selections. We shop at a small greengrocer's for produce and eggs and at a butchery for meat. Many butcheries don't have refrigeration so they have a strong odor.

Nairobi has a modern shopping mall called Yaya. Although it is miniature compared to malls in America, Yaya's shops offer merchandise we can't find other places. Shopping at Yaya almost feels like stepping into another country, but even there we buy our groceries at one store, produce at a greengrocer's, and meat and fish in a butchery. Yaya's butchery, unlike most others, refrigerates its meat. It also sells frozen meat and fish—a rarity here. I almost feel giddy shopping in a non-stinky butchery with such an enormous selection.

We also can shop at *dukas* that line neighborhood streets and country roads. Little stalls built of scrap lumber and corrugated tin, we find them almost anywhere people can find a bit of land; even ten feet by twelve is large enough. *Dukas* sell limited stock—a few tiny three-sided cartons of milk (unrefrigerated); miniature boxes of washing-up powder (laundry detergent); individual rolls of toilet tissue; matches; small packages of flour and sugar; and a couple dozen tomatoes, carrots, onions, potatoes, bananas, cabbages, and avocados.

When I first arrived here, I needed to learn the Kenyan way to shop for produce. Here we don't select our own. Instead, we tell the *duka* operator how many kilos we want—a kilo weighs just over two pounds—and he selects it for us. A number of *dukas* operate near our office and apartment and, since I don't drive, I often shop at a *duka* between trips to a larger store.

We also shop at City Market in downtown Nairobi, but it's not for the faint of heart. To get there we face the challenge of driving around or through those ever-present potholes I've told you about. The second challenge is stopping for red lights because various types of people surround cars. Thieves, for example, reach through car windows and snatch earrings, necklaces, or watches. They're so quick a person doesn't even realize it's happening until it's too late. Our friend Ruth Chapman, visiting from Cameroon, lost her necklace to such thieves. For that reason, we never wear jewelry downtown.

Other people surround cars at intersections, too—crippled people who beg for food or money. One man, without legs, moves himself on his fists. Another has one leg, dwarfed and twisted the wrong direction. He, too, propels himself on his fists. Those are the truly needy and deserving. I look into their pleading eyes, and my heart breaks for them. We gladly give them money or food.

We also see those dear, desperate ones who try to make a living by roasting peanuts. They put a handful into a cone made of used paper, stretch out their sooty hands, and beg us to buy their peanuts for one Kenya Shilling per cone—about two cents. We buy from them because we like to honor their efforts to support themselves, and then we give the peanuts to people who ask for food.

Other times, stopped at a red light, hawkers surround our car. We have little sympathy for them because they dress well and sometimes sell stolen goods—watches, jewelry, telephone books, tools, or magazines. One day a hawker tried to sell a magazine to one of our coworkers. Our friend took a closer look because he hadn't received that issue of his subscription. He looked at the address label—and saw his own name! That guy had stolen his magazine and tried to sell it back to him!

Once we make it to City Market, we brace ourselves because as soon as we open the car door, throngs of people (the destitute, disabled, street kids, refugees—and pickpockets) push against us and call for handouts. First, we lock our car and look over the crowd to hire someone as an *askari* (guard) to prevent thieves from stealing mirrors, lights, or even the whole car. We promise to pay him five or ten Kenya Shillings, but we don't pay until we get back because otherwise he might take our money and run.

After we hire an *askari*, we deal with beggars. We buy bananas, milk, or bread for the genuinely needy, but sometimes a person gets mad because he doesn't want food. He wants money instead so he can buy glue and sniff it to get high.

We dodge trash and spittle on sidewalks, hold our breath against urine smells and even worse smells, push inside City Market, and enter a different world—an explosion of color and tropical scent. First, we come face to face with an enormous display of cut flowers—eight or ten feet high and fifteen feet across. Fragrance fills the air—spicy carnations, seductive tuberoses, fresh mums—a welcome treat after the bad smells outside. Smiling men invite us to buy a bouquet, and we can take home a big arrangement for about three dollars.

Beyond the flowers, we find fruit and vegetables. Each vendor mans his own wooden stall and arranges his colorful produce in tidy squares, row upon row. Their displays almost look like patchwork quilts—squares of red peppers next to squares of broccoli; squares of yellow papayas next to black avocados; squares of eggplants and cabbages, apples and carrots, mangos and red onions, green beans and oranges, tomatoes and pineapples—a treat for the eyes.

According to the local custom, we buy from the same vendor each time. Monico's stall sits in the middle of an acre or so of produce stands.

Monico sees me coming and grins. *"Jambo, Mama! Habari?"* (Hello! How are you?)

"*Mzuri sana, na wewe?*" (Very well, and you?)

"*Mzuri.*"

I hand Monico my large, soft-sided basket and tell him what I need and how many kilos I want. For example, I tell him I need two kilos of onions, and he picks them out for me. I go through my entire list—beetroots (beets), capsicum (green peppers), cauliflower, and so on. If I need something he doesn't have, he gets it from another stall. The occasion involves lots of smiles and pleasantries. Monico always puts extra passion fruit into our basket to thank us for our business, and we give him a few Kenya Shillings as a tip.

"*Asante!*" your grandpa and I call out. "*Asante sana!*" (Thank you very much!)

Monico answers, "*Kwaherini!*" (Goodbye, plural.)

"*Kwaheri!*" (Goodbye, singular.)

We walk back to the car with a heavy basket bulging with fresh produce that cost us the equivalent of less than five dollars.

At one end of City Market, vendors butcher fish and chickens with gusto. Guts and scales fly through the air. Water and blood run across concrete floors and into low spots. With no refrigeration, the stench can be staggering.

Sometimes we also shop across the way from City Market at the blue stalls—rickety wooden stalls crammed together row after row, where Kenyans sell artifacts—wood or soapstone carvings, jewelry, bookends, drums, masks, candleholders, and colorful batiks that portray village life. Narrow pathways—uneven, rocky, and sometimes flooded—connect the maze of stalls.

Proprietors call out in their strong Kenyan accent, "Jambo, Mama!" or "Jambo, Bwana!" And then, smiling, "Buy here! Gooood price! You ah my fost (you are my first) customer!" even if it's four o'clock in the afternoon. We always laugh, and they laugh back, because all of us know we're not their first customer of the day.

If we don't want to buy their goods, we reply *hapana leo* (not today) rather than a definite no. *Hapana leo* gives them hope we might buy another day.

We never pick up an item unless we intend to buy it. Often vendors don't mark their goods with a price, and we never ask the price unless we intend to buy and we're willing to barter. They see our white skin, assume we have money, and plan to charge a lot. Sometimes they ask where we live, thinking we're rich tourists. When we tell them we live in Nairobi, their facial expressions always change, as do their prices—maybe because they recognize we'll know if they try to charge too much. In that case, they might say, "Buy here, Mama! Best price! Best price!"

In bartering, the buyer starts by offering too little and the seller starts by asking too much. Both go back and forth until they settle on a price. We always do it in fun—the seller enjoys bartering and even expects it.

Stepping between those densely packed rows can be intimidating—all of them look the same and there's no easy escape route. Once the vendors know we're from Nairobi, and especially if we buy something, I get the feeling they'd defend us if someone tried to hurt us. I shop there only if I'm with your grandpa, and we relax and have fun. Most Kenyans are kind, fun-loving people. I enjoy their smiles, their bright white teeth, and hearty laughter.

October 13, 1994
Nairobi, Kenya

Dear Maggie,

On our first Sunday back in Nairobi after the orientation course, our coworkers, Marvin and Joyce Hyde, offered us a ride to Nairobi Baptist Church. The next Sunday they offered us a ride, too. After a while, we became such good friends that, even though your grandpa and I have our own car now, the four of us still go to church together.

Let me tell you about one of the greatest delights of my life—listening to, and watching, Africans sing. They have full, strong voices and, unlike many American churchgoers, they sing out with resounding volume. Their music has rich harmonies and distinct, pulsing rhythm. Singing worship songs at Nairobi Baptist is an eye-opening experience for us stodgy white Presbyterians, the "frozen chosen." Africans feel their songs from deep down in the core of their souls all the way to the tips of their fingers and toes. They sway, they clap, and they dance while they sing. King David's dance before the Lord couldn't have looked more joy-filled to God than the Kenyans' dances. Their melodies and ululations fill the sanctuary, bounce off the rafters, and envelop us. I will never, never grow tired of that.

A mixture of Africans and white missionaries make up Nairobi Baptist's choir. When they sing, the African members bounce and nod and swing to the rhythms. They can't help themselves—it just oozes out of their pores. Their grace is a beauty to behold. And the white choir members? Oh, they try, and I give them credit for that, but they can't help themselves—their stiffness just oozes out of their pores. It makes me laugh, though I'm laughing at myself, too, because I'm just as stiff and uncoordinated as they are.

The Hydes always go out to dinner after church. When we lived in the States, your grandpa and I couldn't afford to eat out often, but in Kenya nice dinners cost the equivalent of four dollars or less. Each Sunday the four of us try out a different restaurant. Often we have a choice of farm-grown game meat—zebra, eland, giraffe, gazelle, or ostrich—tender and tasty. Kenyans have fine-tuned the art of gracious dining experiences, and Grandpa and I enjoy the Hydes' company while we explore Kenya.

❖ ❖ ❖

October 14, 1994
Nairobi, Kenya

Dear Maggie,

We have opened our Kiambere home to numerous houseguests, among them your grandpa's cousin Paul and his wife Barbara (missionaries in Zaire), and their boys, who stayed with us for two weeks to have medical work done in Nairobi. We also welcomed newlyweds Andreas and Susanna, friends from our three-month orientation course. Andreas, a Russian-German, and Susanna, a German, work in Bible translation in Ethiopia now. We also welcomed another friend from orientation, Peggy, a retired teacher from Alaska who teaches in Mozambique. I wrote an article about Peggy for Wycliffe-USA's magazine, *In Other Words*.

In May, colleagues from England stayed in our guestroom. Sometimes I perfume our guests' bed sheets and so, on the day of Gordon and Rosemary's arrival, I sprayed, and sprayed, and sprayed, and then realized I'd squirted hairspray on the sheets. We own only two sets of sheets—the other set was on our bed—and with water turned off all over the city, and no clothes dryer—well, Gordon and Rosemary were stuck with those sheets. I just hoped they didn't stick *to* the sheets. Oh, yeah, quaint I ain't.

Gordon and Rosemary had traveled here to attend our annual meetings with directors and delegates from some twenty African sub-Saharan nations. Our international administrators also attend, as do directors from Europe, Canada, Australia, and other places around the world. For two weeks we give reports, make proposals, legislate, strategize, plan, and network. The meetings can be intense, and we cover good, sometimes controversial, issues.

About ten African nations have established their own Bible translation organizations and since we work closely alongside them, their leaders attend these meetings, too. They have seen first-hand the way a person's eyes light up when he hears Scriptures in his own language. They've seen the Bible transform families and communities. I feel both honored and blessed to meet with these men and women, and I applaud their ministry.

Our meetings take place in the highlands forty-five minutes north of Nairobi at an old colonial place, Brackenhurst, surrounded by miles of bright green tea plantations. Brackenhurst dates back to 1914 during the British East African era. Low, whitewashed stone cottages—with red roofs and multi-paned windows—nestle together on a grassy hillside. Rooms are small, spare, and worn, yet charming in an old-fashioned way. At Brackenhurst, we breathe fresh, still air except for the aroma of wood smoke from fireplaces in guest rooms and the dining room.

Brackenhurst is not a luxurious place—except for the eyes. The grounds look like a well-manicured park with emerald grass and lush, colorful flowers: dahlias, Bird of Paradise, philodendrons, ferns, palms, hibiscus, cosmos, jasmine, gardenias, marguerite daisies, bottlebrush trees, banana trees, flame trees, mimosa trees, and many more. Poinsettias and geraniums grow ten or twelve feet tall. One day I paused to look deeply into the heart of a flower, full of intricate detail and shades. I stood back and took in the wider view of the gardens' expanse and the tea fields in the distance, and I marveled at the bursts of color. The scene made me think of God who has given us all this to enjoy. I suspect that He loves color and fragrance even more than we do. In fact, I think the colors and textures and fragrances give us a glimpse of God Himself.

Because of Brackenhurst's elevation, over 7,000 feet, we plan for cool temperatures at night and early morning. We wear wool sweaters, warm shoes, and heavy socks, and sometimes we even take blankets to the meeting room. Besides three hearty meals a day, at mid-morning and four o'clock in the afternoon the staff serves us bracing black tea, freshly baked pastries, cakes, and pies. Life is almost divine at Brackenhurst, serene and gentle, and always a nice break from Nairobi.

On November 11 each year, Wycliffe members set aside the day to pray for our work. Around the world, wherever they gather, they view the World Day of Prayer video so they can link faces and personalities with specific prayer requests. During May's meetings at Brackenhurst, I interviewed several people for this fall's video—individuals from Ghana, Nigeria, Central African Republic, and the Philippines (yes, he came from the Philippines).

One of the people I interviewed, Grace Adjekum, serves as the Director of Ghana's Bible institute. Grace found herself in the midst of brutal ethnic violence in February when your grandpa and I had planned to travel there.

(You'll remember that we received word along the way to skip Ghana so we traveled on to the next country on our itinerary.) When Grace arrived at Brackenhurst, she told us that those clashes had focused on her and Ghanaian Bible translators. Warring factions killed a thousand people, including Grace's adopted son, and destroyed a hundred and fifty villages.

Those two main dissenting groups, the Konkombas and the Nanumbas, expected to receive Old Testaments in their own languages just as the violence broke out. The Konkombas have had the New Testament in their language for sixteen years and have two hundred churches and six thousand Christians. Given that information, some of us muttered among ourselves and wondered how they could commit such heinous acts against each other. Our clucking tongues stopped, though, when we recognized we've had Scriptures in our language for hundreds of years, yet we sin against one another, too. When our knowledge of the Bible remains only a mental, academic exercise, rather than a heart-involved lifestyle, then we, too, hurt others, sometimes with physical violence, other times with cruel words and attitudes. We all need God's grace.

During our stay at Brackenhurst, Grace's sister underwent extensive surgery in Nairobi. She needed a blood transfusion, so Grace asked people with Type O negative blood to donate. Only Bob Creson (the director of Cameroon's work) and I had that type, and we checked out a car and headed down to Nairobi. Along the way, I confessed that I worried about giving blood because of potential exposure to AIDS and hepatitis, but we went ahead with it anyway. Bob watched closely during the procedure and assured me afterward that they had used new, sterile needles.

After two weeks at Brackenhurst we returned to Nairobi, our bodies and spirits refreshed and our heads spinning from the lively meetings, the networking, and new ideas we brought home.

❖   ❖   ❖

October 15, 1994
Nairobi, Kenya

Dear Maggie,
This past summer, your Aunt Karen came to visit us and we loved every precious moment! Just before she arrived, your dad sent an e-mail:

> I hope and pray that the civil unrest in Africa stays far
> from you there in Kenya. Things sound uneasy over
> there, so watch yourselves. I know the Lord has you in

the palm of His hand and there is no place safer. I sure do wish, though, that His hand were not quite so big so we would not have to be so far apart although still in the safe palm of the same hand. I miss you both so terribly sometimes, but then the feeling usually passes and I survive. Having e-mail and getting Dad's vividly detailed journals really seems to help. Jill and the baby are doing great. We are fixing up the kid's room and I can't wait for the little guy/gal to get here so that we can play! Jill sends her love too. I think the kid just kicked "I love you Grandma and Grandpa Thomas." Yes, that was it all right. I spoke with Karen last night and she seems anxious to see you. I hope that someday soon the whole family can be together so that my baby will know how wonderful his/her family really is. Now that would be a good day!

Our safari to Maasai Mara with Karen will always live among my favorite memories. In Kenya, the wildlife reserve's name is Maasai Mara, but in Tanzania, across the border (an invisible line for the most part) its name is the Serengeti. It covers two hundred square miles of plains and forests, and many people consider it the greatest game reserve on the African continent.

In the Mara, life is hushed and wild. We were insignificant specks, intruders on the land. Park employees posted rules for us trespassers:

> Wild animals have the right of way.
> Beware of hippo on road at night.
> Do not disturb elephants by shouting or using motor horns.

We rode in a pop-top van so we could stand up and get a better view. Our driver followed dirt tracks most of the time, but if he spotted an animal that didn't happen to be alongside a road, he drove wherever he wanted to go.

We saw dozens of elephants. I have a warm affection for those colossal creatures because they're family-oriented, relational, and capable of emotion. When an elephant dies, its relatives bury it, shed tears, and audibly mourn. Elephants also mourn if they're taken from their families and put in a zoo or a circus.

Because of their strong emotional attachment to family, especially to their young, elephants can be dangerous. They have killed many people and left survivors with gruesome wounds. A friend told me the story of David Diida, a Borana man of Kenya who spent a month in Nairobi making final corrections on the Borana Bible translation, the culmination of an eleven-year task. Afterward, he took a bus home, but rainy season left the roads oozing with mud. Bad conditions had stopped the bus several times. A two-day trip had turned into a four-day trip, and then the bus came to a standstill again, this time behind forty-four other buses and trucks. The bus driver said he wouldn't continue until the rain stopped and the road started to dry. David had one other option: he could walk the twenty more miles home, a nine-hour trek. He set out at three o'clock in the afternoon and planned to stop after dark and stay overnight with friends.

Seven others walked with him. After three hours, at sunset, they heard an elephant thrashing in the trees, threatening them. It charged and the eight men scattered. David dived off the road to hide under a bush but instead he slipped and fell. He saw the elephant coming for him so he jumped up and sprinted toward a thicker bush—with the elephant right behind him—but he fell again.

David said later that while he looked into the elephant's face, he talked to God. He acknowledged that God, all-powerful, could keep him alive. On the other hand, David also knew that perhaps it was God's will for him to die that day, and if so, he asked God to accept his spirit.

The elephant pushed David around on the ground, dragged him over rocks, and bashed him against bushes. It wrapped its trunk around him—David said it almost crushed him—lifted him into the air, and pounded him against the ground. He cried to God, "I am ready to die!" The elephant hoisted him up again and flung him downward, but it threw David so hard that he flew underneath its body and through the gap between its hind legs.

The elephant stomped the ground, thinking David was under its feet, and trumpeted its victory. David used those moments to crawl through the darkness to the road, and then he forced himself to walk fast despite his wounded body and blood-covered face.

Eventually a group of men found him in the dark and took him to the hospital. Soon David's wife showed up—she had expected him to arrive home two days earlier and, worried, set out to search for him. By the next day, he had recovered enough to walk home. God, who knows the number of our days, had ongoing plans for David. He needed to complete the translated Borana Bible for his friends and relatives, print it, and head up literacy programs so they could read it and other materials in their own language.

Yes, we humans must take elephants seriously. In Maasai Mara with Karen, one day our vehicle drove too close to a mother elephant and her baby. She charged, flapped her ears, lifted her trunk, and let loose a shrill trumpet sound. We knew she was serious so we backed off.

The *twiga*—giraffe—is my favorite African animal. Giraffes move gracefully and their brown and white hides give them a pristine appearance. Most of Africa's animals have cold eyes—buffalo, lion, elephant—but giraffes' long-lashed, soft brown eyes look especially tender. Karen Blixen called giraffes "proud and innocent creatures, gentle amblers of the great plains."[1]

In Maasai Mara, we also saw zebras, antelopes, gazelles, impalas, Cape buffalos, warthogs, ostriches, rhinos, wildebeest, secretary birds, hippos, and topis. We also spotted a bird perched on the top branch of a shrub beside the trail. I'd never seen anything like it—shimmery turquoise and lilac. Our driver stopped so we could snap a picture. I expected the bird to fly away, but it simply sat there, content to let us snap photos. Later I learned its name, a lilac-breasted roller.

One afternoon we came upon five tawny lionesses napping under trees. Our driver turned off the vehicle and, in silence, we watched those great chests rise and fall, rise and fall. The air was still and heavy with heat. We heard only the sound of buzzing flies.

Another time we came upon a pride of lions, both mothers and cubs—twenty-three in all. The cubs romped, wrestled, and tumbled with each other while their mothers patiently herded them through tall grass.

The *simba*—lion—is a regal animal. Some people believe they're the most respected and feared animal of all. These proud animals' muscles bulge as if they were weight lifters. Males can be ten feet long not counting their tails, which are usually two to three feet long. They can weigh from three hundred to over five hundred pounds. At night, the sound of a male's roar can travel up to five miles, a warning to other lions about property and family boundaries. Both males and females stand up to four feet tall at the shoulder, but females are a little smaller than males and have no manes. Female lions usually do the hunting, bringing down large animals like zebra, Cape buffalo, and antelope.

Driving across the hot savannah one day, we came upon a lioness. Rather, she came upon us. With barely a sound, she ran alongside our moving vehicle, using it to hide herself and stalk a wildebeest on the other side. We watched her—just a yard or so away!—watched her instincts, split-second judgments, rippling muscles, and amber eyes riveted on her prey. In the end, the wildebeest got away, but I'll never forget the thrill of that up-close encounter.

One afternoon we almost ran over two male lions napping beside the track. The van's noise awakened them and they lifted their groggy heads. They shook their orange manes, struggled to open their eyes, and posed for a few photos. They kept nodding off, though, so we drove away and left them in peace. So much for their reputation for ferocity.

Later we came upon a cheetah. Long-legged, slim, and lithe, a cheetah weighs about a hundred pounds. When stalking its prey, within seconds a cheetah can run seventy miles an hour, and thus its reputation as the world's fastest land mammal. It can sustain that speed for only two or three hundred yards, though, because its body will overheat. Once a cheetah has brought down its prey, it locks its jaws on the animal's windpipe until it stops breathing. A cheetah begins ripping into the body through the rectum and eats the hindquarters first. It has to hurry to get its share, though, before hyenas, lions, or vultures take over.

That day, our cheetah had killed a Grants gazelle only minutes before we found them in tall grass under a tree. We drove up close—about ten feet away—and again the driver turned off the vehicle. In the silence, the cheetah raised her head, studied us with her copper-colored eyes, and then resumed her dinner. I can still hear the rip of flesh and the crack of bones. I can picture the gazelle's blood on her face. One of the young men with us couldn't stop shaking in his excitement, and your grandpa took an entire roll of film—thirty-four pictures!

In the Maasai Mara, we lived in canvas tents with British Colonial-style safari furnishings, beds draped in mosquito nets, and a modern toilet, sink, and shower. I'll long remember waking before dawn the first morning to a slight noise outside our tent—the rattle of a teacup on a saucer. A Kenyan man spoke in his deep, slow, careful English, "Goood mawning to you. I have brought your tea."

Your grandpa unzipped the tent flap, and there he stood with a linen-covered tray, a pot of Kenya tea, cups and saucers, spoons, cream, and sugar. He stepped into our tent, placed the tray on a small table, and disappeared as silently as he had appeared. The tranquil setting, the cool still morning air, the gracious Kenyan, and the bracing tea created an indelible moment in time, and often I long to live it again. I didn't know it then, but that occasion initiated my quest after serenity and simplicity, my pursuit of a calm and gentle lifestyle.

After we eased into the morning in that fashion, we grabbed binoculars, cameras, canteens, toilet tissue, and hats, and set out for the morning's game drive. The bold African sun arose from low in the east. For two hours, we drove throughout wide-open savannahs and discovered, with childlike glee, an abundance of game animals. Then we headed back to the lodge for a hearty breakfast buffet.

Our driver took us on game drives when the animals are most active, at sunrise and just before sunset. When we arrived back at the lodge at dusk, the aroma of wood smoke signaled that we could take warm showers, and they felt so good after a hot, dusty day. Our slow-paced evenings culminated with a late dinner in the dining room, both rugged and elegant at the same time.

We drove away from Maasai Mara with vivid pictures—in both our cameras and our minds—and with the knowledge that we'd witnessed God's handiwork on a grand scale.

Your Aunt Karen's visit to Kenya felt like a gift for your grandpa and me, and for Karen, too. Only a year earlier we thought our hearts would break apart when we said goodbye for what we thought would be four years, but just think—not only did we spend time together, your Aunt Karen also got to visit Africa! We hated to say goodbye, but Karen had to return to her teaching job. Once again, I pictured that poster in our room in England. I recalled the words from Psalm 126:6, "He who goes out weeping … will return with songs of joy." I realized that God had turned my tears to joy—He brought our precious daughter to us and, in doing so, He showed me that my role as a mother could coexist alongside my role as a wife and missionary.

Karen wrote to us from the Zurich airport on her way home,

> The precious moments with you went so quickly. I can't believe it's already been three and a half weeks and I'm on my way back home again. I wish I could hit the rewind button and make the time keep lasting longer and longer. Thanks so much for everything. I cannot begin to explain what a perfectly blissful, comforting, exciting, safe, loving, adventurous, unforgettable time I had with you. Being with you again was like a wonderfully fresh, safe rejuvenation. I can't tell you how much I had craved, needed your strong, gentle, unconditional love, support, listening, caring, and laughing.

We continued to open our home to various houseguests, among them a young German couple, Ralph and Anetta, friends from our orientation who now work in Bible translation in Tanzania. A friend from Port Angeles, Pete Rennie, also visited. Karen's, Pete's, and Ralph and Anetta's visits overlapped each other. I couldn't have handled all these guests without Elizabeth's help. I can manage grocery shopping, meals, and my work at the office if Elizabeth cleans and does laundry. Bless her.

During Pete's visit, we invited two teachers over for dinner. Both work as tutors, one for a translator family in Kenya and the other for a family in Tanzania. We had no electricity for most of the day, but it came on at four-thirty so I hurried to get meatloaf in the oven. However, fifteen minutes later we lost power again. My cooker (pronounced KOO-kah) has two gas burners and two electric burners, so I took the meatloaf out of the oven, formed it into patties, and fried them over the gas. A few minutes later the power came back on, so I put the patties into a baking dish, topped them with mushroom soup, and popped them back in the oven. Grandpa still raves about how good they tasted, but I hope no one ever asks for the recipe!

Love,
Grandma Thomas

6

Margaret Laura Kathleen Thomas

October 16, 1994
Nairobi, Kenya

Dear Maggie,

We have a telephone in our apartment. Actually, we have two, one on the main floor and one upstairs in our bedroom. Friends tell us people usually wait for years to get a phone.

A phone was very important last July because we were waiting for news of your birth, Maggie. Every time it rang I said, "Maybe this will be news about the baby!" That blessed day arrived on July 31. Over the phone in the corner of our bedroom, I listened to your dad tell us of the birth of Margaret Laura Kathleen Thomas—you had curly blonde hair, dark blue eyes, and weighed eight pounds and eleven ounces. We had a beautiful granddaughter! The next day I wrote this to your mom, dad, and you:

> Dear Matt, Jill, and Maggie,
> We're so thrilled to have Maggie join the Thomas family!
> Welcome, Little One! We're so excited to think of all that your life has in store. I think back to your daddy at your age, and I realize now that I had no idea all the zillions of fantastic experiences he'd have—and that we'd

have with him. I had no way to know then about all the talents and skills he'd have, the laughter he'd bring to us, the joy and pride we'd have in him, his great faith, and the example he'd be to our faith. I had no idea he'd grow to be so tall and strong. And when I think of all these things about him, I realize you, too, will have an intricate and full life and oh, how wonderful it will be! Be assured of my many prayers for you. I'm excited to see how God will grow you up as you blossom into a beautiful young woman, and even into an older woman, too. It's hard to imagine that someday you'll be an old woman like me, but you will. Then you'll know how ecstatic your grandfather and I are right now.

Speaking of your grandfather, he wants you to call him the Swahili word for grandfather, *Babu* (pronounced BOB-oo) because that's easier to pronounce than "Grandpa Big Dog." I don't know what I want you to call me. I just hope you'll see me often enough to recognize me and call me *something*! I suppose just about any name you choose will be fine.

Did you know that your dad's Great-grandpa Thomas had a sister named Margaret Thomas? Your father met her when he was an infant. We have a blue shawl that belonged to her and you might like to own it someday since you share her name.

Your Great-great grandfather, Van Bartholomew, died just a few hours before you were born. I'm sorry you two didn't get to meet, but I plan to tell you stories about a whole bunch of your relatives.

Now, Jill. Sweet, dear Jill. I'm sorry you had such a long, hard labor. Our hearts ached as hour after hour passed and we still had no phone call because that meant you were still in labor. I prayed in every way I could, and when words seemed inadequate, I thought of Jesus at the right hand of God the Father, interceding for you. How thankful I am that He does that for us. We're proud of you for getting through this so well. Last night when we climbed into bed, *Babu* said, "Jill's going to be a great mom." That's right! We're excited that you're the mother of our granddaughter. You'll have such fun with Maggie, dressing her in sweet little dresses, tying ribbons in her hair, and putting lacy little socks on her feet. Some day she'll have a date and she'll ride off in a car with a young man, and you'll be scared to death. Then one day she'll walk down the aisle and get married and, before you know it, she'll present you with a granddaughter, and then you will be "Grandma Thomas."

Hey, Matt, we're proud of you, too, and excited to think of you as a dad now. You'll be a wonderful dad. When I picture you with little Maggie, so sweet and gentle with her, tears come to my eyes. You are the godliest man I know. Maggie possesses a rich blessing in having you for her father. We are rejoicing, and we know God is rejoicing. I saw a poster that said, "God danced the day you were born." Do you suppose God is dancing today over little Maggie? I'm sure He is.

This is the first of many letters we'll send to our little Maggie.

Much, much love,
Grandma Thomas (the new generation of)

P.S. Grandpa and Grandma Crabtree: Enjoy that little gal, and give her twice as much hugging to make up for what we can't give to her. Thanks!

Back in 1967 when I married your grandpa, I became "Mrs. Thomas." That was very new and somehow it didn't seem right, because "Mrs. Thomas" was Dave Thomas's mother. Eventually I got used to it though, and then in 1990 your dad married your mom, and I became a mother-in-law, "Mom Thomas." That was very new and somehow it didn't seem right, because "Mom Thomas" was Dave Thomas's mother. Eventually I got used to it though, and then in 1994 I became "Grandma Thomas." But that seems very new and somehow it doesn't seem right, because "Grandma Thomas" is Dave Thomas's mother.

Now that I'm a grandmother I'm feeling old, but when I told a friend about my first grandchild, she looked at me, paused, smiled, and said, "How wonderful that you can enjoy your grandchildren while you're so young!" Bless her!

On August 3, 1994, I received this e-mail:

Dear Grandma and Grandpa Thomas (*Babu* and Grandma African Violet),

    Thank you for the wonderful letter. I love being here finally. I am happy and big and if I am not eating or smiling, I am sleeping very soundly. I even sleep through my daddy kicking my crib accidentally every time he walks by. I slept 7.5 hours my first night home, and I already know how to raise mommy's voice two octaves every time I eat. I have very smart eyes (so they tell me) and my Grandma 'Tree is always giving me kisses, half from her and half from you, she says. I like to suck on my hand if I could only put it in the same place twice. Grandpa Crabtree is one happy guy and I love it when he picks me up. He says that I am very mature for being only two days old. Mommy and Daddy are very fun. When I wake up we all three just lie on the bed and look at each other and laugh a lot. I think that they are laughing at me, but Daddy says they are just laughing *near* me. Daddy just printed Grandma's e-mail so I can have it for my baby scrapbook. Mommy, Daddy, Grandma, and Grandpa Crabtree are taking lots of pictures and video and will try to send them. All you really need to do though is to look at Mommy's baby pictures; I look exactly like that, except maybe with just a bit of Daddy's cheeks and eyebrows. I love you and I look forward to seeing you in September. My eyes should be focusing by then.

Love,
Maggie

7

Eet Eez A Loooong Sweem.

October 18, 1994
Nairobi, Kenya

Dear Maggie,

I have almost caught you up on the highlights of the last year, but here's a story I don't want to leave out.

Recently our friends Marvin and Joyce asked us to join them for a two-day cultural celebration among the Suba people on Mfangano Island, near the east shore of Lake Victoria. Marvin, who had traveled there before, said he'd arrange our flight, but he wanted the four of us to decide ahead of time where to stay overnight. We could stay with a Suba family, he said, or we could take a small boat to the mainland and stay at a research institute.

I wondered why we'd want to stay on the mainland instead of the island—until Marvin explained the Subas believe it's a blessing to have a rat in one's home. In fact, it's more than a blessing. It's a must. If a house doesn't have a rat, they tear it down. At first, their belief made no sense, but I suppose the real blessing is having food in the house, and the evidence of that blessing is the rat's interest in being there. However, to my way of thinking, a rat is not a blessing—it is a rat. I had read a story in the local newspaper about children with scarred toes because rats nibbled at them while they slept. That settled it. I voted for the boat trip to the mainland, and the other three agreed.

With that settled, on August 19 our six-seater plane lifted off the tarmac at tiny Wilson Airport in Nairobi, and we set out toward the northwest and Mfangano Island, some three hundred miles away. Since Wilson borders Nairobi's game park, we watched out our windows for giraffes, buffalos, or antelopes.

Before long, we approached the east fork of the Great Rift Valley. The morning sun's rays created shadows along the Valley's ridges, like stair steps, and accentuated the way the earth pulls apart *kidogo, kidogo* (little by little) year after year.

In the highlands beyond the Valley, we flew over hillsides and dales, green from recent rains. Small family-owned farms, *shambas*, dotted the landscape. Through our windows, in every direction, we saw thatch-roofed huts, stick-and-mud, the same color as the orange soil. Farmers' crops, laid out in tidy squares, looked like a bright green and orange checkerboard.

And then we saw it—Lake Victoria!—stretched out before us, wide and flat and shiny in the sunshine. It looked almost as big as an ocean. Marvin told us to watch for Mfangano Island off the lake's east shore.

Our little plane touched down on a beach-side landing strip lined with a handful of curious, giggling Suba children. We didn't need our overnight bags until day's end so we left them in the plane and hiked a couple of miles into the hills where the cultural celebration would occur.

Young Suba performers painted white designs on their bodies and wore traditional costumes made of dried grasses, bark, and animal skins. They danced, they beat their drums, they sang their songs, and acted out folk tales. Throughout each event, the Subas laughed—the performers, their parents, grandparents, aunts, uncles, and cousins. Their contagious joy made us laugh along with them.

The fun-loving Subas welcomed us strangers to their island, their celebration, and their homes. I had brought toothbrushes as gifts and handed them out to shy children gathered in the shade of a wide mango tree. We couldn't speak each other's languages, but we communicated with smiles and handshakes.

The celebrations lasted all day—longer than we expected—and at six o'clock the sun set, like it always does on the equator, with only a brief lingering dusk. Festivities continued, though, and minute by minute, the darkness deepened. I worried that a boat trip after dark might not be safe, but our friend Naphtali, a Bible translator for his Suba people, assured us that darkness didn't matter.

After the last of the speeches and awards, a Suba man led us down the mountainside—two miles in thick blackness, around corners, through bushes—to the landing strip and our plane. We loaded our overnight bags, hiked another half mile to the beach in front of the chief's house, and waited for the boat. Our Suba friend stood with us in darkness lit only by the moon on the far side of a thick layer of clouds.

"We should hear the outboard motor soon," Marvin said. We listened, but the night remained silent except for our whispers and the waves that lapped the beach.

We waited.

And waited.

In the faint moonlight, off in the distance we watched a person walk to the edge the beach, strip off clothes, wade out a few feet, and bathe. This provided an interesting diversion, but afterward we remembered our conspicuous lack of a boat.

Out of the corner of my eye, I thought I saw a flash of lightning toward the mainland. My heart sank. A storm! No one else seemed to notice. I hoped that if I didn't say anything, it wouldn't be true. But then I saw another flash, and others saw it too.

The wind whipped up. I pictured our little boat lurching and rolling in a tempest on Lake Victoria, the world's second largest freshwater lake. Only Lake Superior is bigger. Miles of open water separate the island from the mainland. Even in ideal conditions, such a trip would take an hour and a half. A large oceangoing vessel could handle a storm, but we had only a small hand-hewn boat. My stomach knotted.

I stood on the shore and agonized over our options. Which would be better, to venture out on this huge lake in a lightning storm or spend the night with rats? I didn't have to think long. I could live with rat-scarred toes, but I'd never survive a capsized boat in a storm. I wondered—should I say something to your grandpa and Marvin?

Just then, our Suba friend said, "Wait here. I'll go back to the plane to see if the boat went to that shore by accident."

So we waited.

A few minutes later in the hushed darkness, your grandpa pointed. "Look over there. Isn't that a boat?"

In the dim moonlight, sure enough, a long, thin, black line headed toward us, but I couldn't hear the motor. In the shadows, I could see that a man stood in the boat and that he propelled it toward us by pushing a pole against the bottom of the lake. That method would never get us to the mainland.

I could still see the storm in the distance, but it hadn't blown any closer. Maybe we could make the trip after all.

The boat scraped onto the sand in front of us, and the man inside jumped down and disappeared into the bushes behind us.

We waited in silence, though that did not imply patience. About ten minutes later, someone approached from the shadows behind us. He carried an outboard motor.

"Ah," we whispered to each other, "that will help."

To my surprise, no one made any moves to climb in. I wanted to holler, "Let's get this show on the road!" but instead I looked around. Still no one moved. I'm sure God Himself intervened and convinced me to squelch my American goal-oriented compulsions, keep my mouth shut, and watch to see what would happen next.

So we waited again.

Eventually another Suba approached out of the dark carrying a fuel can.

"That's a good idea," we white people nodded in agreement.

It seemed that everyone moved in slow motion but, in due course, the Suba men hooked up the motor and filled it with gas. The time had come to climb in.

Easier said than done. We weren't supposed to touch the water because bilharzia-causing parasites live there and they can cause life-long damage to internal organs. That meant we had to climb up and over the only part of the boat on shore, the tip, nearly six feet off the ground. Marvin climbed in and pulled me up by the arms while your grandpa stood on shore and pushed. Mind you, because I was in rural Africa, I wore a skirt. Hurling myself six feet up and over the edge of that boat in a skirt was not an easy task and I hoped the dark night hid my burning cheeks. Quaint I ain't. Joyce, always ladylike, climbed in with grace and modesty.

We set out into the night with the Suba man in charge of the motor and rudder. The voyage would take an hour and a half, so we settled in. The wind had died down and we saw only an occasional flash of lightning in the distance. We puttered past a couple of little islands. They had no electricity so we didn't actually see them; we only sensed large shadows beside us.

We hadn't traveled long when the motor sputtered. My heart sputtered, too. *Oh, Lord, please don't let us break down.*

We chugged on.

Then it happened. The motor coughed—and died altogether.

We sat there in the hushed blackness. No one said a word.

Then the Suba man's deep, rich voice split the darkness. He drew out each word slowly, "Eet eez a loooong sweem."

I caught my breath. Could he be serious? I don't know how to "sweem!"

I sat petrified in the stillness. Waves slapped against the side of the boat, but no one said anything.

What could I say? What could I do? Swimming to the mainland was not only beyond my ability, it was beyond my comprehension. I struggled to calm myself. Then I devised a plan. If he were serious about swimming, I'd speak up. I'd suggest that we simply drift around in Lake Victoria until morning. When the rest of the world woke up, surely someone would rescue us.

"But," the Suba's slow, velvety voice interrupted my thoughts, "you weel not sweem because the lake eez fool of crock-o-diles!"

We wouldn't have to swim! Thank God! I took a deep breath.

The Suba tinkered with the motor but the boat remained lifeless, sloshing in the waves. I didn't pay much attention because he had given me another thing to worry about: crock-o-diles.

The Suba's voice interrupted my uneasy thoughts. He had found the problem: a fishing net had tangled with the motor. Before long, he unsnarled it. He stood, paused, and yanked the rope. I held my breath for a split second, and—the motor sputtered to life!

An hour later, our Suba friend motored the boat up on the shell-strewn mainland and we hopped down. A few houses had electricity and the glow from their windows helped light our route up the beach. Marvin stooped over and picked up something—wires and vines.

"Duck down. You need to climb under this fence."

We followed Marvin another forty-five minutes through the night until we arrived at an insect research institute where he had reserved rooms. The Swahili word for insect is *dudu*, so we spent the night in a *dudu* research institute. I didn't care what it sounded like—the place resembled paradise.

The next morning we hiked back to the beach for our return trip to the island. In the daylight, I saw what I couldn't see the night before. The boat, made of hand-hewn planks, measured about twenty-five feet long and five feet wide.

This time I had to climb into it in broad daylight. Marvin pulled and your grandpa pushed, and I hurled myself up into the air and over the edge of that canoe with neither poise nor style. The event was painful for all concerned.

An hour and a half later, we pulled ashore on the island. Marvin jumped down and reached up to help me. I tried one position, but that wouldn't work. I tried another position, but that wouldn't work either. Regardless of the position, if I accepted Marvin's help, he'd see up my skirt. Now, if I was a slender, long-legged young woman, Marvin might've enjoyed that experience but, believe me, I don't have good legs. I mumbled something about my embarrassment. Marvin caught on instantly—bless his heart.

He swiveled around and hurried up the beach, leaving your grandfather to help. I can never thank Marvin enough.

Sigh. Quaint I ain't.

❖ ❖ ❖

October 22, 1994
Nairobi, Kenya

Dear Maggie,
Before we moved to Africa, people at headquarters talked with us about potential job assignments. Early on, your grandpa received his assignment to oversee missionary children's education across sub-Saharan Africa. Eventually they asked me what kind of work I'd like to do. I didn't need to think long. I said I'd like to work in journalism. I had studied journalism and creative writing from the age of thirteen. After college, I took writing courses and workshops and got a couple of freelance articles published. I'd always longed for a job that involved writing. I knew that Wycliffe produced several publications and I hoped my life-long dream would come true.

I still remember the day the phone rang and a person on the other end said I could work in journalism—they call it Communications. I hung up the phone, trembling. My dream had come true—but the moment I found out, my heart broke. I seldom cry, but I cried that day. I surprised myself, yet instantly I recognized a problem I hadn't foreseen. Journalism seemed watered down compared to my previous ministries. In the preceding five years, I taught Bible classes. I spent all day and almost every evening, even weekends, studying the Bible and preparing lessons. I worked on the front lines of Christianity—or so I thought—but I could find nothing in the Bible that says, "Go to the utmost ends of the earth to be a Communications Specialist." Journalism seemed out on the irrelevant fringes of real ministry, and that recognition jarred me. My heart broke because I faced a significant loss of meaningful ministry.

I grieved over my job situation for a year and a half.

Then one day, here in Nairobi, I came upon a Bible verse that turned my job around. I had read Psalm 96:3 many times, but that day it took on new meaning. It tells us to publish God's amazing deeds and tell everyone about the wondrous things He does. It suddenly hit me—my job is not about writing articles and making videos. No, it's about telling others the amazing things God does in people's lives once they have Scriptures in their own languages. That's what Wycliffe's magazines and videos are all about! What an honor!

That verse led me to Psalm 9:11, "Proclaim … what he has done." That's what we in Communications get to do. We get to tell people about God's power and blessing in peoples' lives. The message of our stories is, "Look what God has done!"

Because God illuminated those verses for me, I grieved no more. Instead, I was on fire! At that moment, a scene from the past flashed before me. I recalled the old World War II barracks at Wycliffe's center in England and the poster in our room, "He who goes out weeping … will return with songs of joy." (Psalm 126:6). And then, in Nairobi that day I witnessed God at work. He had turned my weeping to joy.

I had always been committed to my job, but after I found those verses, I worked with passion. God has given me a gift, a treasure, a privilege. I get to tell stories about what He's doing across Africa, stories that declare the greatness of our God. They're celebrations of God's blessings for Africans—one person at a time, one family at a time, one community at a time.

In Calgary recently, I shared those Bible verses, and my enthusiasm, with other Communications specialists from around the world. Many found them as meaningful as I had.

Calgary recently? Yes, last month I flew to Calgary, Alberta, to meet with Communications Specialists from around the world, and therein lies another surprise God had prepared for me. He gave me a job that required me to return to the continent where my beloved family lives—and right after my first grandbaby's birth. I'd expected to remain in Africa four long years, the typical missionary term, but after just over a year I found myself strapped in a Boeing 747 on a flight to Canada.

When I first stepped foot on North American soil, I went into a mild reverse culture shock. I had become so accustomed to Kenya's potholes that driving on Canada's roads felt like gliding on air. I needed to reorient myself to driving down the right side of the road. Television programs started on the hour and half hour. I could buy corn chips. Department stores and supermarkets offered vast quantities and selections, and all around me, I saw white people.

In Calgary one sunny, warm evening, I sat in the back seat of a car on the way to a barbeque for the meeting's participants. Tired from days of travel and meetings, I sat back, relaxed, and looked out the window, absentminded. But suddenly I couldn't remember where I was. I had to think hard before I figured it out. It took only twenty seconds or so, but that incident shook me up.

After Calgary, I had business at our southern California office, near your house, Maggie. Since by then I hadn't used up more than a couple of vacation days, and since it didn't cost any more to stop in Seattle between Calgary and Los Angeles, I decided to visit loved ones in Washington along the way.

So, after the meetings, I flew to Seattle where my brother Doug picked me up. Still upset about my memory lapse in Calgary, I told Doug what happened. Being a good clinical psychologist and a good brother, he said, "Let's count how many countries you've visited lately." We counted: United States, England, Scotland, Kenya, Cameroon, Burkina Faso, Niger, Burkina Faso again, Senegal, Ivory Coast, Togo, Ethiopia, Kenya again, Canada, and back to the United States. Sixteen countries in fourteen months. "No wonder you got mixed up," he said.

I spent a few vacation days in Seattle with my mom and your grandpa's parents and in Port Angeles with my precious Karen—such blissful days! Then I boarded a plane toward Wycliffe's southern California office—but before office hours started on Monday morning, I spent the weekend with you and your parents!

A couple of months before your birth, when your dad learned of my upcoming visit, he wrote:

> I am so excited that "the kid" will get to see at least half of the Thomas grandparents so soon! Needless to say, Grandma Kay is excited. Her voice raised two or three octaves. I have not talked with Karen about it. She probably won't give it much thought. Kidding! I know she will be thrilled. Jill said that with Karen coming over to Kenya in the summer, and Mom coming here in September, it wouldn't seem any different for the two of you than the time in between semesters at home/away during college! God sure works things out well.

And I saw that Bible verse again—I, who had gone out weeping, returned home with joy.

I first met you, Maggie, in the Burbank airport. When we arrived at your home and I had my first chance to hold you, you experienced a projectile vomiting episode all over me. Oh, dear! Quaint I ain't! My first thought was, *I hope this doesn't foretell the kind of relationship Maggie and I will have!*

I spent a fun weekend with you, and the next week I worked at our Huntington Beach office. Then, in the Burbank airport on September

25, I cried sad tears and said goodbye to you, your mom, dad, and Great-grandma Kay, who had flown down to visit both you and me.

My plane flew out of Burbank toward Nairobi via San Francisco and Amsterdam. There I spent the night—my first visit to mainland Europe—in a hotel located in a grassy rural area just fifteen minutes from the airport, Schiphol. In the lingering evening sunlight, I took a walk in a green, fresh, crisp Amsterdam. On that nearly-month-long journey, I slept in eight beds—and in numerous cramped airplane seats where, indeed, I had "no place to lay my head."

Well, Maggie, I have long and varied adventures to tell you, but they must wait until another day.

Love,
Grandma Thomas

New baby Maggie
with new Grandma Linda

❖ ❖ ❖

October 25, 1994
Nairobi, Kenya

Dear Maggie,

We heard that a hippo killed a man at Lake Naivasha where your grandpa and I camped during our orientation course. It attacked a family while they slept in their tent, and in order to save his wife and child, the man ran outside to lure the hippo away. He succeeded but, in the process, the hippo killed him. I tremble when I think of all the nights hippos ate grass within inches of our tent window and I snapped pictures of them. God watched out for me more than I knew.

Recently we took a weekend expedition with Marvin and Joyce to Kericho in the highlands toward Lake Victoria, an area that takes more lightning strikes than any other place on earth, or so they say. It's a verdant tea-growing region. The fields look like bright spring-green carpets. Our hotel, upscale at one time, showed its age. The telephones were the old hand-crank type, and the phone book in our room, from 1988, listed Mombasa numbers and Nairobi numbers but no local numbers. Nevertheless, we breathed clean air and escaped the big city—a refreshing break for us all.

Elizabeth and her sister Agnes cover many of their extended family's expenses. Her father and mother separated a few years ago because he's a violent man—he bit off part of his wife's ear and kicked her in the stomach. To this day, she still suffers from that injury, and Elizabeth and Agnes help with her doctor bills. Elizabeth and Agnes also pay their younger brothers' school fees. To make ends meet, the sisters grow maize and vegetables on tiny plots of ground they find in odd spots. They are busy women—after they work all day cleaning other people's homes, in the evening they do their own housework, shopping, gardening, and laundry.

Even though they have jobs, Elizabeth and Agnes can't afford to live anywhere except in a sprawling slum with no running water or electricity. They live next door to each other, and their homes—each merely a room made of rough planks, scrap wood, and corrugated tin—adjoin others just like them in acres of maze-like rows. They have no yards, only narrow paths between the rows where, sometimes, open sewage runs through low spots. Most Americans could never imagine such a place, but it's the best Elizabeth and Agnes can do.

We help Elizabeth with various financial needs such as her daughters' school fees. The girls can look forward to a better life if they have an education so Elizabeth works hard to set aside money to pay for it.

I'd like to introduce you to our coworkers and frequent weekend traveling companions, Marvin and Joyce Hyde.

Nevertheless, sometimes the distance between paychecks "eez a loooong sweem," so we're happy to help. We also help with doctor bills and medicine. It's the least we can do.

Recently your grandpa and I decided we want to help Elizabeth toward financial stability on a long-term basis, so the three of us devised a plan: we loaned her 95,000 Kenya Shillings to buy eight houses—actually, each house is simply one small room, like her own—and she'll rent them out. True to her Kikuyu roots, she's energetic and entrepreneurial. Even though she attended school for only a few years, she's bright and will figure out bookkeeping and other skills a landlord needs. Her income from the houses should total as much as she earns every month cleaning houses so, since she'll continue her cleaning jobs, we expect her income to double. That makes grandpa's heart and mine happy.

I'll write again soon.

Love,
Grandma Thomas

8

B'donk-b'donk Hips, The Apple Lady, Falling Sparrows, and Jitters in Jeddah

November 1, 1994
Nairobi, Kenya

Dear Maggie,

Yesterday you completed your third month in the world. I'm so glad I met you last September! Now I look at your photos and remember special times with you and your parents.

I so appreciate Elizabeth's help in our home. Quite literally, she enables me to carry out my ministry. She's a valuable part of our team of supporters—prayer and financial supporters back home and Elizabeth here in Nairobi.

I've decided that with my big hips, I should've been an African. American men like their women slender, but African men like their women fat. I suppose that way of thinking started when people realized that poor men have thin wives because they don't eat well, and successful men have fat wives because they do eat well. Over time, then, plump wives have served as status symbols for their men—at least that's my theory.

Elizabeth has enormous b'donk-b'donk hips. They bounce like a gunnysack full of wrestling cats. African men go wild when they see hips like that. Women deliberately overeat so they'll get fat—beautiful. Slender

These are the rental houses (one room each) we helped Elizabeth finance in order to increase her income. Friends and family helped her remodel.

Elizabeth is wearing the white dress. Notice her beautiful African ba-DONK-ba-DONK hips.

women struggle with low self-esteem and seek help to gain weight. For the African man, the hips are where it's at, and the bigger the better. And to think that people in America spend millions of dollars every year to lose weight!

I'm a granny with a fanny. I should've been born African.

Quaint I ain't.

I've always assumed that the nice young man I told you about, Wycliffe, works at our Kiambere gate for pay, but recently I learned he's unemployed. Apparently, he volunteers for lack of anything else to do, or maybe he hopes to find work from Kiambere residents. He's a fine young man, kind and quiet. I feel bad that he can't find work.

I've relaxed enough now to walk the two blocks to and from work with a friend if your grandpa can't walk with me. Sometimes I even walk alone if the sun hasn't set. Along the way, I visit every day with a very tall, very handsome young *askari* (guard) who works at the Tamarind business between the Kiambere gate and our office. Andy is a polite, proper man, and I know he'd help if anyone tried to hurt me. So would Wycliffe. Those two men are visible gifts from God when I walk to and from work.

I've become acquainted with a Kenyan woman who sells apples for a living and shows up at our office with a box of them on her head. I call her the Apple Lady but her name is Salome. Kenya-grown apples are small and tasteless, probably because people here don't prune their trees, but Salome's apples come from South Africa and they're crisp and tasty. They cost a bit more than I wish, but sometimes I buy a few because I like to encourage her efforts to support herself—and because we miss our Washington apples! Salome figured out where we live, too, so if she doesn't find us at work, she finds us at home.

I arrived back in Nairobi one month and three days ago, and now I must pack my bags again. Your grandpa and I will work for three and a half weeks in West Africa and then fly to America on business. We'll live out of our suitcases for five and a half months this time. I wonder how many "places we will have laid our heads" by then. Here is our tentative itinerary:

November 13: fly from Nairobi to Accra, Ghana. Sometime between November 13 and 18, we'll either fly in a military plane or take an eleven-hour bus ride from Accra up north to Tamale and then back to Accra. We hope Ghana will be calm at that time.

November 18: fly from Accra to Abidjan, Ivory Coast. Sometime between

November 18 and 24, we'll take a bus to Yamousoukro and Vavoua and then back to Abidjan.

November 24 (that's Thanksgiving Day in the United States): fly from Abidjan to Bamako, Mali.

November 26: fly from Bamako to Dakar, Senegal. Sometime between November 26 and December 3, we'll travel by road to Zigenchour, in southern Senegal, and travel through The Gambia on the way.

December 3: fly from Dakar, through Rome, to New York City.

December 4: fly from New York City to Seattle.

Between December 4 and 7, we'll drive to our office in Huntington Beach, California. While there, we'll spend a few days with your family, Maggie. Your grandpa hasn't met you yet!

Between December and March, our responsibilities will take us to Dallas, Atlanta, Pennsylvania, Quebec, the Midwest, Huntington Beach, and back to Seattle.

March 29: fly from Seattle, through New York City, to Frankfurt, Germany. Your grandpa will attend a conference for educators of MKs (missionary kids), and we'll both attend Europe Area Meetings.

April 29: return to Nairobi.

❖   ❖   ❖

February 13, 1995
Lancaster, Pennsylvania

Dear Maggie,
Greetings from Lancaster, Pennsylvania. I haven't written to you for three months! That's how long we've been traveling on this five-month business trip across Africa and the United States. Currently we're working out of the northeast regional office in this beguiling Amish-Mennonite-Pennsylvania Dutch area. Snow covers the ground and, considering wind chill factors, the temperature feels like fifteen below zero. The sun shines most of the time, though.

Yes, the Lancaster region is a pristine, picturesque part of the world, but it can't erase a troubling image from my mind. Back in November, our plane landed in Bamako, Mali, after dark. We descended the stairs into the night, filed across the tarmac toward the terminal, and stood in a long line waiting to get in. Our only light shone from inside, through the windows. Waiting in hot darkness lent a feeling of otherworldliness to our situation.

Chaos filled the airport because thousands of Zairian refugees had fled violence back home and awaited flights out. One planeload had just taken off, and other refugees awaited the next available plane.

We waited a long time in stifling temperatures, clutching our bags, passports, and shot records, but our line stood still. Colleagues had warned us to expect numerous checkpoints where officials sometimes asked for bribes. Perhaps that, combined with the refugee situation, caused the delay.

I had lots of time to watch a boy about eight years of age in line ahead of us. He stood alone. He carried no suitcase. He held no passport. He owned nothing but faded, threadbare clothes on his little body and oversized, worn shoes on his sockless feet. I suspected he was a Zairian refugee. I wondered why he stood alone. Maybe his family flew out on the plane that just left, or even worse—maybe his family died in Zaire's violence. My heart went out to the little fellow and, standing behind him, I asked God to take good care of him.

A few minutes later, a uniformed man stepped out of the darkness. He, too, had noticed the lone boy. He loomed over the child and mumbled something in French. I couldn't understand any of it. After a brief conversation, the man took the boy by the hand and led him into the night behind a darkened building. What would that man do with the boy? I sensed he had sinister intentions. Alarmed, I prayed even harder. If God knows when even a sparrow falls, then surely He knew about that child. I held tight to the belief that God cared—oh, yes, He cared about that boy!

❖ ❖ ❖

February 15, 1995
Lancaster, Pennsylvania

Dear Maggie, Jill and Matt,

Thanks for sending the Winnie the Pooh Valentine and the snapshots of little Maggie. She has stolen our hearts.

April 30, 1995
Nairobi, Kenya

Dear Maggie,

We arrived back in Nairobi at two o'clock this morning in a warm downpour. We shared the flight from Rome to Jeddah, Saudi Arabia, with a couple dozen Muslim pilgrims bound for Mecca. I suspect they'd never flown before because they were as wound up as thirteen-year-old boys at a Little League championship game. They didn't know they needed to stay seated and wear seatbelts during take-offs and landings, and they didn't speak any languages the flight attendants spoke. You can imagine that those attendants had their hands full on that flight.

Forty-five minutes before we landed in Jeddah, flight attendants told us to put away all books and magazines because when we landed, Saudi authorities would search the plane for materials offensive to their culture. The crew paced up and down the aisles to make sure we put everything out of sight. When we landed, the crew's jitters intensified.

Even though we touched down after dark, through the window I could see uniformed men circled around our plane. They stood about five feet apart and held weapons.

A woman, probably a Saudi official, stood at the back of the cabin and kept watch while others searched the plane. Her tight face and rigid body language revealed her tension.

A couple of rows ahead of me, a woman unfolded a map and had begun studying it when a flight attendant rushed over, scolded her, and told her to put it away.

The Saudis' inspection lasted a long time. After the officials finished and left the plane, I signaled to a flight attendant and asked if I could use the restroom. She wrinkled her brow, shook her finger at me, and said I would offend the Saudis because I wore a sleeveless blouse. She warned me to stay in my seat and out of sight until the plane took off.

During our first twenty-two months in Wycliffe, we have changed countries thirty-nine times. On our recent trip, which began last November, we did business in seven African countries. Then, on December 3, we set foot on three continents: Africa, Europe, and North America. Our work in North America took us to thirty-two states and two Canadian provinces. Over our trip's five and a half months, we slept in sixty-six beds and put about twenty thousand miles on the car.

And now we're back home in Nairobi. For those of us whose assignments require a lot of travel, "home" is the place where you get to unpack your suitcase—all the way. "Home" is where you get to choose which TV program to watch. "Home" is where you make the rules—and take out the trash and make all the meals.

May 5, 1995
Nairobi, Kenya

Dear Maggie,

Recently I received a pleasant surprise. It suddenly occurred to me that dirt, dangers, smells, and inconveniences don't bother me the way they did at first. Instead, I'm more aware of Kenya's natural beauty. I didn't even recognize I had made the transition. This discovery reminds me of Paul's advice to the Philippians—to focus on what is pure, noble, admirable, excellent, beautiful, and worthy of praise (Philippians 4:8).

Every day I see excellence, beauty, and purity, and they are worthy of praise. I know I've said it before, but I can't get over the wide array of plant life that grows here in such abundance and in every color of the rainbow. Between home and the office, tropical flowers and shade trees line the road. Birds sing in their branches and, since few vehicles drive by, the walk to work is almost like a walk through a park. (Remember when I used to be afraid to walk alone to work?) Sometimes I look into the heart of a blossom and think about each flower's perfection. Flowers have no sin. They're pure beauty. It occurs to me that God Himself is even more perfect and beautiful than those flowers.

Besides the lush gardens here in Kenya, vendors sell cut flowers on street corners, in parking lots, and on any piece of ground they can find. For about two dollars, we can buy a dozen rose buds of almost any color. We can also buy lilies, carnations, mums, tuberoses, orchids, daisies, baby's breath, and a long list of others. These roadside displays look like works of art.

Something else thrills me, too. Within ten minutes of home, we can drive through the gates of Nairobi's game park and enter a vast, open landscape—no need to make a long trek to Maasai Mara or another game reserve. Some of our favorite snapshots have captured gazelles, zebras, and even lions, with Nairobi's skyscrapers in the background. Someday I'll show you those pictures, Maggie.

Lots of love,
Grandma

9

Empty Stomachs and God-shaped Holes in Hearts

From everyone who has been given much, much will be demanded.
Luke 12:48

May 7, 1995
Nairobi, Kenya

Dear Maggie,
    This week I received a letter from coworkers in Benin, a small nation in West Africa. They wrote about a situation common in people groups across Africa—they believe in an all-powerful Creator, but they also believe that humans cannot know or have access to Him. Instead, they depend on a fetish—a non-human spirit-being—which, they think, approaches God on their behalf and shows them the way to Him after they die. To win the fetish's favor they hold ceremonies and make sacrifices to it no matter how high the cost. For example, a person might need to buy a goat, for a sacrifice, and enough food and drinks for hundreds of guests. But these Beninese people are poor—they have barely enough food to keep themselves alive from one growing season to the next. Their ongoing sacrifices leave them hungry, poor, and in spiritual turmoil because they never know if they've adequately satisfied the fetish.

Maggie, when you're older, maybe in your forties, look back and think about troubles you've faced in life, and then close your eyes and try to imagine how you could have endured them without knowing God.

I hope you'll always have enough food and money, but what if you had no food for your children? I hope your husband will be faithful to you, but think about women whose husbands are unfaithful. Picture living in a country ripped apart by war, and envision running away from people who want to hurt you and your children.

Then imagine facing those heartaches without knowing God. Imagine never hearing a prayer or a sermon you could understand. Picture living without Christian friends to comfort you or pray for you. What if you did not know that God forgives and that He is a God of second chances? Picture how hopeless you'd feel, and imagine not knowing what would happen to you after you die.

Over four hundred million people live like that every day, year after year, generation after generation, because they have no Bibles in their own languages—a huge hindrance to knowing God personally. If I had to figure out the Bible in a foreign language—Russian or German, for example—I'd be clueless. Even if I had Scriptures in languages I've studied—Spanish, French, or Swahili—I'd still be close to clueless. That's what it's like for that people group in Benin and thousands of others. They have no peace about either living or dying so they exist each day trapped within their fetish system, and that perpetuates their malnourishment, both physically and spiritually.

After people have access to Scriptures in their own languages, they learn about God and that begins to change them from the inside out—He loves them, nourishes their souls, and strengthens their faith. That in turn affects their daily living and relationships with others. The Bible gives them reason to hope when they've nearly lost hope in impossible situations—and believe me, millions of Africans live in the midst of impossible situations, situations you and I can barely imagine.

Here in Kenya, the Sabaot people heard the Easter story in their own language at Easter time. A woman said to the pastor after church, "That was wonderful. We've never heard that story before."

The pastor said, "Yes you have. It's the same story we read every year but in the past, I've read it to you in Swahili. Now you've heard it in your own language."

I heard another story about a church pastor who, for the first time, read to the congregation from the Bible in their own language. A woman stood up and said, "Read that again, it's wonderful. I've never understood that before."

That's why your grandpa and I live in Africa. We want to help people understand God and His Word in their own language so they can have a sweet, satisfying relationship with Him, relaxed in His love.

❖   ❖   ❖

May 30, 1995
Nairobi, Kenya

Dear Maggie,

In Kenya, middle and lower class diets seem plain and sparse to our American way of thinking. People eat lots of *ugali*—stiff white cornmeal—and *chapatis*, round flat breads fried in lard. They also eat what we call Kenyan stew—chopped cabbage, onions, carrots, beans, tomatoes, and maybe rice. Millions of people buy meat for only special occasions.

In my childhood, and in your daddy's childhood, sometimes our family's paycheck ran out before the end of the month. We didn't eat fancy food or wear fine clothes, but we always could find food in our cupboards. Here in Africa, though, too many families can't.

We heard that Japheth, the gardener at our office, had no money for food, or for anything else, because he used it all to pay his children's school fees. The government provides only limited funding so people must either pay fees or go without an education. Dear Japheth—he knows an education could provide his children a way out of poverty, and he's willing to pay their school fees even if he has to go without food for a few days to do so. That reminds me of what Jesus said, "Greater love has no one than this, that he lay down his life for his friends" (John 15:13). Bless Japheth for laying down his life in this way for his children. Several of us have contributed toward a money gift from our staff.

Dr. Harriet Hill, anthropologist and linguist, teaches Bible translation courses at Pan Africa Christian College near Nairobi. Recently she pointed out that people fill up African churches and worship wholeheartedly, but then she told the story of an older woman who has attended church all her life. The woman can recite the Lord's Prayer perfectly because her church requires that for baptism, yet she doesn't know what the words mean because they're not in her language.

Harriet also said that in a region in Nigeria where people attend church every day, a survey showed that over 20 percent could not answer, "Who is Jesus?"

Such stories remind me of words Blaise Pascal penned in the mid-

1600s. He believed that God creates each person's heart with a God-shaped vacuum that only He can fill. Pascal recognized the condition of the human heart, and Harriet recognizes the manifestation of that condition in the hearts of so many across Africa. Because they long for God to fill that vacuum, they take in every morsel of Him available in their churches—and I applaud them for doing so. However, until they have Scriptures in their own heart languages, the God-shaped hole must remain only partially filled.

Harriet's conclusion caught my attention. She wrote, "All this touches our hearts deeply as we realize how rich we are in biblical educational opportunities of every sort, [Bible] translations galore, and clear teaching in our heart language. To whom much is given, much is required."

I agree. I almost weep when I think of all the resources we American Christians have—Bibles, books by the thousands, magazines, Bible studies, Sunday School, Vacation Bible School, summer camps, theological seminaries, conferences, retreats, Bible colleges, Christian radio—yet millions around the world don't have one word of the Bible in a language they can understand. How can we do less than help them translate Scriptures into their own languages? When inconveniences, dirt, or exhaust fumes get me down, I hope I'll remind myself to look at this bigger, more important picture.

Love,
Grandma

10

Moving House

June 26, 1995
Nairobi, Kenya

Dear Maggie,
    The owner of our Kiambere townhouse wanted to move back in so your grandpa and I had to move house, as they say here. We searched hard to find a place both safe and affordable. We now have a "place to lay our heads" in a daylight basement in a brand new house. Our apartment doesn't feel like a basement because the house sits on a hillside and our large balcony overlooks a gully.
    Our new landlord and his family live on the top three stories. He has a Ph.D. from Yale and holds a high government position in banking. I heard that bodyguards escort him everywhere and chauffeurs drive his wife and children around.
    This place has the best security I've seen anywhere here—high iron fences, guards in the front and back twenty-four hours a day, and an electronic alarm system. At night, an additional Maasai guard joins the force with a bow and arrows. Many people believe the Maasai make the best guards because of their ferocity.
    We moved house on Friday afternoon and Saturday. We found the change difficult and that surprised us. We slipped into culture stress—not a good feeling. Water doesn't come out the taps in half of our apartment so we can't use the washing machine, toilet, sink, or shower. Even if the water

worked, the shower stall has no rod for a shower curtain. The kitchen sink gives us cold water but no hot water, and the only electrical outlet in the bedroom doesn't work.

The guards talk all night, but that's both bad news and good news. The bad news: we have to listen to them. The good news: their voices remind us that we have guards and that they are awake.

After Friday night, your grandpa and I agreed that we can live with the guard situation but we can't live with the water situation. We stopped unpacking and decided to hire a truck on Monday, today, and move out. However, yesterday things got better so we decided to unpack after all, and today the landlord promised to fix the water.

June 27, 1995
Nairobi, Kenya

Dear Maggie,

Our water works now, and we've figured out the hot water system, too. In the States, people leave their hot water heaters turned on all the time, but here if we leave a heater on too long, maybe three hours, the water boils, the heater explodes, and boiling water spews across the room.

Some people can turn their water heaters on and off but we can't. Ours is on the ripple system—the city supplies power to a home's hot water tank for about two hours a day in either the evening or the wee hours of the morning. At our new place, the city turns it on from four to six o'clock in the morning.

But, wait! It gets even better! A man installed a shower curtain rod so, with both hot water and a shower curtain, we can now shower!

June 29, 1995
Nairobi, Kenya

Dear Maggie,

After living in Africa almost two years, your grandpa bought a television and VCR—my birthday gift—and paid for them with our income tax refund. Our two television stations show local programs, reruns from the States, and CNN International.

Your grandpa can't make the television work, though. He bought a rabbit-ear antenna but it doesn't help. I suppose it has something to do with its location—tucked in the basement under three stories of stone and concrete. Grandpa thought up a Plan B that should work: he bought a cable that he'll string to the top of the house where there's an antenna.

Nearly every day something new goes wrong in this apartment. A couple of nights ago we awoke to a downpour. We jumped out of bed to investigate. Water gushed from a pipe on the roof of this four-story house and splashed down outside our bedroom window. Eventually it stopped, but it started again in the morning and surged, like a waterfall, into a narrow walled-in walkway—the only route to our car.

When we first moved in and I plugged in our bedside lamp, it didn't work. I plugged it into another socket and it worked fine. Next, I plugged a couple of other appliances into the bedroom outlet, but they didn't work either. I concluded that the electrical outlet was defective. When the Mrs., upstairs, asked how things were going, I told her the outlet didn't work.

The next night when we arrived home, the *askari* (guard) stood in the driveway holding my little pink lamp. He handed it to me and mumbled something about "Mama." I noticed a new, flimsy cord. The Mrs. had replaced it because she assumed our lamp was the problem. That made me unhappy because, first, she hadn't asked if she could make the change; second, the new cord was inferior; and third, even worse, she had entered our apartment while we were not home. I took the lamp inside and tried it out and, of course, it still didn't work in the bedroom outlet, though it worked in the others.

When I arrived home from work last night, for some reason I tried the lamp. It worked. They had entered our apartment yet again and this time they replaced the socket.

When your grandpa climbed into bed last night, it fell apart. Today the Mrs. told us the electrical repairman broke the bed when he moved it. Just how he broke it will always remain a mystery because the bed is sturdy and bolted together. After we crawled into bed for the second time, we wondered aloud, "What will happen next?"

However, we have running water now, which means we can flush the toilet. It works almost every time.

❖   ❖   ❖

June 30, 1995
Nairobi, Kenya

Dear Maggie,
Karen writes, "You sound a bit more miffed than usual." I guess I am. I apologize. I'll work on my attitude.
I wonder—is miffness an attribute of quaintness, or ain'tness?

July 1, 1995
Nairobi, Kenya

Dear Maggie,
Last year at this time, day after day and week after week, people around the world watched television reports and read articles about Rwanda's civil war. Over a three-month period, nearly a million people died unspeakable, gruesome deaths. I nearly grew faint when I saw pictures on TV and heard details. A pilot friend of ours stood beside a river and counted fifty to sixty bodies float past him every minute.
East Africans have a proverb: *Wapiganapo tembo nyasi huumia*—When elephants fight, the grass gets hurt. When the powerful fight each other, they trample on the weak and innocent. That's what happened in Rwanda, and it broke my heart.
Rwanda's atrocities also touched our friend, Sue, a fellow trainee during Kenya Safari. I wrote an article about her experience for this summer's issue of Wycliffe's *In Other Words* magazine. Sue and her coworker, Ann, "moved house" to Bukavu, in eastern Zaire, to begin their work assignments. They had lived there only a week when, on their way to church on Sunday, they noticed people gathered in an open area and sensed tension in the air. After the church service, Sue and Ann saw that Rwandan refugees had set up primitive shelters. By that evening, hordes of Rwandans filled the dusty roads into Bukavu carrying babies, food, and firewood. Day after day, the two women watched thousands of people make their way into town—stunned, exhausted, sick, and malnourished. Some didn't even have shelters.
Sue and Ann struggled with guilt, they said, because they were not refugees themselves, guilt because they had so much and the Rwandans had so little. They wept for the refugees. They prayed for them. They gave them money and food. They befriended them and prayed with them. They listened to weary relief workers, overwhelmed and dazed by the refugees'

anguish. I'm sure those refugees and relief workers sensed that God Himself reached out to them through Sue and Ann. May He bless them all, especially the Rwandans.

❖ ❖ ❖

July 14, 1995
Nairobi, Kenya

Dear Maggie,

One of our television stations shows old *Parker Lewis* programs. Your dad had a role as an extra in one episode of that program. Wouldn't it be fun for us to see him on TV here?

The landlord upstairs tells us we'll have no problem getting a telephone, but I'll believe it when I see it. Everyone else says it takes years to get a phone.

This "place we lay our heads" is located in a quiet pocket of the city. We drive down a winding dirt track to get here so we seldom hear traffic. Our windows overlook a small ravine, and since the closest houses sit on the far side of it, we have a quiet place where birds congregate.

Birds called bee-eaters live around our house. They have orange and lime green bodies, bright yellow throats, and Cleopatra eyes—fluorescent blue stripes across their eyelids and heavy black lines around their eyes. Other birds, which I haven't yet identified, also live here. I love to hear their varied tunes. They sing their little hearts out. I'm pretty sure they're singing worship songs to their Creator.

Living here poses one problem. We must drive across town to get to our office—fighting our way through heavy, snarled traffic and exhaust fumes. Your grandpa decided that to beat the worst of the traffic, we should leave home at 6:30 AM and work until 6:30 PM. By the time we get home, I'm so hungry and weary I can hardly cook dinner—but I always do. Then I fall into bed and start the same routine the next morning. No, quaint I ain't.

Until next time,
Grandma

11

Family Matters

July 31, 1995
Nairobi, Kenya

Dear Maggie,

Happy Birthday, Maggie! Your dad writes in his e-mail, "Today is Maggie's first birthday; in many ways this has been the best year of my life, mostly (obviously) due to her arrival." He calls you "a wonderful little jabbering kid." Grandpa and I wish we could celebrate with you today, but maybe some other year that will work out.

This is our cool season and I struggle with the chill that permeates our offices, our home, and even my bones. By four in the afternoon, I'm not only cold, I'm tuckered out—but my workday doesn't end for another two and a half hours. I've learned to fix myself a steaming cup of strong tea—I've acquired a taste for Kenya tea—with a squirt of milk in it. Besides warming me, it has become, for me, what some people call a comfort food.

On one of those long cold workdays, in the late afternoon I heard a slight noise at my office door. I turned and there stood Sam and Ben Caston and their sweet mother, Jenny. You might remember that Jenny and her husband Brian directed our orientation course when we first arrived in Kenya. Sam and Ben, about seven and ten years of age, reached out and handed me a warm buttery scone right out of the oven. Oh, my heart melted! The four of us had a dear little visit, and I felt so blessed by their thoughtfulness, their visit, and that delicious scone.

When the boys headed for the door, Jenny whispered to me in her delightful New Zealand accent, "Sam said to me today, 'Mummy, David and Linda are sort of like our grandparents, aren't they? Just different from our grandparents in New Zealand.'"

My heart melted all over again. I wanted to cry—tears of love for the Castons and tears of sadness because I missed my children and granddaughter. After the three left, I reminded myself that everyone here experiences the same longing for loved ones and, like the Maasai say, "A child is not owned by one person." Similarly, a mother, grandmother, or grandchild is not owned by one family. Here on the mission field, we stand in for family in each other's lives. The Castons and I had shared a family visit that afternoon.

Elizabeth still works for us. I know the commute makes her days extra long. She leaves home at 5:30 AM, changes buses a couple of times, and walks almost a mile to our house. To show I appreciate her loyalty, I give her bus fare and pay her for travel time. I see weariness in her face and hear it in her voice. God bless her for her faithfulness to us.

I needed minor surgery recently. We have a choice of several good medical facilities in Nairobi. Some hospitals have higher standards than others for sanitation and patient care, so we go to the hospital with the best reputation.

I had always felt safe from exposure to AIDS, but after I learned I needed surgery, I wondered how clean the operating rooms were and how well the medical staff practiced sterile procedures. My anxiety level rose. For a couple of days I sorted through my fears. First, I considered the surgeon, Mr. Patel. (Doctors go by "Mr." here.) He probably went to med school in England and received top-notch training. Furthermore, I had to believe he'd never carelessly risk infecting any of his patients with AIDS—or anything else. Next, I reminded myself that my surgery would take place in the hospital that everyone considered the best.

Then, too, God played a role. Shortly after we arrived in Nairobi, I ran across Psalm 138:8, "The Lord will fulfill His purpose for me." I highlighted those words in yellow and underlined them in black ink. Then I put a bracket around them and wrote in the margin, "This is for me in Nairobi and all across Africa." Back then, and again before surgery, I chose to believe that God had a purpose for my life and that I could trust Him to accomplish it.

I also marked Psalm 139:16, "All the days ordained for me were written in your book before one of them came to be." God knows how many days

I'll live on earth. I knew that if I got AIDS, then AIDS would be part of God's specific plan for my life. I knew He would be my constant companion, like always, and He'd take me to my heavenly home at just the right moment. A peace came over me. And Elizabeth, bless her heart, promised to pray for me.

My surgery went fine, and Elizabeth took good care of me when I returned home. Only time will tell if I've been exposed to AIDS, but I feel no anxiety.

Because I didn't want to worry family at home about my surgery, I didn't tell them. However, little did I realize how small the world now is with this new-fangled e-mail. I had e-mailed dear friends, missionaries in Papua New Guinea, and asked them to pray for my surgery, but I failed to mention that I hadn't told my family. A few days later, I received this e-mail from your Aunt Karen who, I'm sure, smiled while she wrote it:

> I must admit I'm a bit peeved that I had to find out from Britt and Gayle about Mom's surgery. And Jill and I quickly detected your conspiracy of family silence when we realized that you weren't just holding up on communication, you were continuing to e-mail and just not telling us! Sheesh! I'm your *daughter* and I need and *expect to be told* my dear parents' conditions, so don't try *that* stunt again! (*Please.*)

Dear, sweet Karen. I'm sorry I upset her.

August 2, 1995
Nairobi, Kenya,

Dear Maggie,
Here's a glimpse of life for an American in Kenya:

> It's sharing an office lunch table with a Cameroonian man, an English colleague, another from Ireland, a Swiss woman who usually works in Central African Republic, and two Kenyans.
>
> It's getting four punctured tyres in four weeks; the repair costs under a dollar.

It's being an American standing in a Kenyan store owned by an Asian merchant, buying a jar of honey with a label in both English and Arabic which says, "Produce of Australia, packaged in Singapore for Giant Impex of Manchester, England."

❖   ❖   ❖

August 3, 1995
Nairobi, Kenya

Dear Maggie,

A few days ago, we saw our landlord on television giving a speech and meeting with Baroness Lynda Chalker, of the U.K., who works with money donations for developing countries.

We've discovered another problem in this apartment. Spiders. Spiders that bite us while we sleep. Several times, one of us has awakened in the morning with a red, four-inch welt on an elbow. We don't understand the spiders' attraction to our elbows! During daylight hours, we've seen spiders that measure about three inches across, and I suspect they're the culprits. I always spray them when I spot them but, obviously, I haven't found them all. When I think about one of those spiders crawling across me, I get the willies.

I need to pin down several large projects before September 1 because that will be my last day in the office until September 25. Both your grandpa and I are preparing reports for Africa Area meetings September 3 through 15 up at Brackenhurst. I also need to prepare my presentation for the Communications meetings in Dallas and, by September 1, I hope to finalize details for a writers' workshop. After that, I'll have only a few days to catch up with the backlog at the office, close up the apartment, and pack for the Dallas meetings.

❖   ❖   ❖

September 18, 1995
Nairobi, Kenya

Dear Maggie,

Starting tomorrow and running through September 21, I'll host a training-in-writing workshop. We hope it will help increase both volume and quality of materials for publications around the world.

Late Friday afternoon your grandpa and I returned to the city from

Brackenhurst and a couple of hours later, the writing workshop's main presenter, Susan Van Wynen, flew in from the Wycliffe–U.S. office. Before she left home, she hurt her foot but didn't go to the doctor, and now she limps around in great pain. I suspect she broke a bone. I can't imagine how she lugged her bags through the airports.

Two workshop participants—Dottie, who works in Ivory Coast, and Nory, who works in Senegal—were scheduled to arrive at 7:45 AM. In Nairobi when we phone the airlines to ask if a plane will arrive on schedule, they rarely answer. Such was the case this morning, so we drove to the airport only to learn the plane wouldn't arrive until 11:50 AM. We drove back to the office, worked for a while, then trekked back to the airport. Now the ladies have arrived and they're tired. Nory had flown out of Senegal twenty-four hours earlier, and Dottie has fallen sick with amoeba and tummy trouble.

The workshop starts tomorrow morning. In addition to all the serious stuff, I've arranged for shopping, a drive through the game park, and a luncheon at a place called Charlie's. Most workshop participants live in Nairobi, but tonight the three out-of-towners will come to our house for dinner.

In twenty-three minutes, the Pope will land on Kenyan soil. Tomorrow he will speak at 10:00 AM in a church near our office.

My afternoon break is over so I'll sign off for now.

❖ ❖ ❖

September 19, 1995
Nairobi, Kenya

Dear Maggie,

Our writing workshop is progressing well, but I never expected the Pope to shut it down. This morning he spoke at a church less than two blocks from our office. Apparently for security reasons, he arrived in a massive helicopter which hovered low and lingered long right over our office. In our meeting room on the top floor, we could actually feel the thunderous chopping. The noise was so loud that we gave up talking to one another and waited—longer than anticipated—for that helicopter's clearance to land.

Quaint I ain't.

September 23, 1995
Nairobi, Kenya

Dear Maggie,
   Both your grandpa and I feel tuckered out after two packed, invigorating weeks of Africa Area meetings followed by my workshop. The workshop went well and we should see long-lasting, positive effects. Attendees left here enthusiastic about their jobs and eager to have another workshop soon.
   I worry about Elizabeth. She looks exhausted. The three days she works for us are extra-long.
   This week we need to finish our office work, close up our offices and our flat, and prepare to fly out of here October 3.

❖   ❖   ❖

December 18, 1995
Nairobi, Kenya

Dear Maggie,
   I haven't written to you for a while. Grandpa and I just returned to Nairobi after two months in the States on business. By November 30, your daddy's birthday, I had changed countries forty-three times since joining Wycliffe.
   Your grandpa and I are so pleased that you and your parents live near our Huntington Beach office and that we could spend weekends with you. While we were there, your parents announced that in a few months, they will present you with a new baby brother or sister! We are so excited! Recently your dad wrote,

> Each time we go into a book store we go through the
> pregnancy books and find out how far along Andrew/
> Emma/Change-our-minds-on-the-name is, and at this
> point all of his/her organs are in place. His/her little
> eyes are even there and look just like a regular baby's.
> Amazing stuff. God is pretty creative and more than a
> little powerful. I can't even begin to fathom it all, really. I
> love having a family!

December 19, 1995
Nairobi, Kenya

Dear Maggie,

Shortly after Elizabeth started working at our house, she politely hinted—in the subtle way Kenyans make a point—that employers supply their househelpers with a *kanga*, a colorful piece of cloth, to cover their clothes like an apron. We talked it over—should I buy one or give her money and let her choose one for herself? I decided to give her money, the equivalent of only a couple of dollars.

That conversation served as my introduction to a most interesting and essential item within the East African culture. People wear *kangas*—rectangular pieces of lightweight cotton fabric, worn sometimes by men but most often by women—in dozens of ways for dozens of purposes. *Kangas* can serve as aprons, dresses, skirts, head wraps, shawls, baby slings, diapers, tablecloths, tote bags, and blankets. I've even seen women roll them into a doughnut-shape and place them on their heads to balance baskets of produce. In fact, that's how the Apple Lady carries her boxes.

Each *kanga* consists of a bold traditional design in bright colors and a border containing a Swahili saying or proverb. And this is the most intriguing part: the sayings and colors silently communicate important messages to others—personal, religious, educational, or political. For example, they might encourage hard work, good character, and generosity. A woman wears a white *kanga* during the full moon to tell her husband that her heart is pure. A woman's *kanga* can convey that she's happy, sad, jealous, vengeful, ready for romance, ready to marry, or ready to divorce. There are special *kangas* for pubescent girls, brides, newlyweds, the divorced, the dead, and for a woman who has just given birth. With a *kanga*, a woman can tell her mother-in-law to keep her distance or warn her husband he'd better not stray.

Given all that, and since *kangas*' messages are in Swahili and very difficult to understand, I'm glad I asked Elizabeth to choose one for herself! There's no telling what I might have picked out!

Oh, by the way, I hear there's even a *kanga* with a message about the Pope's recent visit. I wonder how they say "helicopter" in Swahili.

Here are a few snippets from our recent everyday life:

Recently a friend told me about her bus ride. Jenny can't be more than five feet tall—just an itty-bitty thing. All the seats were full so she stood in the aisle and held onto a pole to keep her balance. At each stop, people climbed in and crowded closer together.

After one such stop, the bus lurched and an enormous woman staggered against Jenny—and, in the process, she clamped her sweaty armpit over Jenny's arm, the one that gripped the pole. By then so many people squeezed against her that she couldn't move. At the next stop still more people climbed in and the passengers pushed against each other until the pressure lifted Jenny off her feet. She traveled like that—suspended in air and trapped under that sweaty armpit—until she arrived at her destination.

A short time ago I needed a mammogram, but first I needed a breast exam. I opened the doctor's office door, expecting to check in at the receptionist's desk but, to my surprise, I entered the examination room. Dr. L., a Hungarian, sat at his desk wearing a dark suit and tie, smoking a cigarette, and drinking a cup of tea. We talked for a few minutes and then he told me to sit on the examination table next to his desk.

After I climbed up, he asked a few questions. How old was I? Did I have children? How old were they? How long did I nurse my babies? And then Dr. L. said, "Take off your blouse and bra so I can examine your breasts."

I expected him to hand me a gown and leave so I could change, and I expected a nurse to appear, but no, he just stood there and waited.... And so, there I sat, while he reached out with all eight fingers and both thumbs. "Ahhh—nice, young, firm breasts. If I were to look at only your breasts, I never would guess you are so old." Ha! Quaint I ain't.

An article in last night's newspaper reported on a ceremony held by the power company. The Minister for Energy assured everyone that, unlike the past, now we'll experience no power interruptions and failures. The next paragraph said, "The ceremony was interrupted by a blown fuse which plunged the area into darkness."

Love and smiles,
Grandma

12

Merry Christmas and Happy New Year

December 21, 1995
Nairobi, Kenya

Dear Maggie,

Christmas season is upon us, but we have no dreams of a white Christmas. Most Africans have never seen snow or ice. In fact, Christmas is the hottest time of the year—temperatures in the eighties, dry ground, and dry air.

In America, everyone, even those who practice other religions, knows that Christmas commemorates Christ's birth. Some African cultures, however, still know nothing about Him. In Ethiopia, for example, thousands of Surma people have never heard about Christ—even though many Ethiopians have known about Christ since the beginning. (When you're old enough to read, see Acts 8.) For the Surma, Christmas is a day like every other day of the year. Your grandpa and I feel honored to play a wee little part in making the Christmas story available for such people.

We received this e-mail from your dad:

> Dear Mom and Dad,
> I am feeling the blues for not getting to see Karen, Grandma Kay, the Thomas clan, or you two. You are in my heart and my prayers a lot. I miss you and hope your Christmas is good, even though it may be different from

the "good ol' days." Those days will be back sometime, I just know, if not here, then in Heaven. I love you very much. The greatest blessing that God can give us, I have decided, is a good family. Consequently, we have to be the most blessed family that ever lived! Merry Christmas and happy New Year.

All my (our) love,
Matt (for Jill and Maggie and Little Guy too)

❖ ❖ ❖

December 26, 1995
Nairobi, Kenya

Dear Maggie,

My friend from high school, Barb Rowe, her husband Al, and their two college-age kids spent Christmas with us. On the morning of the twenty-fourth, we traveled to Banana Hill at the invitation of Salome, the Apple Lady. Perhaps the invitation was her way to thank us for a loan to open a *duka*—a small store—on Banana Hill. Now she doesn't need to travel to Nairobi every day, and that makes us happy for her and her children.

We drove north about thirty-five minutes, pulled our borrowed van off to the side of the road and, under a bright blue sky, hiked toward Salome's house. Banana trees dotted the hillside, and thus the name Banana Hill. Word of our arrival spread quickly and within seconds, some twenty people hurried down the hill—Salome's children, relatives, and friends.

"*Jambo!*"

"*Jambo sana!*"

Smiling and dressed in their best clothes, they crowded around while Salome, all a-twitter, introduced us.

I had told the Rowes ahead of time that according to Kenyan custom, we should bring gifts of sugar, tea, or flour, so there on the path we handed out our gifts.

Laughing and chattering, our hosts escorted us up to Salome's home. Right away, I noticed that unlike the Nairobi slums where Elizabeth lives, Salome's home sits in a grassy open space. She and her children live in the type of house so common for many Kenyans—one room, about twelve feet square, attached to a row of five or six others just like hers. Salome's house has a concrete floor, cinder block walls, and electricity for one bare bulb in the center of the room. Despite the room's small size, she furnished it with two beds, a small sofa, and a couple of chairs. Salome doesn't have running water, a refrigerator, or a cooker; she cooks on a small charcoal stove that rests on the ground outside.

Salome, like all Kenyans, felt honored to have guests, and a sense of celebration filled her home that day. When we stepped inside, she said, *"Karibuni viti!"* (welcome, please sit down) and she seated us *wazungu* (white people) in front of a low table covered with a nice cloth. She had enlisted help from neighbors who, with big smiles, brought in bowls of food from their own homes.

After her friends left, it seemed important to Salome to shut the door. She and her family sat on stools or stood around the edge of the room, and together we shared a traditional Kenyan meal of rice, beans, and vegetables. While we ate, Barb and Salome talked about the high nutritional value of such a meal. We spent the afternoon visiting with the children, praising Salome for her tasty food, and taking pictures of all of us together. The fun-loving children wanted their pictures taken in front of our borrowed van so they could pretend it belonged to them! I'm sure the Rowes will remember that day. Most tourists can't visit local people in their homes, especially at Christmas. Your grandpa and I will long remember the day, too.

❖   ❖   ❖

December 30, 1995
Nairobi, Kenya

Dear Maggie,

Your grandpa and I just returned to Nairobi after four days in the Kakamega Rain Forest with Marvin and Joyce. We drove six hours one way over potholed roads, but the jolting ride was worth what awaited us—a dense tropical garden reputed for its birds and butterflies.

We stayed at the Rondo Retreat Center. The four of us rented—at the low missionary rate—a quaint little cottage painted pale yellow and surrounded by Rondo's expansive lawns, soaring trees, and lush flower gardens. Inside, handsome antiques furnished the cottage—colonial yet with a distinctly African touch. In the world of interior decorating, this is British Colonial style, a legacy from British East African days.

One sunny morning a guide took us on a nature walk through the rain forest and taught us about birds—over 350 species which attract bird-watchers from around the world; butterflies—40 percent of Kenya's butterfly species live there; and local rain forest vegetation—lush trees, ferns, thick shrubbery, and sixty species of orchids.

At Rondo—so different from Nairobi!—we left our cottage door unlocked all day, and I don't know if we even locked it at night. The tranquil lifestyle at Rondo, its understated old elegance, and the Kenyans' slow-paced, soft-spoken graciousness refreshed us all. I don't think we've ever taken a real vacation in Kenya—only weekend trips. All four of us needed the rest.

One evening before the electricity came on, a dozen tuberose blossoms and I took a long bath by candlelight in the old English claw-foot tub. The flowers' perfume filled the room. But, since that seemed a bit too quaint, before I left the Kakamega Rain Forest I swung on a vine and felt almost like Tarzan's Jane. Quaint I ain't.

❖ ❖ ❖

January 11, 1996
Nairobi, Kenya

Dear Maggie,

I received the following greeting from a Ghanaian I met at our Africa Area meetings. He wrote, "Happy New Year to you and your husband. I realized that you have started the year on a strong note regarding your work. More grease to your elbow!"

Happy New Year to you, too, Maggie!
Grandma

13

Termites, Fresh Monkey, Gazelle, Zebra, Eland, Spiders, and Moving House–Again

January 16, 1996
Nairobi, Kenya

Dear Maggie,
    Once or twice a year, flying termites hatch by the millions and fill the air. The first time I witnessed this, they hatched in the evening and the lights inside our home attracted them. They squeezed through cracks under the door and around the windows and took over our house. I'd never seen anything like it.
    Eventually I calmed down and watched. Flying termites have inch-long bodies and long wings. Once inside, they ran all over the floor. In pairs. The gentlemen flying termites chased the lady flying termites. In the process, their wings fell off and then they mated.
    The other day, though, they hatched in the daytime. At the end of the day when I walked out the office door, there stood the Payton boys, grinning, with termite wings stuck to their lips. They'd feasted on those termites and loved every bite. They'd grown up in rural Kenya while their parents translated the Bible, and since the Kenyan children ate those

termites, so did the Payton boys. I almost gagged when I saw them, but I suppose Americans eat things that would make Kenyans gag, too.

Remind me to tell you sometime about our pothole problems.

❖ ❖ ❖

January 22, 1996
Nairobi, Kenya

Dear Maggie,

For several weeks, our daytime temperatures have risen to around eighty degrees. I'm so thankful for the warm weather—our house and office are now comfortable. Lately we've also enjoyed rain showers at night.

A year ago, we drove with Marvin and Joyce to Thika. You might have heard of the book, *Flame Trees of Thika*, by Elspeth Huxley. Flame trees can grow up to thirty feed wide and scarlet blooms cover their branches.

We had hoped to find a well-known old restaurant with a view of a waterfall that had some connection to the old Tarzan stories. We couldn't find the place, though, and ate in a downright rural eatery instead. It's remained a joke among us since then, but yesterday after church we tried again and this time we found the right restaurant—a posh place during colonial days. I understand the settlers (British colonists and other Europeans) spent a lot of time there.

I found bran cereal in the grocery store! I'm so excited. Now I can make your grandpa's favorite Six Week Tea Muffins.

I enjoy the British-ness of Kenya. Those bran flakes came from England, and Grandpa's right now watching an English program on TV. My pantry has a good supply of Hob Nobs® oat cookies—I fell in love with them years ago on my first trip to Scotland. Our herbal tea came from Edinburgh, and our air freshener and bath soap came from England. Such goods offer me an occasional "escape to Britain" and keep me plugging away in surroundings far different.

Now, if we could just get a phone.

January 25, 1996
Nairobi, Kenya

Dear Maggie,

We heard on CNN that a blinding snowstorm blankets the northwest. We hope loved ones back home will be okay.

The other day Marvin and Joyce didn't have hot water at their apartment so we invited them over for showers and dinner. We also watched a video together, *Ground Hog Day.* Hilarious!

This morning we didn't have hot water here, so we heated water on the stove and sponge-bathed.

❖ ❖ ❖

January 29, 1996
Nairobi, Kenya

Dear Maggie,

A few days ago, about 6:45 AM, we drove by a man killed by a car when he ran across the road. At that time of day, thousands of people fill the roadsides, walking to work, but no one went anywhere near the man. He lay there alone on the side of the road. The impact ripped off part of his clothing but no one cared enough to cover his poor exposed body. Surely, someone could've covered him with something. The police had arrived, but they focused on inspecting the car's damage.

The next day we drove along a hectic city road just after a car struck a child. A group of tattered youngsters picked up his limp little body and stuffed it into the back seat of an old car. I suppose they took him to the hospital.

❖ ❖ ❖

February 3, 1996
Nairobi, Kenya

Dear Maggie,

Your dad tells us you sing, imitate the doorbell and the car alarm beep-beeps, and say, "How funny!" the way your mommy does. He says you play with a baby doll that Great-grandma Kay gave you and you hide it in your parents' roll-top desk. Then you say "Wha baby?" and you lift up your empty hands. Your dad says you repeat this earnestly (he means you say it over and over and over again, the way he did in his childhood) until your mom finds your baby for you. He also wrote that you love to watch Winnie the Pooh videos and you say "Pooh Bear" over and over again—"earnestly." I wish I could watch your videos with you.

Yesterday your grandpa and Marvin played golf at Limuru, and a man named Dave joined them. He didn't know, though, that he had to dress according to the golf course dress code—people can't wear jeans or collarless shirts—and you guessed it, Dave arrived wearing jeans and a collarless shirt. Undaunted, the men dug through the lost-and-found box until they found a pair of slacks and a shirt with a collar. The trousers didn't fit Dave, though, so your grandpa loaned him his. Then grandpa squeezed into the "found" pants—two inches too small in the waist, six inches too short in the legs, and wrinkled. He said both he and Dave looked ridiculous, but they met dress code and got to play golf.

❖ ❖ ❖

February 4, 1996
Nairobi, Kenya

Dear Maggie,

We work among an amusing mix of people on our staff—from Switzerland, the United States, England, Scotland, Canada, and New Zealand. Even among the Americans, some come from the Deep South, others come from New England or California or the Pacific Northwest, and each of us has distinct ways of thinking and living and working. Add to that our different church denominations, different life experiences, attitudes, education, priorities, and prejudices. Each has his or her own expectations, spoken and unspoken assumptions (such as the place or value of women), and unique communication style—though most of us don't recognize we have them. All these factors can cause offense, though I'm sure no one intends to offend. Too often the following is true, "I know you believe you understand what you think I said, but what I don't think you realize is that what you heard is not what I meant" (author unknown). Add to that fatigue, disappointment, sickness, marital issues, culture stress, and homesickness. Some people talk too much and work too little, and others talk too little and work too hard. Add all that up and what do we have? A whole bunch of people in need of God's grace! Only He could accomplish anything through a group like ours.

February 5, 1996
Nairobi, Kenya

Dear Maggie,

Grandpa and I found boysenberries for sale! I could hardly believe my eyes! The greengrocer told us an *mzungu* (white man) grows them near Brackenhurst. For the equivalent of about $2.50, we bought enough berries to make a small pie. Boysenberry pie—heaven on earth! A couple of days later, I found more berries so we bought two little packages. I made one into a pie and froze the rest. The grocer says the berries have only a one-month growing season, so I hope to freeze more to get us through the eleven months without them.

Speaking of food, I received this recipe for "Fresh Monkey" from my colleague Harriet Hill:

> Have the people bring it to you fresh, i.e., without burning the skin off. The female monkey has a very strong taste. You can identify it by its smell even from far away. You can give the hands and feet away. Monkey can be fried like chicken, used in stews, braised, or ground to make "monkey burgers."

This morning on our drive to work, we got stuck in a traffic mess. (Potholes contributed to the problems. Have I ever told you how bad the potholes are here?) To unsnarl the chaos, your grandpa paused to let an oncoming car turn in front of us. Just then, a bicyclist came barreling down beside us and crashed into the turning car. The impact crushed the young man's bike and threw him on top of the car. Only ten feet away, I watched as he rolled onto the ground. For a sickening moment, I watched the car roll toward him but, thank God, the driver stopped.

We pulled over and your grandpa ran to lift the man off the road so traffic could proceed. A crowd gathered, watching the man groan with leg and rib injuries. No one stepped forward to help him, though, so your grandpa did. After all, that's the Golden Rule—we're to do for others what we'd like them to do for us if we were in their place. The young man reached in his pocket and handed your grandpa a card with his name and his employer's name.

Then grandpa began to worry. We learned in our orientation that if you run into someone (which isn't uncommon, since thousands walk alongside the roads), you shouldn't stop because bystanders sometimes take justice into their own hands—they might beat you or even kill you.

Instead, you're supposed to drive to the nearest police station and turn yourself in. Since your grandpa stepped forward to help, and since he took the man's card, would the crowd think he had run into the man? Would they beat him?

The police drove by but they wouldn't stop. We couldn't find a pay phone. The man twitched and trembled, apparently in shock. A huge crowd gathered, and I prayed that no one would hurt your grandpa.

Drivers slowed down to see what happened and traffic backed up. Another car turned at the same place the accident occurred. The oncoming driver, watching the accident rather than traffic, ran into another car. We then had two accidents in the same spot.

Within seconds, another car turned at the same spot and, believe it or not, a bicyclist sped down the side of the road, looking at the accident rather than traffic, heading for the same kind of accident as the first one. I held my breath and covered my eyes—I just couldn't watch. But, by God's grace, the cyclist jerked to a halt only inches before impact.

I looked back at your grandpa, the crowd, and the injured man. A Good Samaritan stepped forward and offered to put him in his car and take him to the hospital. It looked like your grandpa would get away without a beating. *Oh, thank you, Lord!*

Since we had witnessed the first accident, your grandpa gave the driver our phone number and then we drove on to work, where your grandpa called the man's employer about his injuries and trip to the hospital (which Kenyans pronounce OH-spee-tole).

Despite occasional incidents like those, my thoughts most often focus on Kenya's pleasant qualities. We need to know where to find them and then pursue them. Fresh produce, game parks, tropical flowers, birdsongs, the fine Kenyan people—these are some of my favorite things.

When city life gets too stressful, sometimes we escape for a couple of hours on a weekend afternoon. One of our favorite getaways, a borough named Karen, is located a short drive from the city.

Arriving in Karen feels like stepping onto a different continent. European settlers established Karen about a hundred years ago. A few aging shops line one short, curved lane—the kind you'd expect to be cobbled—giving it the feel of an antiquated English village.

Back in 1994, Marvin and Joyce introduced us to a restaurant in Karen, The Horseman—a round, open-air place with a thatched roof. The menu includes a salad bar that we can eat because, unlike some restaurants, they soak their vegetables in chemicals to kill amoebas and bacteria. The Horseman's menu includes a choice of gazelle, zebra, or eland, grilled while we watch, smothered in our choice of sauces. Your grandfather usually chooses their thick, creamy mushroom sauce. Such delightful meals cost the equivalent of about four dollars when we first moved to Kenya, though prices have risen over time.

Dining at The Horseman and other Kenyan restaurants is a drawn-out affair. When we first arrived here, we felt irritated with the way Africans drag out a meal. Soon, though, we learned to appreciate the African way. In American restaurants, waiters hurry us through a meal, eager to shoo us out the door so someone else can use our table. Dining in Kenya, on the other hand, takes all evening, and their way encourages us to slow down and enjoy both the food and ourselves.

As appealing as the village and The Horseman are, the vast countryside outside the town entices me. It's a place of unpretentious, worn estates, a place of long lanes and shade trees and rolling, park-like lawns; a place of horse pastures and tall groomed hedges and manicured English-style gardens teeming with flowers. Karen is a place of open skies and clean air and a life still enough to hear birdsong and the faint rustle of the breeze stirring sun-baked grasses.

Danish-born Karen Blixen owned a coffee plantation in Karen from 1914 to 1931, and it served as the setting for several books she wrote under her pen name, Isak Dinesen. She had a strong affection for the Kenyans who worked on or near her farm. She helped them with medical needs, built them a school, provided them with work, and cared for them in the way Kenyans expected back then, almost like a parent caring for her children.

Karen Blixen's house, a low, spreading stone building with paned windows, is understated yet elegant in the old colonial style. It lies at the end of a long, curved driveway surrounded by acres of lawns, tropical flowering plants, hedges, eucalyptus trees, acacias, cacti, and palms.

I've lost count how many times I've watched the movie *Out of Africa* directed by Sydney Pollack; it's based on Karen's book, of the same title, and several others. Between my visits to her home and the movie scenes shot there, I feel quite attached to the old place. The movie's indoor scenes were filmed nearby at Karen's original house, Mbagathi, but outside scenes were shot at Mbogani, the house Karen lived in from 1917 until she left Kenya in 1931. A wide stone verandah runs across the front and around the side of Mbogani and every time I stand there, I'm aware that I'm standing where Karen hung a lantern to signal Denys Finch-Hatton.

I linger on the verandah on the spot where the movie's stars, Meryl Streep and Robert Redford, dined on a little table covered with a white linen cloth. I hear Mozart's "Concerto for Clarinet and Orchestra in A" drifting from the gramophone Denys gave Karen as a gift, and I picture them sitting there at the table, their longing for each other almost snapping like lightning in the air.

Inside the house, in Karen's bedroom we see her veiled safari hat, safari boots, and riding clothes. We see Denys's books, which he stored on Karen's shelves. He lived at Karen's house between safaris, and Karen said he found happiness on her farm. He loved to listen to her tell stories, and still today we see the fireplace and leather chair where they sat while she wove her tales late into the evening and left Denys spellbound by her charm and imagination.

I've taken the short walk behind her house to see the coffee roaster, still there under the acacias where it no doubt sat when the plantation burned down.

From her verandah and her dining room, Karen had a clear view of her beloved Ngong Hills in the near distance, those hills she mentioned so often. She began *Out of Africa* with these words, "I had a farm in Africa, at the foot of the Ngong Hills."[1] She wrote, "The Mountain of Ngong stretches in a long ridge from North to South, and is crowned with four noble peaks.... It rises to eight thousand feet above the Sea.... To the West the ... hills fall vertically down towards the Great Rift Valley."[2]

The love of her life, Denys, lies buried in those hills. One day we took a ride into those highlands and, driving on a dirt track, we spotted a white sign, about eighteen inches across and a couple of inches tall, nailed to a stake in the ground. Someone had hand-lettered "Denys Finch-Hatton's grave" and an arrow that pointed off in the distance. Now I wish we had followed that arrow, but we were on American time, not African, and felt the need to hurry home before dark.

When my friend Barb Rowe visited us in December, she gave me Karen Blixen's *Letters from Africa*. That book, and *Out of Africa*, have swept me up and carried me into another time in this place. I think of European settlers' lives back then, a curious mix of Victorian gentility and rugged life in the wilds—after all, Karen killed her share of lions. I think of those who frequented places like Karen and Thika, where we dined last month, and I say to myself, *Oh, my, here I am in the very same places.* I'm goofy enough to wonder if I could ever look like Meryl Streep in the movie—gauzy blouse, pith helmet, safari boots—and utterly feminine.... Nah, quaint I ain't!

But, wait! When I stop to think about it, I am acquainted with today's version of a similar lifestyle—like out in Maasai Mara. I'm sitting in a bentwood chair in front of my tent. A Kenyan, handsome and striking in his safari clothes—not unlike Robert Redford in the movie—approaches down the path, hushed. He bows his head and addresses me, almost whispering, in the endearing way Kenyans do, the way Farah spoke to Karen when he said, "*Msabu.*" He bends and places a tray before me, complete with crisp linens, bracing Kenya tea, cream, and scones.

Sometimes I wonder if, fifty years from now, my photos and letters from Africa might inspire your children, Maggie, as Karen Blixen's letters have touched me. Silly me.

❖ ❖ ❖

February 21, 1996
Nairobi, Kenya

Dear Maggie,
Today your dad's e-mail said the doctor believes the new baby is a girl. Your dad says, "We are really thrilled to be having another child. God is very, very good to us and we look forward to meeting our new baby in July." Your grandpa and I will have another precious granddaughter!

❖ ❖ ❖

March 13, 1996
Nairobi, Kenya

Dear Maggie,
The hot, dry season has lasted too long. I can hear the earth groan. This parched and weary land cries out for rain. Farmers cry out for rain, people in the city cry out for rain. I cry out for rain. We look up to the heavens and ask God for rain. Each day we search the skies for clouds. We've watched a few form but, day after day, they drift on over us. Soon the rain must fall. We must have rain.

❖ ❖ ❖

March 16, 1996
Nairobi, Kenya

Dear Maggie,
The rains have begun! When the first drops started to fall, I wanted to run outside from my office and dance in it.

❖ ❖ ❖

March 22, 1996
Nairobi, Kenya

Dear Maggie,

    Your Aunt Karen has been sick for a while and can't seem to get well. Sometimes I haven't known how to balance duties of both a mother and a missionary but, in this case, I know what I must do. Karen needs me and I will be there for her.

    I don't know if people will understand, or accept, why I'm going home. I get the feeling that, now and then, someone back home might think missionaries should tough things out and make sacrifices that the general population doesn't or won't make. (I'm still shocked to think that people used to send missionaries their used tea bags and leftover soap shards.) Our financial supporters might not approve of me spending money for a plane ticket, but our income tax refund equals the cost of a plane ticket, so I'm going. My daughter needs me.

    I e-mailed a friend in Port Angeles, Mary, and asked her to schedule a doctor appointment for Karen. I think again of that Maasai saying—a child is not owned by one person—and I thank God for Mary standing in for me.

    Maggie, bless your dear mother's heart. She sent this e-mail today:

> Dear Ma T.,
>   You are hereby relieved of any and all duties to feel guilty in any way for coming to see Karen. It sounds like she really needs you right now. God has brought missions work into your life right now, but that doesn't mean He has taken your loved ones out of it. Sure, Karen is officially an adult, but sometimes you just plain old need your mom. I have times like that even though my life is full with Matt and Maggie. There isn't anyone else in your life that you can just lean on like your parents and know that they expect nothing in return. Friends and lovers can't do that like parents sometimes. Christ on several occasions spent forty days with just His Father, and He was in His thirties at the time. You have a great opportunity right now to be the real-life arms of the Heavenly Father that give Karen a much-needed hug.

    Your Aunt Karen says that because I'm coming, she feels like a heavy weight has lifted off her. I know I'm doing the right thing. Grandpa's helping me book flights for early April.

❖   ❖   ❖

March 27, 1996
Nairobi, Kenya

Dear Maggie,
　Your sweet mommy writes,

> Emma is growing (and, therefore, so am I) and kicking and rolling around. When we ask Maggie where "Baby Emma" is, she lifts up my shirt and pats my stomach. I'm still afraid she is going to be in for a huge surprise when she comes face to face with ol' Baby Emma.

　Mundara, a coworker of ours, heard I'm going home to help my Karen, and he pulled me aside to remind me of Genesis 32:9 when God told Jacob to go back to his country and his relatives, and that He would make him prosper. What an appropriate verse! I wonder if Mundara knows I worry what people might think of me for going home. Maybe he senses I need assurance that it's okay for me to help my girl. Mundara wanted to send me on my way with that blessing, and I feel doubly blessed because, yet again, God Himself has reached out and blessed me through one of our Kenyan friends.

May 13, 1996
Nairobi, Kenya

Dear Maggie,
　A week and a day ago, I arrived back in Nairobi after spending a month in the States helping your Aunt Karen. If I recall correctly, now I have crossed fifty-three international borders in less than three years.
　Each time we prepare to land at Jomo Kenyatta International Airport, we peer out the window in search of giraffes and zebras grazing across the road from the airport. I get a thrill when I spot those wild creatures coexisting with modern civilization. Eighty years or so ago, Karen Blixen wrote,

> To Denys Finch-Hatton I owe ... the greatest, the most transporting pleasure of my life on the farm: I flew with him over Africa.... You may ... fly low enough to see the animals on the plains and to feel towards them as God did when he had just created them, and before he commissioned Adam to give them names.³

The doctor found that Karen has strep throat, mononucleosis, a sinus infection, and a staph infection. The poor girl has been too busy to take care of herself. She is a middle school English teacher, high school volleyball coach, Young Life leader, and a graduate student working on her master's degree. No wonder she's sick! I'm so grateful I could spend time with her and that God has shown me, again, that my roles as both mother and missionary can intertwine.

When I left Nairobi to go to Karen's, I said goodbye to Marvin and Joyce. They finished their term in Africa and now have new jobs in the Dallas office. The four of us had a great time exploring Kenya together, and your grandpa and I will miss them. They'll always play a large role in our memories of Africa.

A couple of days ago I got this e-mail from your dad:

> May 11, 1996
>   Hello, Mom, and Happy Mother's Day. I hope you know that I feel you are one of the very best moms that has ever lived. It seems that as God continues to mold you into many new and exciting roles, I admire you even more and more. Your commitment to Him, your trust in Him, your trust, love and support of Dad, all are, in my opinion, truly heroic in nature. When I was a kid you were my Mom. That says it all. Every kid loves his mom in a completely unexplainable way. Now you are not just my Mom, you are one of my heroes, someone who challenges me to live up to a higher calling that God has for all of us. I cannot ever repay you for what you mean to me, Mom, nor can I ever express accurately how much I love you. I love you very much. I hope that you have a great Mother's Day and that you realized that if you were going to get an e-mail from me you would have to come

in to the office during the weekend to get it. Sorry about that. (Maybe you did go wrong somewhere.)
Happy Mother's Day!

Matt

While I helped Karen in the States, your grandpa moved us out of our apartment. Now "the place we lay our heads" is an apartment at Cassia Court. Spiders in the other place kept biting us while we slept. On the morning of my flight to Karen's, I awoke to yet another spider bite, this time on my face. At work that day, two colleagues with medical expertise looked at the four-inch welt around my eye. One whispered to himself, "It's too bad it's so close to her brain!" Alarmed, I asked what he meant. He explained that the poison could easily get into my brain. Yikes!

That did it. Grandpa said he'd find us a new place to live, and he did, even though he was sick at the time. Doctors treated him for typhoid, but later lab results didn't confirm the diagnosis. Whether your grandpa had typhoid or something else, he suffered for weeks. Even so, he hauled our entire household out of the old place, across town, into the new building, and up three flights of stairs. Bless his heart. Elizabeth set up the kitchen, arranged furniture, made beds, organized, and stocked linen closets. When I walked in the door, I found everything in place and running smoothly. Now, that's how I like to move house!

From our new home, we walk to work in five minutes—a major improvement over our long drive across town. I'm so relieved to have a normal work schedule now.

Our apartment building stands on a hillside and, from our third floor unit, we look across much of the city and toward the airport. The edge of Nyayo National Stadium's parking lot begins about two hundred feet from here, on the other side of a narrow road, a railroad track, and shrubs. These days military and police bands practice their marching and music in the stadium in preparation for Madaraka Day, a commemoration of the date in 1963 when Kenya attained the right of self-governance, just prior to independence from Britain.

Love to you,
Grandma

14

Literacy

Defend the cause of the weak and fatherless;
maintain the rights of the poor and oppressed.
Rescue the weak and needy.
Psalm 82:3–4

May 19, 1996
Nairobi, Kenya

Dear Maggie,

    A merciless drought ravages several regions of Africa and thousands of people have died. A friend told me a story that broke my heart. In one of those places, children cry because they're hungry, but their mothers have no food. Even so, they build a fire in the evening and put on a pot of water. This makes the children think their mothers will cook dinner, so they stop crying. The mothers let the fire burn until the children fall asleep for the night. Then they put out the fire.

    I ache every time I think of that story. I pray for those dear, desperate people. Maggie, we must never take our food and clothing for granted, and we must share with those in need.

❖ ❖ ❖

May 20, 1996
Nairobi, Kenya

Dear Maggie,

One day I heard someone ask, "Why do we work so hard to help people groups translate the Bible into their own languages if they can't read it?" Good point. If people can't read, their Bibles will just get dusty on a shelf. That's why literacy—teaching people to read—is a necessary part of the Bible translation task. We have a saying, "Translation gives people the Bible, and literacy opens it."

Literacy helps people in other ways, too. More than 90 percent of the world's poor can't read so, to help them escape poverty, our literacy specialists teach more than reading—they also teach writing and math. Literate people can read newspapers, vote, and participate in local and national affairs. They can read instructions on medicine bottles, fill out forms, and manage their finances.

Recently I met a woman who teaches literacy classes for a language group in West Africa. The people had trouble learning so Esther investigated and found the problem—hunger. People can't learn to read and write if they go to bed hungry and awake the next morning with nothing to eat for breakfast.

Esther looked into why they were hungry. She discovered that the soil was so poor that it couldn't produce good crops, so she and her husband taught the people to compost—it increases the soil's yield, it works for three years compared to chemical fertilizer, which stays good for only one, and it costs less, too.

Next Esther taught them to raise small animals because they provide compost material as well as meat and eggs. Disease, however, kept killing the animals, so she taught them to give their animals injections.

Esther also looked at how the people used the grain they grow. Millet is the staple crop in that region but instead of eating it, they use most of it make beer for their annual funeral festivities. This leaves the people hungry for much of the rest of the year. Now Esther and her husband are teaching people how to use less millet for their beer so they can feed their families better.

Your grandpa and I have heard numerous stories about the way literacy improves women's lives in particular. We hear a saying across Africa, "Teach a man to read and you have taught one person. Teach a woman to read and you have taught a family." In too many cases, African men either abandon their families or fail to provide for them. Women, then, often become the providers, the stabilizers, the dependable ones, in both families and communities. Because they understand the importance of education, they attend literacy classes, and as women learn to read, write, and do math, they gain a sense of their own worth and ability to help themselves and their families.

Health improves among literate women because they learn better methods of sanitation, hygiene, and nutrition. One woman said that before she attended literacy classes, "I did not know what a balanced diet meant. I now know that I need a balanced diet so I can grow properly and be healthy."

Literate people can plan and budget for the farming year, study agriculture journals, learn improved methods of agriculture, and keep records so they can grow better crops the next year.

When women develop math skills, they can set up income-generating projects—selling rice and corn, for example, and making and selling bean cakes, peanut cakes, jewelry, baskets, crocheted doilies, tie-dyed cloth, and other crafts. I often purchase their products because I admire those women and want to support their efforts.

When women learn those skills, the entire community can benefit because often women turn around and teach others, both adults and children, how to read, write, and do math. With their new skills and confidence, communities have built schools, started businesses, and drilled boreholes for safe drinking water.

Literacy classes often operate in partnership with local churches and include Bible studies in the people's own languages. In the same way that women teach their children to read, write, and do math, they also teach them what they learn in Bible studies.

In all these ways, literacy helps people—helps them join in local and national affairs, grow spiritually, and escape poverty. Literacy has a far-reaching impact for generations to come and is one way we extend God's love to people in tangible, practical ways. Through literacy, we lend a hand to the widowed and the fatherless, the poor and oppressed, and the weak and needy. It's hard to live so far away from you and our loved ones but we also thank God that we can, in our own small ways, help with these causes.

Love and prayers,
Grandma

15

Monkey Business, Presidential Pageantry, and A Trip to The Emergency Room

May 26, 1996
Nairobi, Kenya

Dear Maggie,

These are exciting days for your grandpa, and for me, too, because West Nairobi School will open in September! Over the past couple of years your grandpa has e-mailed your parents about the ways God has helped him start this new school for MKs—missionaries' kids. Because he has already written so much about that, I'll let you read his letters for yourself when you're old enough.

Since your Aunt Karen has taught at her school in Port Angeles for three years, she's eligible to take a leave of absence and—your grandpa and I are so excited!—she will teach at West Nairobi School next year! Just think—she'll teach at WNS its very first year!

Recently we bought a bed for Karen to use when she gets here. We can buy furniture made by craftsmen alongside the road but, because they build it on rocky dirt, neither they nor we can tell if the furniture is level. We found a bed, made of a wood that resembles pine, which seemed sturdy and level. We couldn't buy it, though, because the man had just varnished it, so we agreed to return the next day. Rain started falling just as we drove off, and it poured for hours. We weren't sure what to expect when we returned, but the bed seems okay. We also found a bookshelf and bentwood chair for Karen's room.

On our way home, we stopped at Nakumatt and bought a mattress—a foam rubber pad with a lightweight cotton cover. I'll need to have sheets made because we can't buy fabric wide enough for sheets. Actually, we can buy ready-made sheets, but they're three feet too short. On Biashara Street, a block lined with Asian cloth merchants, we can buy fabric in any of the stores and they'll make sheets, at no extra charge, by sewing three long strips of fabric together lengthwise.

The electric company has turned off our power for several hours on three of the past five days. We never know when they will turn it off and that's disastrous for anyone working on the computer. I think every person on our staff has lost important documents—forever, apparently.

These power outages have forced a different rhythm in our office routines. When we have electricity, we use the computer and other things that require power, and we save meetings, filing, and organizing for those times with no electricity.

❖ ❖ ❖

June 3, 1996
Nairobi, Kenya

Dear Maggie,
From our apartment, we watched a line of limos deliver President Moi and other dignitaries to Nyayo Stadium for the Madaraka Day celebration. During the ceremonies, fighter jets flew low overhead in daring formations. We watched all this from our balcony, but we couldn't actually see into the stadium so we watched the singing, parades, and speeches live on television. Pretty neat!

❖ ❖ ❖

Monday, June 10, 1996
Nairobi, Kenya

Dear Maggie,
I heard another story that makes me glad we can help people

have access to Scriptures in their own languages. Sometimes when a congregation doesn't have a Bible in a language they understand, the pastor reads one verse or passage at a time, and an interpreter translates it for the listeners. In Ethiopia one Sunday, the pastor read a passage in 1 Timothy that teaches Christian women to care for widows in their families. The interpreter, however, translated incorrectly. He told the congregation that Christian women should slaughter widows and not burden the church with them. This mistake wouldn't have happened if they'd had the Bible in their own language. Apparently, someone caught the error before anyone hurt their widows, but this incident makes me wonder how many other misinterpretations occur.

July 1, 1996
Nairobi, Kenya

Dear Maggie,

For my forty-ninth birthday, your grandpa took me on a weekend safari to Amboseli National Park near the foot of Mt. Kilimanjaro. We didn't realize the road would end before we arrived at the Amboseli Serena Safari Lodge, and we had driven our city car! The road turned into a track strewn with boulders, and though your grandpa agonized mile after mile after mile, he kept driving—over heaps, around sharp stones, and through ruts—ever so slowly, and we got there okay.

We took fun game drives, spotted numerous animals, and took in views of Kilimanjaro, a mindboggling hulk of a mountain. It stands so tall that even the equatorial sun can't melt its glaciers. Clouds usually blocked Kili from sight, though, except for brief periods in early morning and late afternoon.

In the lodge, we ate our meals at an assigned table beside a window, and a small black-faced monkey always sat on the ledge outside, her face about ten inches from mine. Often here in Kenya, window openings have glass slats (jalousies) which we can open or close. That monkey—with a mean look in her eye—kept reaching through the slats to snatch our food. To discourage her one time, I closed the slats and pinched her fingers. That made her hopping mad—I saw fire in her eyes! I'm sure she would've attacked me if the window hadn't separated us, but since it did, I pinched her fingers any time she got too aggressive. She would then glare at me, but I reminded her that thanks to Harriet's recipe, I knew how to fry her like chicken, make her into stew, braise her, and make monkey burgers out of her. No, no, no, quaint I ain't.

One morning we meandered through the colossal breakfast buffet and loaded our plates as if we hadn't eaten in a week. We carried them to our table and returned to the buffet for juice and coffee. When we got back, food and broken dishes covered our table. That monkey had squeezed through the window and helped herself to our breakfast. Just then, a waiter hurried over and suggested we dish up our breakfast over again—and promised to seat us at a different table. I guess that monkey got the last laugh.

❖   ❖   ❖

July 3, 1996
Nairobi, Kenya

Dear Maggie,

Elizabeth still works for us three days a week and, like me, she's thankful she has a shorter commute now that we've moved house. She takes such good care of us. Her singing, energy, and bubbly presence multiply the well-being in our home. She constantly worries, though, about rumors that her neighborhood will be bulldozed down. My heart nearly fails me at the thought of millions of Kenyans losing their homes and their few possessions. May God have mercy on them.

A college guy named Ted lives with us now. He came over for the summer to work in one of our offices and the housing coordinator asked if he could live with us. He reminds us of our own kids—he has a great sense of humor, excellent manners, and a positive attitude. And he calls me "Mom." I love it.

When Ted got up his first morning, he asked why a man had been singing in our stairwell so early in the morning. Your grandpa and I looked at each other, puzzled. We told Ted we hadn't heard anything, but he assured us he heard a man singing and that the noise echoed through the stairwell. Now, our building's stairwells echo because the walls and floors are stone or terrazzo (stone chips and concrete with a smooth, hard surface), so we could understand that Ted might have heard an echo. But, a man singing in the stairwell? Just then, we realized that Ted had heard the Muslims' pre-dawn call to prayer from a nearby mosque. Their calls occur five times a day starting about 5:30 AM, even before sunrise. Grandpa and I had become so accustomed to hearing them that we'd tuned them out.

One Saturday morning we took Ted downtown to City Market—dodging potholes—but he has never traveled to a country so different from his own and apparently the crowds and new ways of doing things were too much for him; often it takes people time to appreciate the positives within cultures new to them. Now Ted doesn't want to come downtown with us anymore, but that's okay. As long as he calls me Mom, he can get away with almost anything.

Ted knocked on our bedroom door one night and when I stepped into the hallway, I could see his body trembling. He said he felt chilled and that he had diarrhea and vomiting.

Your grandpa and I talked it over but weren't sure what to do. In the States, we would've driven him to the hospital emergency room, but here in Nairobi, because of crime and carjackings, people don't go out at night unless it's an emergency. After your grandpa and I hurried through our short list of options, he drove to our office, two blocks through our relatively safe neighborhood, and used the office phone since we don't have one of our own. He called friends, a doctor and nurse couple, and they said Ted's condition warranted making the risky trip to the hospital. Our friends promised to pray for them and, of course, I prayed too.

After a couple of anxious hours, I heard them climbing the stairs and I flung open the door. Once inside, they told me lab tests revealed a bacterial infection, the typical "tummy trouble" that bothers so many people. The doctor prescribed antibiotics, but the hospital pharmacy had closed for the night. They phoned a different pharmacy, one that stayed open until midnight, and even though it was already midnight, the pharmacy stayed open a few minutes longer so your grandpa and Ted could get there.

The next morning I wondered how Ted caught that infection; he knew he could use only filtered water for drinking and brushing his teeth. Then I got an idea. I asked if he ever let water into his mouth in the shower. Ah, that was the problem. Ted showers more carefully now.

(Our friend Marvin brushes his teeth with tap water, but he has lived in or taken business trips to several dozen foreign countries and has developed an incredible digestive system. I've urged him to donate his body to science when he dies. His innards must be amazing.)

A few days ago, we walked downstairs on our way to work and noticed a pile of rocks on the front steps. I asked the guard about them. He said thieves broke into our compound overnight and he had collected those rocks as his only defense. In this neighborhood when trains rumble through at night, thieves take advantage of the noise to muffle the sounds of their break-ins.

Another night recently, we awoke to blasts nearby. We're accustomed to noises through the night, but we'd never heard anything like that before. We jumped up and looked out the window. Red flashes lit up the night sky, one after another, each one accompanied by an explosion. We felt sick when we realized the blasts were occurring between the airport and our apartment—was a coup d'état underway? Our office administrators have a message system for such times and we soon learned that an oxygen tank facility had caught fire, and each time a tank exploded, it sent out a blast and red flames.

Whew!
Grandma

16

Emma Elisabeth Anne Thomas

July 11, 1996
Nairobi, Kenya

Dear Maggie,
    These days we wonder when we'll hear news of Emma's birth. My mother phoned me at work yesterday to say she tried to call your parents several times but since no one answered, she wondered if they had headed for the hospital. We're all eager for the good news!

    I love to arrive at our office early in the morning and find Japheth sweeping the grounds with his broom of herbs. He always smiles and greets me in his hushed voice, "Goood mawning to you." I sense God's gentle grace in Japheth's being.
    Our Swiss colleague Luise has trained Japheth in the gardens' design and care. They're a riot of color and texture all twelve months of the year—cannas, lantana, periwinkle, lobelia, impatiens, bamboo, ferns, aloe, banana trees, bougainvillea, oleander, frangipani, hibiscus, African lilies, African daisies, eucalyptus trees, bottlebrush trees, jasmine, and geraniums, among others. One day a friend introduced me to a delightful shrub covered with hundreds of flowers about an inch across. In the evening, those flowers give off a heavy perfume. On the first day a blossom opens, it's a dark purple color; by the next day it's light purple; and the third day it's pure white, and thus its name—Yesterday, Today, and Tomorrow. One of my favorite

plants, a vine covered with long clusters of deep violet blossoms, climbs up and around our office building. Japheth, a loyal, hard-working employee, cares for them all.

We just learned that medical bills for Japheth's son left the family without money or food. Some of us donated money to help. May God have mercy on them.

We see needy people all around us. A white-haired man works as a guard at our apartment compound. He walks slowly and his bony limbs protrude through his tattered clothes. Guards earn about eighty Kenya Shillings a day, a little more than a dollar. Perhaps he, like many others, sends some of his paycheck upcountry to a wife and children. Because we look for ways to help the needy earn money, your grandpa hires the guard to wash our car once a week.

❖ ❖ ❖

July 18, 1996
Nairobi, Kenya

Dear Maggie,

I just got off the phone with your dad. Your sweet mom gave birth to Emma Elisabeth Anne twelve and a half hours ago, July 17 your time. Your daddy says Emma wants to eat all the time, she has good color and reflexes, and she looks around a lot. She's fair and blonde, like you, Maggie. She weighs eight pounds, seven ounces, and she measures just over twenty inches long. Your grandpa and I thank God for Emma Elisabeth Anne's safe arrival and can't wait to meet her! Meanwhile, we'll look forward to photos.

Your daddy's Great-great-grandmother Thomas named her girls the same names your parents have chosen for you and your sister: Margaret Thomas and Emma Thomas. I don't suppose your parents did it on purpose—I think they didn't even know. What a coincidence!

July 21, 1996
Nairobi, Kenya

Dear Maggie and Emma,

My mother, your Great-grandma Kay, sent me this poem she wrote for wee baby Emma:

Dear Lord, bless sweet Emma Elisabeth Anne!
We know for her life you've a wonderful plan.
How we'll love her, enjoy her, and play with her too—
Her Mommy and Daddy will tell her of You.
They'll help her to walk and to talk and to pray,
And big sister Maggie will teach her to play.
So, Lord, thanks for Emma Elisabeth Anne,
She is welcomed with joy by the whole of our clan!

Great-grandma Kay
July 1996

Your grandpa and I can hardly wait to see pictures of baby Emma, and we hope you're in some of them, too, Maggie!

Love,
Grandma

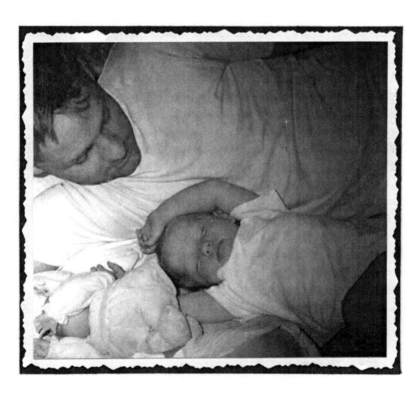

Matt with new baby Emma Elisabeth Anne

17

West Nairobi School

July 22, 1996
Nairobi, Kenya

Dear Maggie and Emma,
    Your grandpa and I had never seen flamingos so we took a day trip to Lake Nakuru National Park and invited our college boarder Ted and a gal named Jan to join us. She attends our Seattle church and came over for a couple of months to help get West Nairobi School up and running. Even more than seeing flamingos, we wanted Jan and Ted to fall in love with Kenya. I think that, down deep, I also wanted to make up for the cockroach Jan found in her pizza in an upscale restaurant.
    On our game drives at Lake Nakuru, we spotted hartebeest, giraffes, warthogs, antelopes, gazelles, monkeys, baboons, Cape buffalos, zebras, a group of five white rhinos—and flamingos, too, of course. We also saw water buck, handsome animals we'd never seen before.
    Midday we stopped at the lodge for lunch. We chose to eat at the bar because meals there cost the equivalent of under $3 while meals in the dining room cost over $17. Outside on the patio, we sat in a line beside each other so everyone could enjoy the view of the lake. A row of low tables sat in front of us.
    Eventually the waiter stepped out with our meals. He had started placing them on our tables when he screamed and flung his arm toward your grandpa. Startled, we jerked our heads to look at him when an

enormous baboon dropped from the roof onto your grandpa's lap. It grabbed a handful of food and knocked the plate to the ground. The waiter hollered and waved his arms, but the baboon looked him in the eye—arrogant and defiant—turned, and pounced on Jan's plate, then my plate, and then Ted's, all the while stuffing food into its mouth. Dinner plates and drinking glasses shattered on the patio. Food splattered every direction. Suddenly, it seemed, the baboon tired of us and ran off across the field.

All this happened in about thirty seconds. Afterward the four of us laughed, but the episode could have turned dangerous. Baboons are mean, tenacious, and strong, and they've even snatched small children. This guy was a big one. Grandpa estimated it weighed over fifty pounds.

The manager hurried to apologize, but he also explained that we humans were guests in the baboons' territory. He sent us off to the dining room to eat the $17 meals, but charged us for only our original order from the bar. The total bill came to under $15, but we ate $68 worth of meals.

July 30, 1996
Nairobi, Kenya

Dear Maggie and Emma,

A year and a half ago, West Nairobi School existed as only a misty dream. When your grandpa presented the initial idea to our boss, we worried that he might not like it, but he did. At his advice, your grandpa took the idea to the next level, and then the next, knowing it could be vetoed at any point. To our amazement, the school idea got one green light after another. Then it faced its toughest hurdle: it became official business at our Africa Area meetings last fall. We knew that God could either make it happen or bring it to a halt. Delegates debated and discussed the plan. A couple of people voiced concerns, but nothing came up that your grandpa had not already thought through. Next, it went to committee. Soon it came back for the vote—and the school received the official okay!

Despite official approval, one man thought your grandpa couldn't pull it off. "It'll never happen," he scoffed. A couple of people called him crazy to try to open the school this year and urged him to aim instead for next year. Nevertheless, God and your grandpa have accomplished the seemingly impossible—West Nairobi School will open this fall!

Grandpa can hardly contain his joy—he has leased a facility for WNS, and the principal, James, has arrived. He's working like crazy to orient

James and work through stacks of paperwork. Parents love the school's location, and increasing numbers of students have enrolled. Two of my life-long friends, Barb Van Winkle and Barb Rowe, shipped boxes and boxes of books to the school library. Bless their hearts!

The school sits on two and a half acres of land. The gardens need attention, but your grandpa hired a gardener. Do you remember the nice young man named Wycliffe? For a long time he has looked for a job but, in the meantime, he has volunteered at our apartment gate. Well, Grandpa hired him to maintain the school's grounds and hired his wife Hellen to cook lunch for the school's cleaning staff. For a long time now, I've hoped

Wycliffe and Hellen
at West Nairobi School

and prayed someone would give Wycliffe and Hellen jobs, but little did I know your grandpa could help answer those prayers! Now they live in a nice little house on the school grounds. They're fine Christian young people, quiet, hard working, and dependable.

Life right now is wild but wondrous. New teachers and school-related people fly in one after another after another. We just learned that a teacher family will arrive Thursday—we hadn't heard a date before—and another teacher will arrive Thursday, too. Another, scheduled to arrive Thursday, hasn't received her work permit yet. She might have to wait another two weeks.

On Sunday, a young teacher arrived from England. John—tan and blond with aqua blue eyes—looks like the young Paul Newman. He'll be here for three weeks to set up play fields and sports facilities at WNS. Another teacher and the dorm parents will arrive on Saturday, and the schedule goes on like that for a couple more weeks. Your Aunt Karen arrives August 13, and school begins August 19.

The arrival of each person or family involves a run to the airport, meals at our house, stacks of dishes—no dishwashers here—and orientation. We take them to church and acquaint them with the city and its ways. We teach them sanitation, hygiene, how to soak vegetables in chemicals, and how to filter drinking water. We also do a few fun things with them because we want them to fall in love with Kenya. I help your grandpa with all these on top of my full-time job so I feel like I'm swirling in a whirlwind, but an exciting one. This school is a dream-come-true for your grandfather.

At this wild and crazy time, I'm so thankful for Elizabeth's help at home. I couldn't do all this without her. Sometimes I ask her to buy a few items at a *duka* nearby, and other times I ask her to chop vegetables for a pot of soup. She does all kinds of chores that I don't even ask her to do, and she lets me know when I need to add something to my grocery list. "Leen-dah," she says, "we need more OWN-ee-owns" (onions).

The other day a friend suggested that a working woman needs a wife. Amen! Quaint I ain't!

Love,
Grandma

18

Job's Perspective

August 1, 1996
Nairobi, Kenya

Dear Maggie and Emma,
Nairobi houses an interesting mix of people, cultures, and religions. When we drive around town, we can see any number of churches, mosques, cathedrals, and temples.

A significant number of Nairobi's citizens are of Indian heritage, descendants of immigrants who helped build the railroad from Mombasa, on the Indian Ocean, to Kampala, Uganda, starting in 1896. Referred to here as "Asians," they tend to work as shop owners, businessmen, and doctors.

Numerous international agencies and corporations headquarter in Nairobi, too, as do embassies and a United Nations office, so people from around the world live here. Most dress in either Western or African clothing, but it's not unusual to see an Arab man dressed in a traditional long white robe and flowing red and white headpiece—seated in the back of a chauffeur-driven Mercedes Benz.

Nairobi has several universities and colleges, and many Kenyans have a good education, hold responsible jobs, and dress well. They tend to make up the small middle class.

Nevertheless, the unemployment rate is about 55 percent, a staggering figure. But it's more than a statistic. Real people have no way to feed their families, real people feel real hunger, and real people need medical help. They love their children just as much as we love ours. Can you imagine their desperation? For more than half of Kenya's people, poverty and malnutrition are ongoing, everyday realities.

For generations, many Kenyans have lived on family farms and survived on their own grain, vegetables, fruit, chickens, goats, and other animals. Traditionally, when a man dies his children subdivide his *shamba* (farm) but, inevitably, plots have grown smaller and smaller until some aren't large enough to divide any more. Coupled with severe drought, living off the land has become increasingly difficult.

To support their families, thousands of Kenyan men have moved to Nairobi to find jobs, leaving their wives and children upcountry to work the *shambas*. The men send money back home but, considering some of them earn only a couple of dollars a day and must pay for their room and board (often in one of Nairobi's slums), they don't have much left to send home. Nevertheless, because they love their families, they do the best they can.

Many of Kenya's citizens get up before dawn, splash off with water—often from a neighborhood tap—and sometimes eat nothing for breakfast. When the sun comes up at six, we see thousands of people on the streets walking for miles to get to work; most can't afford the bus. Too many wear worn clothes and tattered shoes, often the wrong size, sometimes without laces. Many work for the equivalent of less than eighty dollars a month, and yet they are the blessed ones—they have jobs. The unemployed look for jobs but, all too often, they simply can't find work.

Our friend Bernard (pronounced BARE-nard) has more training than many and works as a driver in Nairobi. Like thousands of other men, he sends money home to his wife and children upcountry, where they farm their plot of earth. He told us he sold his maize crop for a few hundred dollars, an amount he depended on to cover most of his family's needs for an entire year. The buyer took his maize, and that of many other families, but never paid for it. This left those families on the verge of starvation. After months of controversy, the buyer said they could have their maize back—if they came and got it. These families are so poor they can hardly feed their families, let alone hire a truck to transport grain, so now they have neither their maize nor their money for it. For several weeks, we have watched Bernard turn increasingly gaunt. We worry and wonder if he's going without food so his children can eat. Or, maybe it's something else, like AIDS. We don't want to pry, but we hope that soon he'll let us know how we can help.

One Monday morning, Elizabeth arrived with a sad look in her eyes and said, "Leen-dah, my daughters and I have had nothing to eat all weekend!" She shook her head. "Nothing!" Shocked, I pulled open my cupboard and insisted that she eat.

While she ate, she explained that she and her sister Agnes—both widows—sold almost everything they owned so they could pay a hospital bill for another sister. Can you imagine such loyalty and generosity? Jesus told the rich young man to sell everything he possessed and give the money to the poor (Mark 10:21), and Elizabeth and Agnes literally did that!

I wonder—would I do that for one of my brothers? Elizabeth and Agnes have shown me what genuine sacrificial love looks like. I can't get it out of my mind.

I think a lot about those Kenyans who live every day on the edge of desperation. Half of Nairobi's three million people live in one of three hundred densely packed slums. One of them, Kibera, is considered the largest on the African continent. These people carry the constant burden of worry—worry about violent crime and threats to bulldoze down their neighborhoods. But, most important, will they have food for their children?—money for medical help?

Why has God blessed me with abundant material possessions and the benefits of the modern world but withheld such things from vast numbers of Africans? I've searched for answers. My heart aches for so many souls across the continent.

When our friends explain their current crisis and ask for help, sometimes I see dark desperation in their eyes. Too many live always on the edge, always on the brink of malnutrition, clinging to their unadorned, spare existence, fighting against unrelenting poverty. Even with help from Kenyan churches, programs, and organizations, their lives are so fragile, so precarious. I see a flicker of hope in their eyes when we give them a job, money, or food. Our help seems like a small thing, but for them, it is an answer to prayer.

My heart cries out for justice. The Bible says God is good and just, but why do I have so much while many of my Kenyan friends have so little? They're good, hard-working people who love God and serve Him, and something within me expects that good things should come to them. They must cry out, like David, "How long, O Lord? Will you forget me forever? How long will you hide your face from me?" (Psalm 13:1).

I search Scripture, I pray, and I ponder. What is poverty? What is wealth? Our Maasai friends believe your grandfather lives in poverty—only one wife, only two children, and no cattle. Who is rich, and who is poor? Compared to many of our Kenyan friends, your grandpa and I look rich in material goods, but compared to our friends and family back home, our missionary income makes us look poor. And, as poor and desperate as some of our Kenyan friends are, they're rich compared to millions of people living in places like Zaire and Sudan. It's all so confusing.

I know that sometimes people suffer because of their sins—they must live with the natural consequences of their bad choices. However, all too often someone else's sin inflicts hardship on people. When a man runs off with another woman, for example, he leaves his wife and children to fend for themselves, and often they struggle to make ends meet.

In other cases, choices made by previous generations cause children and grandchildren to suffer. Other times a government's decisions cause adversity.

Perhaps in the case of our African friends, all those reasons contribute to their plight, but that's not the whole answer. I'm searching for more than that.

Why do I have so many blessings and so little heartache? Several reasons. Many of my blessings come from the hard work, sacrifices, and wisdom of the generations who lived before me in both my family and my nation. I enjoy the benefits of my country's long heritage—political stability, technology, schooling for all, medical and scientific advances, established churches, and God's Word in my own language. I did not ask for these blessings—many of which Africans don't have. Africans did not ask for their hardships—many of which I don't have. But I still want a more complete answer.

Jesus' disciples assumed sin caused illness and suffering, and in John 9:2–3, they asked Him whether a certain man's blindness resulted from his own sin or his parents' sin. Jesus answered that sin had not caused the blindness. It happened, He said, so that God could display His work in the man's life.

I had to stop and read that again—so that God could display His work in the man's life. Wow! Only a person of great faith can, in the midst of his afflictions, wait and trust God to display His work in their lives. Those words tell me I must cling to the hope—no, I must believe—that these needy ones' troubles will reveal God's work in their lives. May He grant them endurance and faith while they wait and watch for Him to act.

But, when I think more about the meaning of those words, even now I see God's work in my friends' lives. Every time someone gives them food, a job, or a place to live, we see God at work—since He often uses human beings to answer prayers. The Bible tells us He will care for us, but He does not knock on a person's door and hand him a check to cover his rent. He does not place a roasted chicken on the dinner table. No, almost always God uses other people in the process of answering prayers. He knows how comforting and encouraging it is to look into someone's eyes and see kindness and concern. He knows how good a hug feels, and how cheering a friendly face can be. So, He gives us each other. He works in and through other human beings who serve as His representatives.

I also see God's works every time I see the faith of those dear people. When they tell me of a crisis or heartache or fear, in the same breath they say they trust that God will help them—not that they hope He will, but that they believe He will. Their words give me pause. In the midst of their unrelenting hardships year after year, when most of us would lose hope and give up, they still trust God. Like Job, they place their faith in God not because of material things He gives them, but because He is good. Whether they are hungry or well fed, God is good. They love God for Himself, not for what He can do for them. They know God never promised to remove every hardship and sorrow, but He promised always to be with them—and that is sufficient. Job never gave up on God, and my African friends have not given up on Him.

Would I have such faith if I were in their position? Would I, like Job, refuse to charge God with wrongdoing? Or would I cry out, "Curse God!" (Job 2:9) in the way Job's wife did?

I must bow down before these honorable people. They show me that God is good—and in that way He displays, even now, His work in their lives.

God has given me a rare privilege to know people with faith like Abraham's. I've always marveled that "Against all hope, Abraham in hope believed" (Romans 4:18). I'm astounded every time I read that verse. Against all hope!

"Without weakening in his faith, he faced the fact[s].... Yet he did not waver through unbelief ... being fully persuaded that God had power to do what he had promised" (Romans 4:19–21). Our friends here face the facts the way Abraham faced the facts. They have no reason to think their lot will improve. They foresee only ongoing poverty, hunger, and sickness. Nevertheless, like Abraham, against all hope, in hope they believe, fully persuaded that God has power to help them. I pray that He will honor their faith. I feel humbled and thankful to glimpse real faith in action. I hope God will help me remember their faith when mine is weak.

When my heart breaks over the plight of our needy friends, I take comfort in Bible verses such as Psalm 10:17–18, "You hear, O Lord, the desire of the afflicted; you encourage them, and you listen to their cry, defending the fatherless and the oppressed." Those words assure me that ultimately God will make all things right. Until then, my friends trust Him, and God asks me to entrust them to Him. Someone once said that God's purpose might not be for us to understand, but His purpose is for us to trust Him.

My search for answers has led me to other Bible verses. Jesus, reiterating Old Testament teaching, said the poor will always be with us (Matthew 26:11, Deuteronomy 15:7–11). God wants us to share food with the hungry, provide shelter for those who need it, and clothe those who need clothing (Isaiah 58:7).

And with those verses, my search for answers has led me to myself.

In the Parable of the Sheep and the Goats, Jesus said we each have a responsibility to help those in need:

> When the Son of Man comes in his glory ... he will put the sheep on his right and the goats on his left. Then the King will say to those on his right, "Come, you who are blessed by my Father; take your inheritance.... For I was hungry and you gave me something to eat, I was thirsty and you gave me something to drink, I was a stranger and you invited me in, I needed clothes and you clothed me, I was sick and you looked after me, I was in prison and you came to visit me."
>
> Then the righteous will answer him, "Lord, when did we see you hungry and feed you, or thirsty and give you something to drink? When did we see you a stranger and invite you in, or needing clothes and clothe you? When did we see you sick or in prison and go to visit you?"
>
> The King will reply, "I tell you the truth, whatever you did for one of the least of these brothers of mine, you did for me."
>
> Then he will say to those on his left, "Depart from me, you who are cursed, into the eternal fire prepared for the devil and his angels. For I was hungry and you gave me nothing to eat, I was thirsty and you gave me nothing to drink, I was a stranger and you did not invite me in, I needed clothes and you did not clothe me, I was sick and in prison and you did not look after me."
>
> They will also answer, "Lord, when did we see you hungry or thirsty or a stranger or needing clothes or sick or in prison, and did not help you?"
>
> He will reply, "I tell you the truth, whatever you did

not do for one of the least of these, you did not do for me" (Matthew 25:31–45).

Sobering words. A sobering message. God has allowed your grandpa and me to come into these Africans' lives, and our response to their needs reveals to God—and to us, if we'll pay attention—the state of our hearts. God wants us to help them, but He gives us a choice. Will we be part of His answer to their prayers? Or not?

It occurs to me that coming to Africa isn't all about Bible translation. It is about Bible translation, yes, but it is about more than that. In my mind, I hear the words of Esther 4:14. Maybe God brought your grandpa and me to this place for just such a time as this, to help Him fulfill His purposes for this handful of Kenyans—Elizabeth, Japheth, Enoch, Salome, Wycliffe, Hellen, Bernard—and fulfill His purposes for us, too. My heart overflows. *Thank you, God, for letting us play a small role in Your work in their lives.*

I take comfort in Romans 8:18, "I consider that our present sufferings are not worth comparing with the glory that will be revealed in us." I try to picture the stunning glory God will reveal in them someday. I hope He encourages them by keeping the glorious end in view. However, it occurs to me that, even now, I see God's glory in them—they are bright examples of how to know and love God. I feel honored to know them, and I look forward to spending eternity with them.

I'll never know all the reasons I have so many blessings and too many Africans have too many sorrows. I do know that God wants me to trust Him and to help my African friends. To whom much is given, much is required. Somehow, God turns that around and puts it into our hearts, and it wells up in the form of joy.

And there it is again—God has turned my tears to joy.

Grandpa made an important point the other day while we talked about the needy people we see here in such great numbers. He said that despite their hardships, Africans also know joy. They love to laugh—and they have such hearty laughter! They love to sing and dance and, oh—they are so good at both! They especially treasure gathering with friends and loved ones, and those are riches of the highest order.

Love,
Grandma

19

Hospitality

'Tis good to give a stranger a meal, or a night's lodging....
and give courage to a companion.
—Ralph Waldo Emerson

August 5, 1996
Nairobi, Kenya

Dear Maggie and Emma,
    Remember Jan who traveled with us to see the flamingos and survived the baboon incident? Jan hit the ground running and has never let up the two months she has lived here. If she saw a need, she didn't wait for someone to ask her—she took care of it. On Tuesday, her fortieth birthday, I rounded up a few of her friends for lunch at an Ethiopian restaurant, and that evening she joined us at the airport to say farewell to our summer boarder, Ted. Your grandpa and I had grown close to him, and we felt sad to say goodbye.
    The next morning we returned to the airport, dodging potholes, and picked up a new WNS teacher, Don, his wife Sam, and their three kids. That day I also readied Ted's room for our good friend Marvin, who used to work here with us and was scheduled to arrive Thursday. At the last minute, however, we learned he couldn't get on that plane and would arrive Friday morning instead.

That night Don, Sam, and their little ones came over for dinner along with John, the young Paul Newman look-alike. After dinner, Sam told us their apartment didn't have blankets or breakfast food, so we loaded their arms and Grandpa drove them home.

John didn't have a place to stay that night and so, since Marvin's arrival had been delayed, I told him he could sleep in Marvin's room. After Marvin arrived, John still didn't have a place to stay, so we put a mattress for him on our storage room floor.

Saturday morning we got up early and I made buttermilk pancakes, scrambled eggs, and bacon for Marvin, John, and your grandpa. Then we literally dashed from the table and hurried to the airport, swerving around potholes, to pick up Gary and Char, the new dorm parents. Another couple, Tim and Sharon, met them at the airport, too. The two couples had worked together in South America so we invited everyone to our house for coffee and a visit—until I shooed them out the door in order to serve lunch to Marvin and your grandpa. (John spent the day sightseeing with another family.) I felt pressured to hurry because we wanted to take Gary and Char grocery shopping and because I had to get home in time to make Swiss steak for a table full of guests that night. I was scurrying, therefore, to get lunch on the table when Joel, a man on our staff, stopped by to talk to Marvin. I invited Joel to eat lunch with us but he declined so we ate while he and Marvin talked business around the lunch table.

While they talked, I counted the hours left in the afternoon and the number of hours Swiss steak needs to cook, and my heart sank. I realized I would have to change my dinner menu. I sat there and wracked my brain—what could I fix for our dinner guests?

When I saw Marvin sink his teeth into his last bite of sandwich, I leapt up, cleared the table, and apologized to Joel because we had to leave. I hope he understood.

We took Gary and Char shopping, and when we got back, I washed a stack of dishes and then searched for, and found, old curtains from one of our other apartments and hung them, wrinkles and all, in the storage room John would occupy that night. Sometime during that afternoon, Marvin locked my keys in the office, and I noticed I had blisters on my feet.

I scrubbed another stack of dishes while I prepared dinner for Marvin, John, Gary, Char, your grandpa, and myself. I can't remember what I served, but no one left the table hungry.

After dinner we hurried Gary and Char out the door because the rest of us had to drive to the airport—for the second time that day, the third time in less than twenty-four hours. We were to pick up a lady named June, flying in from the States to work at the school, and Marvin was to meet a crew of thirteen from Charlotte who came for a ten-day building project among the Suba people on Mfangano Island in Lake Victoria.

On our way to the airport, we stopped at the office to pick up a bus Marvin had pre-arranged to transport his group. When we got there, though, the bus was smaller than he had asked for. It would work okay for the airport run that night, but it wouldn't work for the trip to Suba-land. He stood there in that parking lot and realized that with such late notice, he had only one option for the next morning's journey—he'd have to sign out one of our office vans and travel caravan-style with the bus.

At the airport, one of June's bags failed to arrive. Since she couldn't file a claim until all passengers had claimed their luggage, we didn't get home until 1:00 AM. While we stood around and waited for June's bags, Grandpa and I invited John to live with us the rest of his three weeks here. His original housing arrangements had evaporated so we're happy to offer him a room.

We picked up June's missing bag at the airport after church the next day, and then we and our crowd—Gary, Char, John, James (the new principal), June, Marvin, and his thirteen—dined at the edge of Nairobi's game park at Simba Saloon, a place famous for game meat.

Before Gary and Char arrived in Nairobi, we had bought an entire household of second-hand stuff for the dorm. We couldn't unpack it before they arrived, though, because the landlord hadn't finished painting their apartment. Then the moving guys broke the refrigerator, and today is their third day without it. They've also had trouble wiring their stove, from the States, for the different electricity here. I've given them food for the past couple of days, and I made them coffee cake for breakfast today. I admire their patience and good attitude, but this is a tough situation. It's a good thing no dorm kids have arrived yet.

I got a phone call this morning from a book editor and line manager at Tyndale House, a man who teaches journalism courses this term here at Daystar University. Since I've offered local writers' workshops for the past year, I asked if he could teach one for us. Today he tells me he'll present a workshop Friday. I'm so pleased! Now I need to make the arrangements.

Today I also took a phone call from Pierce and his wife Carma, teachers on their way to West Nairobi School. They received a call Friday from the Dallas office and learned they couldn't leave the States as scheduled on August 8, three days from now, because they lacked $600 a month in their pledged financial support. They canceled their plane tickets but, over the weekend, their supporters pledged almost that entire amount. Now they have clearance to come and they've booked tickets as far as London on August 12, but they can't find a flight from London to Nairobi.

Well, Maggie and Emma, now you've seen a glimpse of our lives over the past couple of weeks. This lifestyle will continue until all the teachers arrive—airport runs, dinners, orientation, and whatever help our new arrivals need. I've scaled back my Communications job for a couple of weeks so I can help with your grandpa's Children's Ed department. It's a wild but exciting time for him, and therefore for me.

❖ ❖ ❖

August 21, 1996
Nairobi, Kenya

Dear Maggie and Emma,
Your Aunt Karen arrived a week ago and we love having her here with us! The doctor says her sore throats won't go away until she recovers from mono. Maybe hanging out with her mom and dad will help.

On Saturday, August 17, we hosted a dedication ceremony for West Nairobi School—a great celebration! Nearly 150 people attended, twice the number we anticipated. Several families joined the festivities even though their children attend another school or are home-schooled. Others came who have no children but wanted to celebrate with us. Afterwards one family told us that their daughter, enrolled in another school, wants to attend WNS instead.

The school looks great. It used to be an empty old stone house on two and a half acres of overgrown land, but Wycliffe has worked hard and now the school sits amid groomed flower gardens, shrubs, and lovely old jacaranda trees. Wycliffe looks so happy these days. Like Japheth, he's a soft-spoken, reserved Kenyan, but his smile lights up his face and his eyes twinkle. And, like so many Kenyans, he has a deep hearty laugh that I love to hear.

Inside, colorful, cheery school stuff fills the building—bulletin boards, maps, hand-made desks and chairs, and book-lined shelves. The school even smells shiny—all waxed and polished. Marvin said it looks like a real school now, summing up what all of us think about the before-and-after contrast.

Marvin, as you know, brought a group to Kenya for a couple of weeks to put up a building for the Suba translation project. They also brought over all the school's textbooks—not only did they get the books here on time, they saved the school thousands of dollars in shipping costs. They finished their Suba project and arrived back in Nairobi on Friday night, so

Karen with Benson and Wycliffe, the two hard-working gardeners who transformed the grounds at West Nairobi School

Marvin brought them to the school dedication on Saturday.

When they arrived, I took one look at Marvin and knew something bad happened. He told me their borrowed van blew a head gasket upcountry and they had to leave it alongside the road. All the people, and their gear, squeezed into the too-small bus and, behind schedule, they were hurrying toward Nairobi in the dark when a car drove over a hill, lost control, and ran into their bus. No one received serious injuries, but they spent two and a half hours settling everything with the police. The unexpected challenges left Marvin shaken. Mostly he worried about leaving the van unattended because, by the time someone got back to repair it, thieves could have stolen or stripped it.

Saturday after the dedication, we showed Paul Newman—I mean John—a couple of tourist spots because he has barely had time to look around. We couldn't let him leave Kenya without seeing a few sights! That evening John made savory crepes for dinner—tasty British fare.

We said goodbye to Marvin and his group Saturday night on their way to the airport, but Sunday afternoon we heard a knock on our door and in walked Marvin. The airline had bumped their entire planeload.

Sunday we skipped church and took John and Karen to the game park and Karen Blixen's house. Yesterday we drove John to the airport for his return to Bristol, England, for the start of his third year teaching Geography. We all said a sad goodbye—we had enjoyed each other so much.

The first and second grade teacher hasn't arrived yet so on the first day of school, August 19, the principal taught her students, and Grandpa helped with the principal's administrative duties. This situation is common on the mission field, so *hakuna matata*—no worries! Missionary flexibility is both necessary and lovely, and besides, I'm glad your grandpa had an excuse to be on campus. He and God have worked so hard to develop West Nairobi School, and I know he really wanted to witness the first day's excitement.

Tomorrow another new family arrives. They're not connected to the school, but our administration asked us to serve as their hosts. That means we'll pick them up at the airport, take care of their meals for a few days, and orient them to life and work here. We've had a little experience with that lately!

I'm exhausted.

❖ ❖ ❖

September 2, 1996
Nairobi, Kenya

Dear Maggie and Emma,

Your grandpa has filled in as one of the bus drivers since the first day of school. He just finished his morning route and popped into my office, grinning, because six more children have registered since Friday. WNS has twice as many students as he anticipated.

Besides teaching all day, Karen also drives a school van. What a heavy responsibility! She's an excellent driver but traffic here is so different from what she's accustomed to back home, especially driving on the left side of the road. I'm confident of Karen's skill and judgment, but I worry about other drivers and the damage they could inflict upon those precious little lives Karen drives to and from their homes.

I've used up my coffee break time so I'll sign off.

September 4, 1996
Nairobi, Kenya

Dear Maggie and Emma,

I could hardly believe my ears the other day. But first, some background. A number of Africans want to work in Bible translation, and nearby Pan Africa Christian College offers Bible translation courses.

So, let me tell you the story I heard. A man arrived at PACC the other day, unexpected. He had walked all the way from Burundi in central Africa. Because of civil unrest, the journey took him an entire month. When he arrived and people asked what motivated him, he said he wants to attend PACC and learn how to translate the Bible. Every time I think of that man and his story, I get tears in my eyes.

Recently a colleague, Rosemary, asked me to rate my job satisfaction on a scale of one to ten. I didn't even need to think about it—I rated it ten.

With Rosemary's question and my answer, in my mind's eye I saw our room in England, on our way to Africa, and the poster that read, "He who goes out weeping … will return with songs of joy" (Psalm 126:6). I had arrived in Africa weeping because I thought my job lacked meaning, but God turned around my attitude and has given me joy in two ways. First, I get to play a role in Bible translation, and second, through my job I give people opportunities to praise God because of what He does here in Africa. I consider my job an honor and a blessing. God used Rosemary's question to show me, once again, that He has turned my tears to joy.

September 29, 1996
Nairobi, Kenya

Dear Maggie and Emma,

Today your Aunt Karen celebrates her twenty-fifth birthday. She has adjusted well to life on this side of the world. At school, she has learned to change the questions she usually asks her students. Instead of, "What is your favorite TV show?" which she might have asked her students back in Port Angeles, she asks her missionary-kid students, "How many countries have you lived in?"

I just read a newsletter she sent to her prayer and financial supporters back home, and it allowed me to see Kenya again through a newcomer's eyes. Karen writes that by now, five weeks into the school year, they can flush the toilets without dumping in a bucket of water, and they're working on a water-filter system so she can have her daily dose of coffee at school. She says she's adjusting to driving one of the school buses, sitting on the right side, driving down the left side of road, dodging a variety of moving or stationary obstacles, learning the unwritten rules of the road, and avoiding accidents.

Karen also says students and faculty have adapted to operating without electricity. The city turns it off every day from 8:00 AM until 2:30 PM. Just think—for almost the entire school day they can't use computers, copy machine, VCR, coffeemaker, or refrigerator. No one complains, though. Everyone knows life can be a challenge here sometimes.

Karen studies Swahili, too. She's learned important phrases like *mimi nina penda kahawa moto* (I like hot coffee) and, for Fridays, *tunienda weekendi* (it's the weekend).

At home, she's learned how to spray Doom mosquito spray without even waking up at night and how to sponge bathe when we have to ration water—or when the water comes out of the tap scalding hot. She writes in her newsletter, "I've almost forgotten what a phone is, since I rarely see one, not to mention use one. I've managed to make one bag of jellybeans from home last this whole time. And I've already grown to love the gracious kindness of this country and its people."

I will attend meetings in Calgary soon, and your grandpa and I both have business to do in the States. I feel bad leaving your Aunt Karen here alone, but I'll hurry back. I'm glad she has lived here long enough to feel settled in her school routine, driving, and shopping.

❖   ❖   ❖

November 2, 1996
Nairobi, Kenya

Dear Maggie and Emma,

I just returned from the States and Canada. In Calgary, I attended the annual worldwide Communications meetings, a valuable time for us to strategize how best to tell the world about the great things God does in and through Bible translation. Grandpa remains in the States recruiting teachers for MK (missionary kid) schools across Africa.

The most exciting part of our trip was meeting sweet Emma Elisabeth Anne Thomas! She's a beauty—soft fair skin, blue eyes, and silky blonde hair. I still marvel that God gave me a job that requires me to travel to our southern California office from time to time!

Your dad wrote us this note:

> Thank you so much for driving down here to visit us on your busy trip to the States. It has been great to see you and to have you see the girls. I love them so much and I love you so much, that it satisfies my heart greatly when you and they can be together too.

In London on my return trip, our British friend and former boarder, John, met me at Heathrow and drove me through the English autumn countryside on the way to Gatwick and my connecting flight to Nairobi. Along the way, he took me to lunch in a quaint (*quaint!*) country pub. I enjoyed seeing our good friend John again!

Your grandpa usually drives me downtown to City Market on Saturdays but since he's still in the States, Karen—bless her heart—drove me. She handled traffic challenges of all sorts and maneuvered around and through potholes. I'm impressed.

Daytime temperatures now hover around eighty degrees and purple blossoms cover jacaranda trees all over the city, right on schedule. Dusty season has arrived, but last night rain fell for half an hour and your Aunt Karen whooped in delight. She says she misses the rain back home.

Love,
Grandma

20

Zaire, and More Lessons on Hospitality

Offer hospitality to one another.
1 Peter 4:9

November 18, 1996
Nairobi, Kenya

Dear Maggie and Emma,

    Unspeakable brutality rages again in Zaire and Rwanda. For the past few months, people around the world have watched television reports of the violence. I'll never forget some of the scenes, especially pictures of children. They're so horrific I will not—cannot—write words to describe them. The International Red Cross reported that terror spread like wildfire and that in the midst of panic, violence, and bloodshed, people by the hundreds of thousands fled to the hills for safety. All of our personnel assigned to Zaire remained here in Nairobi after their recent annual conference so for now, at least, they're not in danger.

    This unthinkable violence and its ramifications have shaken all of us. Since our colleagues can't return to Zaire, many of us have offered to house them. A woman named Jan lives with us now. She recently arrived in Kenya and planned to travel on to Zaire and teach at Rethy Academy, a school for missionary kids, but the turmoil has kept her in Nairobi. She needed a place to live so we invited her here, and now she teaches at West Nairobi School.

Sometimes for weeks on end, only a trickle of water runs through our pipes, and that causes vapor locks in our hot water heaters—no water comes out even if the tank has water in it. A couple of months ago, the water heaters in both the master bathroom and Karen's developed vapor locks. Before your grandpa left for the States, he fixed ours but he couldn't fix Karen's. Now she uses the master bathroom shower, but I don't know what we'll do when your grandpa returns because the heater doesn't hold enough water for three showers.

The city turns on our water heaters between two and five in the morning. Saturday the city must have turned them on for just an hour because only lukewarm water came out. Sunday morning the city didn't turn them on at all so we couldn't take showers.

We decided to go to church anyway, but just as we headed for the door, Jan said, "Oh, no! My toilet's leaking!" Water covered the floor. *Fundis* (repairmen) don't work on Sundays but the apartment manager looked it over. He couldn't figure out the problem, though, so we skipped church to tinker with it. To my surprise, I fixed it. (Nope, quaint I ain't.)

We have heard amazing stories surrounding the recent crises in Zaire. For example, Dr. Jo Lusi, a Zairian Christian and orthopedic specialist, stayed in Goma, Zaire, when relief agencies and almost everyone else evacuated across the border to safety. He has gained notoriety as the only surgeon in the Baptist hospital, the one functioning hospital in the entire vicinity. Perhaps your parents saw a CNN report about Dr. Lusi who works eighteen-hour days in the operating room.

Dr. Lusi and the hospital staff had an urgent need for medicine and food so on November 8, one of our pilots, Dennis, and an AIM-AIR pilot, Jim, flew some two tons of medicine to Kigali, Rwanda, the airport nearest Goma. Both Denny's children and Jim's are West Nairobi School students—Jim's daughter, Kristi, is one of your Aunt Karen's students. During the men's trip, all the students and teachers prayed for them.

In Kigali, Denny and Jim hired two vans and loaded them with the medicine, over four hundred pounds of food, and two drums of diesel. Then they drove four hours to Gisenyi, Rwanda, separated from Goma by two steel barriers and fifty yards of no-man's land.

Dr. Lusi planned to meet Denny and Jim at the border to help get their supplies across but an early curfew kept them from doing so. Instead, they spent the night in a hotel in Gisenyi. By the time they arrived, however, the press corps had already packed the hotel to overflowing (no doubt people in the States were watching many of them on television), so Denny and Jim slept on the floor.

At the hotel that night, journalists learned of the men's association with the famous Dr. Lusi and asked many questions. One European journalist, skeptical that Zairian rebels would let them cross the border, said, "The UNHCR [United Nations High Commissioner for Refugees] has not been allowed to cross, the Red Cross has not been allowed to cross, Doctors Without Borders has not been allowed to cross, and you won't be allowed to either."

Jim replied, "We'll pray about it."

"I know about you Christian types." The journalist turned and walked away in a huff.

The next morning Denny and Jim were among the first to arrive at the heavily guarded border. The rebels didn't let them cross so, with those curious, skeptical journalists watching, Denny and Jim waited. They talked with officials. They prayed. They watched for Dr. Lusi on the other side.

Mid-day they spotted him. He had brought two ambulances to transport their supplies to the hospital. Dr. Lusi spoke to rebels on one side and Rwandan soldiers on the other, but they wouldn't let the men proceed.

Just then, a soldier showed up on the rebel side. He recognized Dr. Lusi—the doctor who had treated his wounded daughter that morning. Within minutes, the soldier arranged for Denny and Jim to cross. Correspondents from CNN, NBC, *Time* magazine, and other news agencies had to wait behind the barricade. They could only watch—and film for the world to see—the two vans drive across the border and reload supplies into Dr. Lusi's ambulances.

November 22, 1996
Nairobi, Kenya

Dear Maggie and Emma,

Your grandpa's cousin Paul and his wife Barbara are among those stranded in Nairobi due to Zaire's civil unrest. They received word that looters broke into their house in Lubutu, Zaire. Church leaders heard ahead of time about the planned break-in, so they broke in first to carry out and store everything valuable. Paul and Barbara hope that includes their translation materials and computer equipment. Paul suspects that after their church friends left, rebels stole the rest of their possessions.[1]

Since your grandpa hasn't returned from the States, last Saturday night

Karen and I invited friends over to watch the *Babe* video. Tomorrow night a few of us will watch *Out of Africa*. That movie captures both Kenya's natural beauty and the spirit of Africa's people. One of our coworkers is an extra in the film—a jolly man with red hair and a red beard—and he even has one line.

November 29, 1996
Nairobi, Kenya

Dear Maggie and Emma,

We have never celebrated Thanksgiving here because it's not a Kenyan holiday. It's a regular workday for us, but this year I yearned to come home after work and feast on a Thanksgiving dinner. Turkeys here are expensive, but the thought of no special dinner left me feeling blue. Yesterday, however, Thanksgiving Day, your Aunt Karen drove me to the store after school. I brought home a whole chicken and, while it roasted, I prepared stuffing, mashed potatoes, gravy, green beans, and a salad. Just before we sat down at the table, Karen remembered that the last time I returned from the States, your great-grandma sent a can of black olives back with me. Then we remembered that on another trip your grandpa brought a can of cranberry sauce—two perfect additions to our meal. Karen, Jan, and I enjoyed a delicious candlelight Thanksgiving dinner with soft music in the background.

Our Zaire director arrived back in Nairobi late yesterday after a few days there. His safe return must have been a special Thanksgiving gift for his family. Evacuations have begun for the few remaining missionaries in Zaire including teachers and students at Rethy Academy. I understand Zaire's president has cancer and people expect civil war will break out when he dies—though it appears to have already started. Given that information, Jan will live with us for an extended time.

If Jan needs to live here after our friend Randy arrives for Christmas break, we'll make our storage room into a bedroom for him. That should work fine as long as (1) Jan's toilet doesn't break again; (2) the city turns our water back on (we've been carrying water from the office but the city has turned off water at the office, too); (3) our water filter somehow fixes itself; (4) we can get Karen's hot water heater fixed; and (5) we can find gas cylinders so we can cook. Nairobi frequently has no gas cylinders for weeks or even months on end.

My friend Nancy belongs to a book club here in Nairobi along with Dr. Lusi's wife, a British lady. Mrs. Lusi recently flew to see her husband in Zaire and when she returned, she told Nancy that soldiers wouldn't let her through the gate at the hospital. When Dr. Lusi came to talk to her from the other side, she heard a voice, "Mrs. Lusi, we'd like to talk to you." She turned and saw a familiar face—Christiane Amanpour, the CNN reporter. Nancy didn't tell me details of the interview, but this story made me realize that some of our colleagues live in the midst of, or on the fringes of, news headlines around the world.

I received this letter from Denny, the pilot who flew supplies to Dr. Lusi. He wrote:

> Dr. Lusi shared how these necessary supplies had arrived the very day his previous supplies ran out. God's timing is never too late. I am not aware that any of the major news agencies reported what had happened that day. But I am confident that many of them had to do some thinking to understand why the U.N. and the Red Cross were not able to accomplish what these silly missionaries had just done.... God is the one who did it. The Red Cross, MSF [Doctors Without Borders], and the U.N. were there watching as we crossed the border. All they could do was watch. God opened the door for us to cross. A few days later when the border was finally opened under international pressure, the press reported that "the first supplies to reach Goma had crossed the border." This was not true. A week before that God had opened the door (the border) for supplies for the Christian hospital to cross. The Christian hospital is staffed with an effective Chaplain, and I am confident that the hospital has been a testimony to suffering people in Goma, and through numerous press agencies to others around the world.

❖ ❖ ❖

December 2, 1996
Nairobi, Kenya

Dear Maggie and Emma,

We have invited a friend, Douglas, to spend Christmas Day with us. He works in Bible translation in Zaire and, like his colleagues, he's stranded here in Nairobi because of the hostilities there. He heard that burglars broke into his house in Zaire and took most of his worldly possessions, and he told us of his need to heal from so many losses—personal things, sentimental things, and work-related equipment.

Mostly, however, he mourns the loss of his translation materials. When I listen to Douglas talk, I can read between the lines. He has invested more than just time and effort to translate the Bible with and for a group of Zairians—he has invested his heart, his soul, his all. Now he worries that perhaps his efforts and prayers have come to nothing.

On the other hand, it's too early to know how this will end. Maybe in time Douglas will get good news about his materials and can resume his work. Right now, though, he grieves.

Douglas said that even though he feels like a homeless person, he has chosen to count his blessings—friends and a place to live in Nairobi, a visa so he can remain here, friends and family back home who pray for him, and people who have offered to help replace what others stole.

Dear Douglas. I marvel at his perspective and his faith. If ever I suffer great loss, I hope God will remind me of Douglas and his example.

December 19, 1996
Nairobi, Kenya

Dear Maggie and Emma,
Warm Christmas greetings from Nairobi—"warm" meaning something in the eighties today. Around here the locals are saying, "It's beginning to look a lot like Christmas."

West Nairobi School is a busy place these days—and bulging! Even more students have applied for the new term in January, and thirteen kids evacuated from Rethy Academy have enrolled as well. Four teachers from Rethy now teach at WNS, too—two with AIM (Africa Inland Mission) and two with Wycliffe. (Rebels seized Rethy. No one knows its condition.) Given the added numbers, your grandpa has arranged for an additional two-classroom building and more chairs, desks, and textbooks.

But we're not complaining! Not at all! Actually, we're thankful that WNS can help these families and play a small roll in answering their prayers. I think back to that guy who called your grandpa crazy for trying to open the school this year, but God must have known that these thirteen kids and four teachers—and all the families they represent—would need WNS *this* year.

I just received an invitation to fill an extra seat on a little plane flying to a nearby country for the dedication of a newly translated New Testament. For years, civil war has torn apart that region and, because of fighting in that area last week, a commander in the rebel army will accompany us to secure the area. Can you believe it?!

We'll fly out on Sunday morning at six and arrive back in Nairobi on Monday before dark. Just five of us will fly in, and we'll sleep in a tent overnight.

❖   ❖   ❖

December 21, 1996
Nairobi, Kenya

Dear Maggie and Emma,

In the end, I could not go on that trip. An official in a downtown Nairobi office had almost finished filling out my travel papers, using an electric typewriter, when the power went out. He refused to fill in the rest by hand—and it was late Friday afternoon. He said, "You'll have to come back Monday," but that was the day of the return flight.

Love,
Grandma

21

The Verge of The Unknown

Today, dear friends, we stand upon the verge of the unknown. There lies before us the new year and we are going forth to possess it. Who can tell what we shall find? What new experiences, what changes shall come, what new needs shall arise?[1]

January 10, 1997
Nairobi, Kenya

Dear Maggie and Emma,

We enjoyed a nice Christmas with your Aunt Karen and several friends. Over the school break, she and three friends went on a real safari. They didn't stay in a safari lodge, the kind with a fence to keep out people-eating animals. No, they camped under acacia trees on the wild Kenyan plains!

She and a friend also took the train to Mombasa, on the coast of the Indian Ocean, where they played volleyball on the beach and rode camels. She showed me her photos, and the sand down there is powdery white. People on the coast had a white Christmas!

On New Year's Eve, 1996, my mother (your Great-grandma Kay) wrote me a long letter about the trip you girls and your mom and dad took to Seattle for Christmas. Lots of snow fell and she took seven rolls of film. She wrote,

Those sure are sweet girls with such pleasant dispositions. I had gotten Maggie a paint-with-water book and thought a small bowl of water and cotton swabs would work best, and they did quite well—Maggie called the swabs "cute-tips!" We had fun frosting little sugar cookies: green frosting with chocolate bits or cinnamon bits on top. She was quite serious about it. I had made her a little apron. She looked very sweet.

I asked if her daddy had measured her on the wall

Maggie's Great-grandma Kay wrote about Christmas, 1996:
"We had fun frosting little sugar cookies—green frosting with chocolate bits or cinnamon bits on top.
She was quite serious about it.
I had made her a little apron. She looked very sweet."

behind the basement door, where we record such things, and asked if he had told her how tall she was. She didn't seem to know how to answer so I asked, "Three feet?" She looked at me with absolute amazement. "No, just two feet!" she said, looking down at her feet to be sure she was right.

Doug impulsively bought her a little brown bear with a red hat and scarf. It had real character! She seemed shy of Doug so he didn't realize that she really appreciated the bear. A bit later, she whispered to me, "I never had a bear with a scarf." Then, as the day went by, she consistently referred to it as "Unca-Doug-Bear."

January 14, 1997
Nairobi, Kenya

Dear Maggie and Emma,

In addition to a full teaching load, your Aunt Karen drives students to and from school in either a van or a station wagon, and we have asked relatives and friends to pray for her while she drives that precious cargo around town.

After I got home from work one day, I heard a knock at our door and opened it to find Christa, a WNS elementary student. She asked, "Is Karen okay?"

Karen hadn't returned home yet. What did she mean, *is Karen okay?*

Christa asked, "Was she hurt in the accident?"

An accident! I fought to stay calm. I asked Christa a few questions, but she knew only that Karen had an accident while she drove students home after school. Without a phone, I could only pace the floor and pray.

Before long, though, the door opened and in walked Karen. Thank God! She explained that she had dropped off a station wagon full of kids and then turned the wheel over to Patrick, a Kenyan employee training to take over a school bus route. Patrick second-guessed the driver of a huge city bus but guessed wrong—and stopped only after he had driven part way under the bus. Its back corner broke through the car's windshield but, *by God's grace*, Patrick stopped only inches before the bus hit Karen's head. (Patrick will find a different job!)

Karen sent a newsletter to her prayer and financial supporters back home and her words touched my heart:

> One of the most tremendous things I've experienced this year is praying with my students. Every morning the eighth graders and I start out by making a list of all our praises and requests on the board and then we pray for each one. It's been amazing. We've prayed for the safety of Kristi's father who was trying to fly emergency medical supplies into the fighting zone of Zaire. He made it in and back unharmed, undelayed. We've praised God for the completion of Daniel's family's translation of the New Testament into the Sabaot language. We've prayed for God's wisdom and guidance in the school and seen it become a great help to many more than even dreamed. We've prayed for safety on the bus routes and seen God make at least four near-disasters on the road turn out safely.

Not long ago Karen asked her students what they've learned here. Their answers tickled me:

> I've learned that chickens are in many ways like people.
>
> I've learned how to recognize a jigger (bugs that lay eggs under your toenails).
>
> I've learned to watch a Maasai warrior kill a goat without throwing up.
>
> I've learned that the roads in Kenya are really bumpy.
>
> I've learned that Kenya is really different than the Netherlands.
>
> I've learned how much fun it is to get mail.
>
> I've learned that having friends helps a lot.
>
> I've learned to drink dirty water.
>
> I've learned to get along without HubbaBubba.
>
> I've learned to walk and walk and walk and walk.
>
> I've learned to bring my own toilet paper on trips.

I've learned that people smell different because of the food they eat.

I've learned that if you turn Africa sideways it looks like a horse.

I've learned to be careful with the flashlight in the *choo* (outhouse/toilet).

I've learned to expect to run two hours late when you're on African time.

I've learned that beauty depends on the person who is seeing it.

February 20, 1997
Nairobi, Kenya

Dear Maggie and Emma,

    Your grandpa's brother and sister-in-law, John and Shelly, visited us for a couple of weeks. It's great to have family visit us! They might work at West Nairobi School next year so they wanted to check out what it's like to live and work here.

    We wanted to introduce John and Shelly to Kenya's natural beauty so we took them on safari to Maasai Mara. I could never grow tired of the Mara. Life is serene there in the animals' own kingdom—where they reign. The Mara seems untouched by the evils of mankind and I'm sure that makes God smile.

    There's something about Maasai Mara, and Amboseli (where your grandpa took me for my birthday, at the foot of Mt. Kilimanjaro), and even Nairobi's game park—something that has worked its way into my heart and spirit and being. I'm not sure I can explain it, but the land and animals called to me and I answered. I am hooked.

    Africa's animals roam freely throughout a seemingly limitless land of unspoiled savannahs and escarpments and wilderness. I look around and see them as they existed in ancient times. I see the same lean, boundless scenes that Teddy Roosevelt and Ernest Hemingway saw, a timeless, expansive landscape shimmering under Africa's burning sun. In it all, I see God's hand.

    I'm tempted to say that at the Mara we saw all the usual animals, but those animals never have been and never could be "usual." Rather, we saw the usual assortment of those mighty creatures, including *kifaru*—rhino. In 1909, Teddy Roosevelt set out on the most enormous safari carried out in East Africa, and he said this about his experience with a rhino:

> Suddenly ... there was a succession of snorts like a steam-engine blowing off steam.... While a rhinoceros's short suit is brains, his long suit is courage, and he is a particularly exasperating creature to deal with, because he has not sense enough to know that you can harm him, and he has enough bad temper to want to harm you....[2]

We took pictures of animals in all their untamed beauty—lion, giraffe, warthog, secretary bird, guinea fowl, ostrich, zebra, wildebeest, baboon, gazelle, eland, topi, and impala. We also experienced an up-close moment with one snorting, bad-tempered Cape buffalo. I snapped a quick picture of him twitching and drooling, enraged that we would invade his domain. Grandpa took pictures of hippos in the Mara River and of crocodiles, maybe fifteen feet long, congregated on the river's banks lying in wait for their next victims.

We also took John and Shelly on a weekend road tour around Mt. Kenya, crossing into the northern hemisphere on the east side of the mountain and back into the southern on the west side. We stayed overnight at The Outspan, an old traveling lodge from British colonial days. Much like Brackenhurst, The Outspan's low, whitewashed stone buildings sit among thirty acres of rolling lawns, tropical vegetation, and old-English flower gardens. Each of our rooms—white plaster walls and red tile floors—had a fireplace and pleasantly worn British colonial furniture. Through our French doors, we looked across those lush gardens and indigenous forest toward Mt. Kenya, soaring more than 17,000 feet into thin equatorial air. Stepping into Kenya's unpretentious, charming past always has a soothing effect on me.

The staff, dressed in crisp white shirts, black ties, and black trousers, served morning and mid-day meals on a wide verandah with the same view as our rooms. We enjoyed leisurely morning and afternoon tea on the verandah, too.

In the evening, though, we moved inside to a large dining room with dark wood-paneled walls, a high ceiling, and tables set with fresh white linens, crystal, and candles. Dining in Kenya is tranquil and unhurried. Both diners and waiters speak softly, and the atmosphere leaves me relaxed—body, soul, mind, and spirit. Nights are cool at that elevation, and when we returned to our rooms after dinner, the staff had already lit the fires and turned down our bed linens. The Outspan offered a blessed respite from the rush and noise of Nairobi—all for the price we'd pay at a cheap motel in the States.

Your grandfather needed to drive down to George and Wendy Payton's place on business and decided to make the trip when John and Shelly could join us. The Paytons live at Malindi, north of Mombasa on the Indian Ocean, where they help translate the Bible. Our drive jarred our bones, but your grandpa skimmed over the tops of the washboard-like road the way Brian taught him during our orientation.

When we visit the coast, we step into yet another distinct world—another culture—within Kenya's borders. Arab traders founded Mombasa around the eighth century. In 1498, Portuguese explorer Vasco de Gama landed on Mombasa's shores, and in the 1500s Mombasa served as Portugal's trading headquarters along Africa's east coast. From there sailing ships traveled to and from ports at the farthest ends of the earth, their holds packed with ivory, spices, gold, frankincense, myrrh, and other treasures.

In 1840, the sultan of Zanzibar took control of Mombasa but, in 1895, the British took control, and it served as the capital of the British East Africa Protectorate until 1907.

Nowadays, Mombasa is a blend of all those cultures in its architecture, art, ancient buildings, and population, though most people are of Arab origin. Muslim mosques outnumber Hindu temples, and I've heard that Muslims along the coast pay school fees for children if they convert to Islam. People believe that an education will help their children escape poverty and, since many families cannot afford their children's fees, the Muslims' offer is attractive.

Mombasa is a paradise of white sandy beaches, coral reefs, and aqua-colored ocean that goes on forever. Heavily scented tropical plants thrive in the moist, warm salt-sea air. Enormous old mango trees and their thick, dark leaves provide a shady place where people socialize, get haircuts, and buy melons, tomatoes, pineapples, or chickens.

Teddy Roosevelt said of the trip between the coast and Nairobi, "I really doubt if there is a railroad trip in the world as well worth taking as that railroad trip up to the little British East African capital of Nairobi.... It was much like going through the garden of Eden with Adam and Eve absent."[3]

Well, Maggie and Emma, it's time to get ready for bed, but I'll write again soon.

Love,
Grandma

22

Hurling Through The Valley of The Shadow of Death

The Lord is my shepherd.
Psalm 23:1

February 25, 1997
Nairobi, Kenya

Dear Maggie and Emma,
 Saturday morning a van full of West Nairobi School's teachers left on a day trip around Mt. Kenya, the same loop we drove with John and Shelly recently. Your Aunt Karen couldn't make up her mind if she wanted to go but when the doorbell rang at six-thirty that morning, she told the others she had decided not to go.
 Around six that evening Gary, the dorm dad, knocked on our door. Gary and Char have a phone and we don't, and they received a call with news that the teachers had an accident in Chogoria, about three hours north of here. Gary passed on reports of a broken rib, broken pelvis, and several minor injuries.
 Your grandpa made phone calls, formulated plans, and signed out a van. Since it's not safe to drive at night, we left the next morning at sunrise, 6:15 AM. Grandpa drove the van and Karen and I followed behind in our

car (with Karen at the wheel since I don't drive here) so that if one of the teachers needed to lie down in the van, we could put a couple of passengers in our car.

Forty-five minutes into our trip, your grandpa braked ahead of us. His van blocked our view so we couldn't tell why he slowed down, but then we noticed broken glass on the road.

Just then, Karen said, "Look, an accident just happened! Look at the dust still swirling in the air."

From my seat on the left side of the car, I saw a white car lodged in a wide ditch to the left. Between it and our car, a man—clutching an assault rifle—charged toward me, ten or twelve feet away. For a sickening second or two, he and I made eye contact. I yelled at Karen, "Keep driving!" and she did. About two seconds later she said, "Mom, look!" Dozens of people ran for shelter.

I found an article in this morning's paper about this incident and learned that three people died. Four gangsters, driving the white car, which they had stolen, shot at a pickup in front of Grandpa. The shooting happened only seconds before we got there, but we were around a curve in the road and didn't see it happen. The pickup had veered off the road to the right but Karen and I didn't see it because we were looking at the car on the left—and at the thug with the assault rifle. Officials suspect the truck transported drugs.

Part of the article makes me shudder. It confirmed what I suspected: the gangsters stopped a car at gunpoint and fled. That man who charged us, that man with the assault rifle, that man just ten feet away, that man who looked me in the eye—that man intended to carjack us! But, by God's split-second grace, Karen kept driving and the gangster stopped the car behind us instead.

When we arrived at the PCEA (Presbyterian Church of East Africa) mission hospital at 9:15 AM, everyone told us that if our teachers had to have an accident outside of Nairobi, they chose the best place because Chogoria's hospital is the finest of those upcountry. The staff included a young Canadian doctor and his wife, three interns from the United States, an Egyptian doctor, a dear gentleman from England, and a kind, helpful Kenyan staff.

We could tell the accident left the teachers shaken, but most of them had only minor injuries. However, we had to wait for reports on the two most seriously injured, Bridget and Shelley.

Meanwhile, we listened to the teachers explain how the accident happened. Their van was traveling downhill along a steep, zigzagging road when a *matatu* (a mid-size heavy bus), packed with passengers, lost its brakes and crashed into the back corner of the school van. The bus shoved the van down the rest of the hill, curves and all, across a short bridge at the lowest spot—with a drop-off of a couple hundred feet on one side—and part way up the hill on other side. Our van's driver, Pierce, actually steered for the bus because it had literally attached itself to the van.

Both doctors and police told us that the teachers' van, and Pierce, saved the bus passengers' lives. They emphasized that every accident on that stretch of road—and there have been many—has resulted in fatalities, except for this one. *Matatus* here have their own names painted on them and the name on this one was from Psalm 23, "The Lord is My Shepherd." I marveled at those words' appropriateness: God had shepherded passengers in both vehicles as they hurled through the valley of the shadow of death.

While we waited in the hospital's halls, the teachers told us that people in a Toyota Land Cruiser stopped and pulled out the wounded—some unconscious, others in and out of consciousness—and crammed them into their vehicle. Imagine all those broken people packed in the Land Cruiser!

Those Good Samaritans said, "We are Christians. Don't worry about your possessions. We'll collect them for you," and they drove to the PCEA mission hospital only eight minutes away—another of God's provisions.

The *matatu's* passengers remained stranded at the accident scene. They built a fire and sat around it all night, singing hymns and praying for the injured—they knew the teachers had saved their lives. In the morning, a number of them made their way to the hospital to pray for our teachers.

Everything moved slowly in the hospital. By midday, I started to worry about our return trip to Nairobi—we prefer not to travel after dark because of carjackings and bad road conditions. I wanted so much to arrive home before sunset; my stomach still churned over that morning's incident.

Eventually we learned that Shelley received head and neck injuries, but she'd recover. Bridget, who evacuated from Zaire a couple of months ago and joined the WNS staff, received the most severe injuries. She had sat in the back corner, the point that took the *matatu's* impact. She has a broken pelvis on both sides, a shattered hip joint, and damage to internal organs. Can you imagine what she must have felt when those people pulled her out of the crumpled van and loaded her into their Land Cruiser? I nearly faint to think of it.

The PCEA doctors said Bridget needed to fly to England immediately for proper care—she'd suffered grave injuries—but we couldn't get her to Nairobi, let alone to England. People back in Nairobi could find neither an ambulance nor a helicopter that could accommodate stretchers. We offered to transport her in our van, but the doctor said she'd never survive the long drive over bumpy roads. My heart nearly failed me.

What were we to do? I could think of nothing. Nothing.

I could pray, though, and I did. Nevertheless, from my human perspective, I could see no way to get Bridget out of Chogoria.

After a long, painful wait, we received good news! Someone back in Nairobi had arranged for a German AmRef doctor to fly up on a Kenya Wildlife helicopter large enough to transport a stretcher. If ever there was a time to sing a doxology, that was it. "Praise God, from Whom all blessings flow!"[1] We would have to wait for their arrival, but at least they were on their way.

Jan, the teacher who lived with us for a couple of months, had been sitting next to Bridget in the van, but her injuries were less serious.

Before the trip, while Karen debated whether to go, she told me, "I know there's room for me—I can sit in the back with Jan and Bridget—but I just don't know if I want to go." When we arrived at the hospital Jan said, several times, "I'm so glad Karen didn't come! She would have sat between Bridget and me and would have been badly injured!" It shakes me up to think what could have happened to my Karen. I can only thank God over and over and over again.

Doctors tended to the wounded until after 5:00 PM. Meanwhile, for two hours I stood on an enormous field adjoining the hospital—along with Grandpa, Karen, doctors, interns, nurses, and a couple of teachers who were healthy enough to stand—to await the helicopter and help with crowd control. Over fifteen hundred people gathered to see the tin bird land in a cloud of orange dust. They didn't seem to understand the danger of standing too close, so we held them back.

A hush fell when the hospital staff wheeled Bridget, and later Shelley, across the red dirt field. When the helicopter lifted off, I had mixed emotions. I felt sad about the ladies' injuries but delighted and thankful for the German doctor and the Kenya Wildlife helicopter. God had enabled someone back in Nairobi—a blessed someone—to find them both and bring about what had seemed impossible only a few hours earlier.

With a four-hour trip ahead of us, we drove out of Chogoria half an hour before sunset. We had to trust God rather than daylight to get us home safely—and He did.

Pierce and his wife Carma rode in our car and the rest traveled with Grandpa in the van. Karen and I dropped them off at their home and arrived home about nine-thirty. Grandpa delivered his passengers to their homes, except for Jan. He checked her into the hospital and then received an update on the two who flew down, Bridget and Shelley.

When he arrived home at 1:00 AM, he said that even though Bridget had needed to fly to England, by the time she landed in Nairobi her internal injuries were so serious that they took her directly into emergency surgery. As I type, she's in intensive care, and I haven't heard if they'll try to fly her to England. Shelley is in intensive care too.

The other teachers—bruised, stitched up, and shaken—will recover at home.

With a troubled yet grateful heart,
Grandma

The teachers' accident

23

Houseguests

*I hope to visit you and talk to you face to face,
so that our joy may be complete.
2 John 12*

March 5, 1997
Nairobi, Kenya

Dear Maggie and Emma,

    I'm taking my fifteen-minute coffee break and want to catch you up.

    We hear that Bridget will travel to England for a long recovery. Shelley is well enough to remain here but faces a slow recovery, too. The other teachers are mending well.

    On the morning after we brought the teachers back, our pastor and two friends from Port Angeles arrived amid several days of protests in the city. We had looked forward to our friends' visit but, when they arrived, I felt miserable because I had no clean sheets, no pillows, and a long grocery list—I had originally planned to take care of those things the day before, the day we helped the teachers. If George, Vern, and Pastor Mike noticed my lack of readiness, they didn't let on, but I still felt bad. I don't usually treat guests that way.

    Pastor Mike, the devotional speaker at our staff retreat, shared insights and messages that blessed us like holy vitamins. We returned home refreshed and invigorated.

After the retreat, we told Mike, Vern, and George (who call themselves the Three Amigos) that they couldn't come all this way without going on safari to Maasai Mara, and they didn't argue with us. When they returned, those three goofy guys demonstrated that they'd perfected the screech Maasai women make when they dance—high-pitched, off-tuned, and ear-piercing.

After our staff retreat, three girls moved in with us for two weeks. Their parents' visas expired and they had to leave Kenya to renew them. With the Three Amigos plus the girls, nine of us occupied our apartment.

Last night, to my surprise, another girl moved in with us. The girls told me she usually spends Tuesday nights with them because she lives too far from school to come every day. Instead, she travels to town and attends school on Tuesdays, stays overnight, attends classes Wednesdays, and then returns home. That means ten of us occupied our apartment last night.

I just found out that school dismisses at noon today so I'll need to make lunch for everyone. I've been wracking my brain, but I can't think of anything to feed them. We have food—that's not the problem—but I need something quick so we can get back to the office and I need enough for ten people. *Ten people! Dear Lord, what will I feed them?*

March 10, 1997
Nairobi, Kenya

Dear Maggie and Emma,

The city now turns our electricity off every afternoon and that makes it hard to get our work done at the office. Sometimes we work evenings and weekends to catch up.

The three little girls still live with us, and less than twenty-four hours after they move out, your Great-grandparents Thomas will occupy that bedroom. The city announced they would turn off water in our neighborhood, and they did in about half of the city, but we still have water! I'm so thankful! God knows that with up to ten people in our house, we really need water.

We plan to drive your great-grandparents around Mt. Kenya and stay overnight at The Outspan. I'm nervous about traveling up there, though, because last month on the same road, that gangster—that murderer!—almost carjacked us.

March 17, 1997
Nairobi, Kenya

Dear Maggie and Emma,
　We received word that you and your mom and dad plan to move to Kansas City this summer. How exciting! You'll live close to your Grandma and Grandpa Crabtree—oh, that does my heart good!—and your dad will work on his Ph.D. We are very pleased!

March 21, 1997
Nairobi, Kenya

Dear Maggie and Emma,
　Greetings from overcast, cool Nairobi. It feels like any moment our first rain might fall, and we really need it.
　Your great-grandparents Thomas have arrived and we're excited—we love them so much! We have enjoyed introducing them to Kenya's natural beauties and to Nairobi, our home for almost four years. (I wonder, though, what they think of the potholes.) We took them on a trip around Mt. Kenya and, even though we got a punctured tyre, we ran across no carjackers or accidents—unlike last month's journey.
　After your grandpa shows his parents the school this morning, we'll drive to the airport to pick up John, our Paul-Newman-handsome British friend. Next week for three days, your great-grandparents and John will go on safari to Maasai Mara. I'm sure it will be a grand adventure for them.

March 24, 1997
Nairobi, Kenya

Dear Maggie and Emma,
　Today I received this e-mail from your dad:

The girls are doing wonderfully. I am very anxious for you to get to see them and spend some time with them. They are growing up so fast and they are so much fun. Maggie is just like my little friend; we do so many things together, and now Emma is getting to be a whole ton o' fun too. I can't wait for you all to see them again. I love you and miss you a lot.

MT

❖   ❖   ❖

April 13, 1997
Nairobi, Kenya

Dear Maggie and Emma,

Every day I look at your pictures on my refrigerator and count the days until we see you in person. I can hardly believe we're nearing the end of four years and preparing for furlough in the States.

Rainy season has started! We often have thunder and lightning storms at night. The rains have cooled temperatures and greened up grasses and other living things.

Do you remember that trip Grandpa and I took to Mfangano Island in 1994 for the Subas' cultural celebration? Recently I learned that after they heard a portion of the Bible in their own language, one of them said, "Yes! Finally, the Suba people can hear God speaking in their own language. He has ceased to be a foreign God. He is our God!"

With a happy heart,
Grandma

24

Silly Foreigners!

April 15, 1997
Nairobi, Kenya

Dear Maggie and Emma,

Next Sunday we'll leave for a two-week trip to Chad, Cameroon, and Congo, but even though our plane tickets say that, we don't know how our itinerary will actually turn out.

For example, two weeks ago our boss, John, bought tickets to travel the same route as ours—Nairobi to Addis Ababa, Ethiopia, for a change of planes and a flight to N'Djamena, Chad. At the Addis airport, they took John's bag and checked him in. Just before departure, however, they told him the plane wouldn't land in N'Djamena because too few people wanted to get off there; instead, the plane would fly from Addis directly to the stop scheduled after N'Djamena. In the end, John couldn't go to Chad at all because the flight was only once a week and he had business in Cameroon the following week—just like our itinerary. Instead, he returned to Nairobi and, a few days later, flew directly to Cameroon.

Then there's Ed. He wanted to travel from Ouagadougou, Burkina Faso, to some other African country. (I can't remember which one, but it doesn't matter.) In Ouaga, he confirmed his flights and flew to Abidjan, Ivory Coast, where he spent the night. The next morning he arrived at the airport, ticket in hand, ready for the next leg of his trip. They said, "Sorry. That flight left yesterday."

He said, "How can that be? You sold me this ticket and you printed today's date on it."

"That's right," they said, "but yesterday we decided to send it a day early." Because that, too, was a once-a-week flight, Ed had to fly back to Ouaga and try again another week.

Then there was the time your grandpa and I had tickets to fly out of Niamey, Niger, but airline officials bumped everyone and, instead, filled the plane with pilgrims bound for Mecca.

In addition to airline adventures, our travels can be impacted by our miniscule knowledge of French, health concerns (mainly gastro-intestinal upsets and malaria), and potential unrest. Zaire's civil war still rages and by all accounts, rebels expect to seize the capital city, Kinshasa, within the next couple of weeks, about the time we'll be working in Brazzaville, Congo. Only a river separates the two cities, so that situation has us a bit concerned.

April 29, 1997
Yaoundé, Cameroon

Dear Maggie and Emma,

Greetings from Yaoundé, Cameroon. My friend Ruth Chapman said I could use her e-mail to send a couple of messages to Dallas, which I did, and it occurred to me that I could send a quick note to family as well. Our trip so far has been perfect. We'll leave here Thursday for Brazzaville, Congo, and fly back to Nairobi on Sunday, May 4. We haven't heard much recently about Zaire's civil war, but Kinshasa sits right across the river from Brazzaville, and we wonder what we might see.

May 5, 1997
Nairobi, Kenya

Dear Maggie and Emma,

We returned home yesterday from our two-week trip to Chad, Cameroon, and Congo. Once again, God gave us a smooth trip and good health. We had some late flights but, considering all that could have gone wrong, we have no complaints.

N'Djamena, the capital of Chad, is an exotic desert city, a marketplace for cotton, dates, livestock, salt, and grain. The city is home to both black Africans and Arab Africans, a city where some people gather at mosques and others meet in a cathedral. N'Djamena reminds me of Bamako, Mali. Both are located in the Sahel, a swath of arid land that borders the Sahara Desert and stretches from the Horn of Africa across the continent to the Atlantic Ocean. Increasing drought and famine have caused the Sahara to claim more and more of the Sahel and that makes life there precarious, especially for subsistence farmers.

In N'Djamena, we lived in the home of a family on furlough. Tall stucco walls surrounded their boxy stucco house. All the houses and offices seemed to look alike, and everything wore the color of the sun-bleached sand that covered the streets.

A man named Bashir guarded the house. He wore a long white robe and wrapped his head in a traditional white turban. He also tended the grounds inside the walls—no lawn, only hot sand and a handful of hardy shrubs.

Bashir and his wife lived in a small house within our walled yard. I looked out the window one day and spotted Bashir's young wife—very tall and very graceful and very topless.

I learned that a large number of people in that region belong to a sect of the Islamic religion. Because they want God to forgive their sins and help with their needs, they carry out their religion's practices, including animal sacrifice. However, in case that's not good enough, they also carry out another religion's ritual that requires them to pay money. But in case that's still not good enough, they also pray to the God of Christians.

While we worked in N'Djamena, temperatures rose to a hundred and fifteen degrees or more in the shade. After sunset, the temperature dropped slightly outside but not inside. To maximize air circulation, we opened the metal louvered window slats, but even a slight breeze was rare. To make matters worse, our bed's mosquito net hindered any breeze that might have come through the window, and the temperature under our net was even higher than in the room.

Since most of the time we had neither running water nor electricity, we couldn't seek relief from showers or fans. Water came on sporadically, usually in the middle of the night. We learned to open the shower spigot and place a bucket under it before we went to bed so that when the water came on, it splashed into the bucket and the noise woke us up. Then we bolted out of bed, grabbed another bucket, and filled it, too. After that, if the taps still gave us water, we enjoyed the total luxury of a shower—sweet!—even though it was the middle of the night.

My friend Barbara Trudell travels to the same African nations we do and she wrote this about buying breakfast in N'Djamena:

> Swathed in white robes, the bread seller sits under a neem tree at the side of the road. His weathered face broadens into a smile as he sees potential customers—us—approaching. My French is terrible; I say, "We wants to buy two of bread." He laughs and breaks into a stream of Arabic. I don't speak Arabic, but I am dead certain that he has just said, "Honey, I don't speak French! Just buy my bread and we'll both be happy."
> So I look in his cardboard box and pick out two long, slender loaves of white French bread (the breakfast staple in Western Africa). I'm sure he's telling us what they cost, but we remain clueless. He laughs again—silly foreigners!—and motions for me to show him my money. Five, six coins in my palm: he picks out four and nods his head. "That'll do it," he says (I think). He shakes our hands, and we turn back down the dusty road towards our house. The language barrier, broken once again with a smile!

The intense heat and shortage of water quickly took a toll on my health. I sensed that if I had stayed one more day I'd become sick, yet our colleagues live in those conditions day after day, night after night, month after month. As if those weren't challenges enough, they were so short of personnel that several Bible translators had set aside their work in order to fill administrative roles. Without at least a minimal administration, no one could work there, so, bless their hearts, the work goes forward, even if slowly.

We worked with them in their offices during the day and sat around their dinner tables in the evenings—and not one person complained. No one complained about the personnel shortage or about setting aside translation programs. No one complained about the heat, the lack of electricity, or their inability to use computers, fans, photocopy machines, or other electrical equipment. They were great role models for me. I have the utmost respect for those folks.

Last Thursday and Friday were national holidays here in Kenya. That gave your Aunt Karen a four-day weekend so she traveled to Egypt. Can you believe it? Egypt! A WNS teacher, Sally, who retired from teaching last spring, invited Karen to join her. They arrived home this morning at six-thirty. Karen said the men were especially flirtatious and aggressive so I'm glad she and Sally traveled together. They said they had a great time, and I'm eager to see their pictures.

Speaking of pictures, I hope your mom and dad are showing you girls our pictures so we won't seem like complete strangers when we arrive. We'll leave for furlough in just a few weeks. Yikes! I'd better start sorting and packing! For now, though, I need to go to bed.

Hugs and kisses,
Grandma

25

More Accounts from The Heart of Africa

May 6, 1997
Nairobi, Kenya

Dear Maggie and Emma,
 I want to tell you more about our recent trip. In Yaoundé, Cameroon—green, humid, and a welcome contrast to Chad—we lived with the director and his wife, Bob and Ruth Chapman.
 Around their breakfast table, Ruth told us that she and Bob, their daughter Erin, and their sons, Ross and Tim, traveled to Kenya in 1989 before flying home to Canada for furlough. While they vacationed on the Indian Ocean, malaria mosquitoes bit the boys, though they didn't know it at the time. Tim, age five, fell ill on the flight to Ontario, and the next day Ross, age ten, got sick, too. The doctor prescribed antibiotics for strep throat but a few days later, he sent Ross to the hospital's emergency ward with a misdiagnosis of hepatitis. Tim checked into the hospital at the same time. On June 23, 1989, six days after they arrived in Canada, Ross and Tim died of cerebral malaria, only one hour apart.
 The boys' deaths traumatized Bob and Ruth and she told us they wondered if they could continue their work in Cameroon. Over time, though, she and Bob came to believe God had allowed their tragedy for a purpose and that He would not waste it. Mostly they wanted to live in the

center of God's will for them and, from that viewpoint, they knew as surely as before that God had called them to work in Cameroon. Though they didn't know specifics then, God still had plans for them: Bob now directs our work in Cameroon.

At Rain Forest International School in Cameroon, we met up with Reuben, the school's principal, and his wife Judy, the office manager.

After they retired a couple of years ago, they contacted Wycliffe about contributing in some capacity—they had good health and a wealth of skills and professional experience they wanted to share.

I recall our first meeting with Reuben and Judy. We knew immediately that we liked these two. Reuben explained that he and Judy spent several years planning for their retirement—but not in the way most Americans do. They searched the Bible for guidance, Reuben said, and they found no instructions about retiring from ministry. Instead, they found plenty of evidence that they should continue using their God-given talents and experience. That's why they contacted Wycliffe.

Over lunch, we answered their questions about working at a school for missionary kids, addressed their worries about cross-cultural living, and told them they could expect some delightful surprises on the mission field. We encouraged them to continue their application process. They responded with enthusiasm, and we knew they could fill important roles.

Then they dropped the bombshell. They said they couldn't leave the States for more than a couple of months.

I'm sure they saw on our faces what we felt in our hearts—a sinking feeling. Educators usually need to spend at least a school year on the field.

No one said anything for a few seconds.

Then Reuben spoke. He explained that their adult daughter, going through a rough time, needed their stabilizing influence. Our hearts went out to them—we knew, firsthand, how much parents want to help their children when they're in need—and we suggested that perhaps Wycliffe could find a job to fit their time slot.

Then Reuben and Judy looked at one another and said, "Maybe we should think about this some more. Let's pray about it. Maybe we could leave home for a whole school year." I could hear the worry in their voices, so their willingness to consider a longer assignment touched my heart.

We enjoyed Reuben and Judy so much and, as we went our separate ways, we promised to pray for them, knowing the next weeks and months might not be easy for them. We didn't know what they and God would conclude, but from our human perspective, we wanted to snatch them up and take them back to Africa with us!

A few months later, we heard that Rain Forest International School had indeed snatched them up—for two years!—so we enjoyed visiting them a couple of weeks ago and seeing how well they are doing. They told us about the new friends they've made, both Cameroonians and fellow missionaries, and—especially important to them—they've received numerous e-mails showing the ways God is caring for their family back home.

Our third stop was Brazzaville, Congo, separated from Kinshasa, Zaire, by only the Congo River. Rebels have taken control of all of Zaire except the capital, Kinshasa, and everyone expects them to arrive there at any moment.

I know almost nothing about Zaire's history, its president, the rebel leader, or the complicated political contexts of the civil war. I do know, however, that Zaire's situation is many-faceted and thorny—and beyond my comprehension. My heart aches for the country's people—I hope they can live healthy and peaceful lives soon.

President Bill Clinton appointed the U.N. Ambassador, Bill Richardson, to serve as the President's special envoy to Zaire and to help arrange talks between the two sides. According to a newspaper article, Richardson, now in Libreville, Gabon, says the Zairian president will resign. We hope and pray this will lessen violence in the transition, but the situation remains unpredictable and, in fact, Richardson said the rebels will take Kinshasa by force if necessary.

If that happens, millions of people—Zairians, missionaries, aid agency workers, and government officials—will likely flee across the river to Brazzaville. Five million people live in Kinshasa but only 900,000 live in Brazzaville so if Kinshasa falls, Brazzaville will have a hard time keeping foreigners out. Troops from France, Britain, Belgium, the United States, and Portugal are now on the ground in Brazzaville.

Because that scenario would destabilize Brazzaville, missionaries and other foreigners have packed one suitcase per person in case they need to evacuate. Now, from here in Nairobi, we watch the news every day to see what happens. We worry about our colleagues there and pray for God's protection.

Love,
Grandma

26

Am I A Real Missionary?

May 8, 1997, your Great-grandma Kay's birthday
Nairobi, Kenya

Dear Maggie and Emma,
 We heard that the two sides in Zaire's civil war planned to hold talks on a ship off the coast, but we don't know the outcome.

May 12, 1997
Nairobi, Kenya

Dear Maggie and Emma,
 I recently heard a story that shows how much Africans want the Bible in their own languages. When a church pastor asked the congregation to help financially with a local translation project, an elderly man walked forward with a couple of eggs in his hand—he had nothing else to give. He said, "I probably will not live long enough to see the Bible in my own language, but I want to give these eggs so my children will be able to read God's Word."
 That dear old man must sense, as Blaise Pascal did, that his children's hearts have a God-shaped hole that only He can fill. The man knows,

too, that until they have Scriptures they can understand, that gaping hole remains only partially filled.

I received this e-mail from your dad:

> Dear Mom:
> I guess it is probably Monday morning for you now and Mother's Day is past. I still wanted to wish you a happy day and tell you that I love you very much. I am so grateful to God and to you to be blessed with having you for my mom. Your courage and character are great inspirations for me, Mom. I really don't take for granted the fact that you and who you are really has made me most of what I am. Thanks, Mom, for everything. I love you very, very much. Have a great day.
>
> Love,
> Matt (for Jill, Maggie, and Emma too)

May 15, 1997
Nairobi, Kenya

Dear Maggie and Emma,
One of our churches in the States asked me to submit a newsletter article about what it's like to be a missionary. I wrote:

It's looking up on my wall and gasping at the sight of a putty-colored mini-dinosaur with bulging black eyes.
    And yet, it's discovering that geckos eat mosquitoes and are therefore welcome visitors in our home and office.

It's looking out the window at another smog-filled morning.
    And yet, it's noticing that the smog has lifted and there's blue sky and sunshine up there!

It's carrying a heavy ring of keys to open doors at the office and at home. It's re-locking the doors behind me after I go in.
    And yet, it's being thankful for money to buy keys and

locks, knowing that some people are too poor to buy them.

It's choking on a cloud of black exhaust spewing out of the truck ahead. It's getting "ring around the collar," by 10:00 AM.
    And yet, it's owning soap and a change of clothes so I can scrub away that "ring around the collar."

It's finding foreign substances in the sugar—insect parts, insect droppings, and other unidentifiable and perhaps even worse substances.
    And yet, it's having enough money to buy sugar.

It's filtering my water so I won't get diarrhea, vomiting, typhoid, and any number of things. It's getting tummy trouble anyway, despite my best efforts to avoid it.
    And yet, it's having enough money to buy water filters, and it's having doctors and good medicine when I do have tummy troubles.

It's arriving at the office and finding that thieves stole computers and other equipment.
    And yet, it's receiving donations from people back home so we can buy new equipment.

It's taking forty-five minutes to place one phone call across town.
    And yet, it's having a phone.

It's frequent power outages, usually just after I've typed a long e-mail but just before I've hit the "send" button.
    And yet, it's appreciating the electricity when it is on. Our colleagues in Zaire have electricity only a couple of days a week.

It's having no water in the taps for days on end.
    And yet, it's realizing that I've managed okay anyway.

It's using plastic-wire twist-ems over and over and over again.
    And yet, it's the joy of having twist-ems.

It's calling my daughter in the States and knowing that she's crying even though she thinks I can't tell.

> And yet, it's knowing that God knows how much our hearts break. It's committing our daughter's tears, and ours, to Him and trusting Him to work things out. It's having our daughter come teach at the new school here and live with us again for one brief but blessed school year.

It's living half a world away when grandchildren are born.

> And yet, it's receiving a letter from a dear friend saying, "I gave new baby Emma lots of hugs and kisses for you." It's cuddling a friend's newborn here in Nairobi, and it's the privilege of standing in as a substitute grandma because her own grandma lives half a world away.

It's longing to be with loved ones for holidays, birthdays, and family reunions.

> And yet, it's having several homesick young adults call me "Mom." It's making new friends that become like family and who spend holidays and birthdays with us.

It's being aware that I'm the only white-skinned person in sight.

> And yet, it's discovering that most Africans are genuinely friendly and feel honored when we visit their homes.

It's receiving a letter from a church at home asking, "What is it like to preach across Africa? How many souls have you saved?" It's being a support worker, not an evangelist or church planter, and asking myself, *Well, then, am I a real missionary if I only provide services for those on the cutting edge?*

> And yet, it's visiting a place where Bible translation is progressing and seeing that for the first time, people can hear Scriptures in their own language and begin to understand who God is. It's knowing that those Scriptures form the necessary foundation for evangelization and church planting. It's knowing that my very small role contributes daily toward filling a God-shaped hole in the hearts of millions of people across Africa.

Love,
Grandma

27

The Stuff of History Books, Recipe Books, Video Cameras, and Photo Albums

May 17, 1997
Nairobi, Kenya

Dear Maggie and Emma,
    South African President Nelson Mandela hosted talks a couple of days ago between Zaire's president and the rebel leader, and we're eager to hear the outcome. First-hand accounts from Kinshasa include trash-covered streets, armed soldiers, and heavy automatic weapons fire. Each day on TV, we watch as one government comes to an end and another takes shape. This is the stuff of history books.

❖ ❖ ❖

May 21, 1997
Nairobi, Kenya

Dear Maggie and Emma,
    CNN reports that rebels took over Zaire's presidential palace in Kinshasa and that the rebel leader declared himself president on Saturday.

Now a new flag flies in the nation he re-named The Democratic Republic of Congo, the country's former title after its independence from Belgium in 1960. Yes, this is the stuff of history books. Maybe someday, Maggie and Emma, you will read about this in school.

CNN showed pictures of smoke rising over Kinshasa—pictures taken from the same spot in Brazzaville where we stood just three weeks ago and took pictures. According to the Red Cross, two hundred people died in disturbances over the weekend. I can't help but worry that this will—or has already—set off the mass exodus across the river to Brazzaville. *Dear Lord, please keep the violence in check! And please take good care of our friends in Brazzaville!*

❖   ❖   ❖

May 22, 1997
Nairobi, Kenya

Dear Maggie and Emma,
We have heard no more news out of Kinshasa, but of course we wonder if Zairians are fleeing to Brazzaville.

This afternoon Karen returned from a camping trip with middle-school students, and tomorrow videotaping begins for West Nairobi School's teacher-recruitment video—starring Karen! (I had no part in that decision!) I first met the photographer, Dave, when he and his wife worked in Cameroon, and now he works out of the Calgary office. He's living with us while he videotapes for WNS and takes photos for Wycliffe-Canada's magazine.

I recently found this recipe. Do you think your Mom would be interested in it? (Just joking!)

    WATER BUFFALO DINNER

    10 medium-sized water buffalo
    2 rabbits (optional)
    salt and pepper

    Cut water buffalo into bite-sized pieces. Add enough
    brown gravy to cover. Cook over kerosene fire about two
    weeks. This will serve approximately 580 people. If more

are expected, two rabbits may be added, but do this only in case of emergency as most people do not like hare in their stew.

❖ ❖ ❖

May 25, 1997
Nairobi, Kenya

Dear Maggie and Emma,
 We still hear nothing about Zairians fleeing to Brazzaville. We hope our friends there are okay.
 Friday and yesterday, Dave shot footage for the WNS video. Today he'll tape Karen at home curling her hair and making espresso. He'll continue filming this afternoon and all day Monday. We want to give potential teacher recruits a glimpse of everyday life in Nairobi—but we'll edit out the potholes!

❖ ❖ ❖

June 3, 1997
Nairobi, Kenya

Dear Maggie and Emma,
 Riots have disturbed downtown Nairobi for a couple of days. Crowds swarmed from Uhuru Park into the center of downtown and smashed store windows, looted, stoned people, and set cars on fire. We were driving home from the store when it began. We heard the rioting but couldn't see it. Problems continued the next day on a smaller scale, but the city seems okay now.
 Speaking of riots, I think your grandpa might start one over the potholes around here.

 Your Aunt Karen will fly out of Nairobi on Friday, but I think she wants to keep it a secret from Port Angeles friends so she can surprise them. She has had a good year here. She says she wouldn't have missed it for anything, but now she is eager to return home. Her seventh grade English position awaits her at Stevens Middle School. She has blessed Grandpa and me and, I trust, her students and their parents.
 On Sunday, Karen suggested that we skip church and drive around

Nairobi's game park since this would be her last chance to do so—and probably the last chance for your grandpa and me, too, before furlough.

We had hardly driven through the gate when we spotted a lion—*simba*—sprawled across the road, sunning himself. Another car came along, though, and scared him into the brush.

A few seconds later, we came upon another massive lion strutting down the middle of the track as if he owned the whole world. We followed him, ten or fifteen feet behind, for almost two kilometers as he sauntered down the road, stopping now and then to mark his territory. We took lots of pictures and hope some turn out okay.

I look back over these four years and laugh because on my way to Africa, I memorized my friend Esther's instructions for staring down a leopard—but I've never seen one!

That doesn't mean a leopard hasn't seen me, though. During our three-month orientation, the Maasai spotted one in our vicinity and we know, too, that animals roamed throughout our camp at night. I'm sure we've driven by leopards in game parks but failed to spot their long tails hanging down from tree branches where they perch to enjoy, in leisurely fashion, their latest kill and an afternoon nap.

Even though we haven't seen a leopard, we've seen lions, elephants, Cape buffaloes, and rhinos—the other four of Africa's "Big Five." To this day, I still have to pinch myself to be sure I'm really in Africa. Africa! Yes, I'm really in Africa!

❖   ❖   ❖

June 6, 1997
Nairobi, Kenya

Hi, Maggie and Emma,

Today I met a blonde, blue-eyed little angel from Switzerland. She will celebrate her third birthday in November so she's a little younger than Maggie is. Her parents work in Central African Republic so little Christine speaks French (the language of CAR), Swiss German, and English. They say she counts from one to five in Swiss German, and six to ten in English.

This afternoon Christine, slightly disoriented in our office's park-like grounds, called out in perfect English, "Where's my mommy?" I took her by the hand and we walked around—actually, Christine skipped—looking for her mommy. When we found her, she whispered in Swiss that she needed to use the bathroom. I wonder—how did she know to speak to me in English? Anyway, I enjoyed holding a little girl's hand and skipping around. Only holding Maggie and Emma's hands could have been better. Soon I will!

Our lives are frantic these days. I don't know if I'll ever complete my projects and clear out the office before we leave for furlough. I think I can handle our apartment, but my office is a disaster. I have piled stacks of files on my desk and on top of my file cabinets—and now on the floor, too. (I know this doesn't surprise your dad.) I take work home in the evenings and weekends, and I pray I'll finish well.

Hugs,
Grandma

28

Of Elephants and Grass

When elephants fight, the grass gets hurt.
East African Proverb

June 7, 1997
Nairobi, Kenya

Dear Maggie and Emma,

For months we've watched, and agonized over, Zaire's civil war. We've housed, helped, and prayed for missionary families forced to leave their homes and their work. We've watched the rebel leader and his troops march throughout Zaire and take over the country.

One month ago, your grandpa and I stood on the banks of the Congo River in Brazzaville, Congo, and looked across to Kinshasa, Zaire's capital, knowing that rebels planned to seize the city any day and potentially cause millions of people to flee to safety in Brazzaville.

Knowing that, we were stunned when civil war broke out—not in Kinshasa, but in Brazzaville, the city everyone looked to as a safe haven. The government's military is battling against the militia of a former president, and our colleagues now find themselves in the midst of war on Brazzaville's streets.

Among them are our friends Alec and Marie.[1] When they furloughed a couple of years ago in Quebec City, your grandpa and I stayed with them for a few days to recruit French-speaking teachers to work in francophone African countries. Several feet of snow covered the ground and temperatures dropped to thirty-seven below zero. On one of those bitter cold days, Marie served us her Sweet and Sour Meatloaf and it instantly became one of your grandpa's all-time favorites. Every time I make that recipe, I think of Alec and Marie. They were delightful hosts so we enjoyed meeting up with them again last month in Brazzaville. Now the chaos of civil war surrounds them.

That familiar East African proverb comes to mind, *Wapiganapo tembo nyasi huumia*: When elephants fight, the grass gets hurt. Alec sent an e-mail yesterday and as I read and re-read it, I thought of the "grass"—the dear Congolese people and the colleagues we worked with just a month ago. When the powerful fight, the weak, poor, and innocent get hurt.

Alec says they're safe, but international phone lines are down, and cannon fire and gunshots must be unnerving. I worry about the Wilsons whose fifth child is due at any moment.

The U.S. Embassy invited people to evacuate on an Air France plane that's there on the ground, but the flight crew can't reach the airport.

June 8, 1997
Nairobi, Kenya

Dear Maggie and Emma,

Moment by moment we agonize for our colleagues in Congo. We seem helpless to do anything but pray. The U.S. Ambassador to Congo heard that no one should expect a resolution any time soon so the U.S. Embassy is now transporting people to the airport where planes will fly them across the river to Kinshasa, Zaire. But remember, rebel forces overthrew that government only a couple of weeks ago and the situation there sounds precarious.

We long for more information and news trickles in from various sources—CNN, newspapers, e-mails, staff meetings, and word of mouth. This morning, rebels detained a Marine and a U.S. Embassy consul. The hostages are now free, but two embassy vehicles were destroyed and another's tires were blown out.

The French military brought in armored personnel carriers and the U.S. Embassy issued a mandatory evacuation that affects almost everyone we know there. They won't have an easy time, though, because fighting on the road to the airport has left it impassable, and the airport remains closed. A few days ago, we heard that an Air France plane was on the ground but the flight crew hadn't reached the airport. Today we learned that the plane took off without most of its crew.

Colleagues are trying to make radio contact with four women, Liza and Betty in a remote place in the interior and Sue and Elaine in another. I heard a report of tanks in Brazzaville's streets but have heard nothing about Joanie Wilson, our pregnant colleague.

My heart breaks for the Congolese people. I lift them up to God. "You hear, O Lord, the desire of the afflicted; you encourage them, and you listen to their cry, defending the fatherless and the oppressed" (Psalm 10:17–18). I don't understand God's purposes, but I trust His goodness and His work on their behalf.

❖   ❖   ❖

June 9, 1997
Nairobi, Kenya

Dear Maggie and Emma,

I am so behind at my office! Today I must read almost ninety e-mails. I don't know how I'll close things down before we leave for furlough. I sent two boxes home with your Aunt Karen when she left Friday night, so I've made a little progress.

❖   ❖   ❖

June 10, 1997
Nairobi, Kenya

Dear Maggie and Emma,

This morning, CNN International reported that fighting in Brazzaville is out of control, bodies cover the streets, and French soldiers tried to take a group to the airport but had to turn back. We picture the city as we saw it last month—full of sunshine and lush tropical vegetation—and try to juxtapose mental pictures of the devastation there now.

A number of people were hiding in the U.S. Embassy but this morning's news reported that many evacuated yesterday to Kinshasa; most of our people hope to arrive there by today. Can you imagine evacuating from Brazzaville to Kinshasa when people in Kinshasa thought they'd have to evacuate to Brazzaville?

Three of our Brazzaville personnel were attending meetings here in

Nairobi when the disturbances broke out and they can't return home because the airport there remains closed. We give them our listening ears, our prayers, and the use of our computers and e-mail.

One of them, Harry James, has not yet contacted his wife and children. They planned to evacuate to Kinshasa two days ago and take the first available flight to Nairobi, but they have not arrived. Brazzaville's international phone lines are down so Harry knows nothing about his family's whereabouts. The violence rages on and Harry is panic-stricken. When I imagine this happening to me and my children, my heart aches for him. Last month in Brazzaville, the Jameses invited us to their home for lunch one day. They are a nice young family with two children, a girl about six and a baby around a year old—Emma's age. May God have mercy on them.

Tonight I've been thinking about a couple of times when a situation has devastated my world. In the early hours, still stunned, shocked to the core, I sensed God's voice assuring me that "in all things God works for the good of those who love him" (Romans 8:28). I think, too, of Joseph's words to his brothers who tried to kill him, "You intended to harm me, but God intended it for good to accomplish what is now being done" (Genesis 50:20). In ways I'll never fully understand, God works in the midst of our desperate days to bring about something good. I think of that old saying: Every cloud has a silver lining. Even when a cloud blocks the sun, if we look carefully we can see the sun's glow along the edges—the silver lining. The dark cloud still exists but, when we look at the bigger picture, the sun's rays coexist with the cloud.

At times like this when people live day to day with upheavals in Zaire and Congo, I believe God has a silver lining in mind. He strengthens, hones, teaches, sharpens—He refines individuals, families, groups, organizations, ministries, and even nations. He separates wheat from chaff and blows the chaff away. He polishes rough edges. He separates dross from silver. In the midst of these heart-crushing wars, who knows what God is doing behind the scenes within individuals and families? Who can say what He's doing within our organizations and ministries, within governments and nations?

I know God will not waste this suffering. He will bring about any number of good results that we cannot imagine right now.

June 11, 1997
Nairobi, Kenya

Dear Maggie and Emma,

This morning at our staff meeting, we heard details from Brazzaville about the Wilsons and their new baby. Joanie, her husband Jake, and their four children evacuated from their home to the World Health Organization (WHO) yesterday for a flight to Zaire—though we're supposed to call it the Democratic Republic of Congo now, or DRC. While they awaited the flight, though, Joanie gave birth in the WHO compound. Afterward, she decided she needed something back at home—it must have been very important!—so she, Jake, and their five children returned home, despite the mayhem of civil war and bodies in the streets. When they returned to WHO, everyone had evacuated and they'd taken the Wilsons' luggage with them. Just imagine! Now they have a new baby, four other children, and no possessions except for the clothes on their weary bodies.

From a human perspective, so many situations look impossible, but we trust God knows each person's circumstances and that He is, in an ongoing way, choreographing the various ways these events will end.

❖ ❖ ❖

June 11, 1997, 11:30 AM
Nairobi, Kenya

Dear Maggie and Emma,

A stunning bit of news arrived one hour ago. During coffee break, I visited with Harry James, the young man stranded here while Brazzaville's turmoil surrounds his wife, Ingrid, and their children. He confessed that he was falling apart—he didn't know if they were safe or where they were.

Just then, a shout interrupted our conversation. "Harry, Ingrid is on the phone!" You can't imagine Harry's excitement! Ingrid and the children are safe in—Switzerland! They had indeed evacuated to Kinshasa and almost immediately left on a flight to Switzerland rather than Nairobi. Harry will fly there tomorrow night. He said, "I'll be there with them for lunch on Friday." Bless his dear heart. These have been excruciating days for him.

June 12, 1997
Nairobi, Kenya

Dear Maggie and Emma,

Two colleagues assigned to western Zaire are also stuck here in Nairobi. I received an e-mail from one of them, David Morgan, a delightful Englishman and the director of our work in western Zaire—a hot spot right now, as you know.

> From: David Morgan, West Zaire/DRC Group Director, currently in Nairobi
> Date: June 11, 1997
>
> Dear Friends,
> The stress factors have certainly upped now that we are dealing with two crises....
> Our new truck [in western Zaire] was kept safe by Pastor Sanguma; he drove it and despite being chased by soldiers managed to keep it, though they apparently took the batteries out. Our old truck is reportedly in Imese. Sadly the area around Imese is still out of communication. Our Guest House in Gemena was destroyed and all of ... our goods stored there likewise. Everything has been taken from it. Books, papers, everything; toilets and bathrooms have been broken, water consequently got everywhere and flooded the place. It is quite uninhabitable....
> These are not easy times. Things seem to be getting worse and worse. Yet we rest on the everlasting arms and know the One who holds everything together.
>
> Still with you in Jesus,
> David and Sharon

The Washington Post reports that additional French troops arrived in Brazzaville and airlifted over 350 foreign nationals. Rocket and artillery fire continue. In fact, one shell strayed across the river and landed in Kinshasa in a Nigerian diplomat's garden!

According to CNN, Brazzaville's airport houses hundreds of stranded evacuees. Both of the warring sides are trying to take control of it and exploding shells light up the night sky. On Monday and Tuesday, French military forces transported 1,500 people, by boat or military convoy, to the airport. About half of them flew to Libreville, Gabon, or Pointe-Noire on Congo's coast. I suppose the other half flew to Kinshasa. A U.S. military plane flew more than fifty people out of the country on Tuesday, some Americans and some of other nationalities.

This is starting to seem like a bad dream. I'm not even on the front lines yet sometimes I feel dazed, and I'm not alone—friends around the office sometimes walk around like zombies, too.

My thoughts return to my Old Testament friend Habakkuk, troubled by conflict, destruction, and injustice. He cried out to God, and He answered, "Just watch—you'll be amazed! I'm going to do something you'll have to see to believe!" (Habakkuk 1:5 paraphrased). So, once again, I'll follow Habakkuk's example—I'll spread my concerns before God and watch for His answer. Can He once again do something utterly amazing?

❖ ❖ ❖

June 13, 1997
Nairobi, Kenya

Dear Maggie and Emma,

Today we heard from the Jim Smith family, among the first Americans evacuated from Brazzaville on Saturday night. Now safe in North Carolina, Jim e-mailed that while confined to their home in Brazzaville on Thursday night, they listened to gunfire, artillery, and grenade blasts.

On Saturday, the U.S. Embassy set up a car convoy and military escort to transfer Americans to the airport. The convoy arrived at the Smiths' gate at 3:00 PM and then—they had to leave behind their Canadian, British, and Swiss friends. Their own embassies were arranging their evacuations, but I'm sure it pained the Smiths to leave ahead of them.

Their convoy encountered only sporadic gunfire while they picked up embassy personnel, missionaries, and Peace Corps volunteers. Two hours and only a few stressful moments later, Jim wrote, they arrived at the airport where their group boarded two small planes; they could bring only one small bag each. After a fifteen-minute flight across the Congo River, they landed safely at the N'djili Airport near Kinshasa. U.S. Embassy officials welcomed them with soft drinks and potato chips.

United Nations Ambassador Bill Richardson (and President Clinton's special envoy to Zaire) "just happened" to be in Kinshasa—though I'm sure it didn't "just happen." I'm sure God had something to do with it!

Richardson planned to fly to Andrews Air Force Base, Maryland, the next day on an old Air Force One and he offered seats to anyone who wanted to join him. Thus, the Smiths evacuated in style!

We received incorrect information at our staff meeting a couple of days ago. When the Wilsons' baby was born, their luggage did not leave without them. Jake explained in a message today that he and Joanie had planned to deliver the baby at home but at 1:00 AM on Tuesday, WHO urged them to get to the clinic. Jake said they had to cross two roadblocks but arrived okay, and Joanie gave birth to their healthy baby girl shortly after 3:00 AM. A couple of hours later, with mortars landing near WHO, and worried about their safety, the Wilsons returned home and, exhausted, slept for three hours. During that time, evacuees at WHO left the country.

Eventually a French colonel let the Wilsons join a convoy. Imagine their relief! Along the way, heavy gunfire detained them for nearly an hour, but finally they arrived at the Aeroclub, located at the airport, and fighting broke out there as well. Cement debris peppered Joanie's face when bullets struck a wall nearby, but she's okay.

Now safely evacuated, in Zaire—DRC—the Wilsons are having trouble getting a passport for the baby because in the midst of that chaos, no one filled out a birth certificate. To complicate matters, the baby was born in Congo, not DRC, and until she has a birth certificate and passport, the family can't leave. I can hardly imagine the moment-by-moment challenges those dear ones face.

Last month in Brazzaville, your grandpa and I enjoyed getting better acquainted with Marcus Miller and his wife, Krissie. In addition to working with them around their office, we enjoyed a leisurely dinner in their home one evening and, on our final night in Brazzaville, we stayed overnight with them—well, sort of; we got up at 2:00 AM and Marc drove us to the airport. We traveled on the same flight as their daughter, returning to Rift Valley Academy after spring break. Even though she's a teenager, she's already a seasoned international traveler and took good care of us.

A couple of weeks ago Marcus, Krissie, and their son flew to Nairobi for our meetings, and one afternoon we took them to a mall and showed them around. It seemed like a little thing to us, but they were effusive with thanks.

Now civil war tears Brazzaville apart and the Millers have had to stay here. They're nearly sick with worry over both missionary colleagues and Congolese friends. They don't know what has happened to their home or their dog. Throughout this past week, I've seen agony and apprehension on their faces. At least once a day Krissie comes to my office to use my computer, e-mail, and telephone, and sometimes to shed tears.

In the midst of this heartache, we've received some good news! As of yesterday, all our Brazzaville-based personnel have left Congo! From here in Nairobi, we have watched and prayed—and day after day, we've witnessed gigantic feats that God and His human helpers have pulled off to evacuate our fellow workers to safety.

Even though all our colleagues have left the capital city, a few people remain in other parts of Congo. Thirteen missionaries await evacuation from Impfondo, up north on the eastern boundary with Zaire. Four others—Liza and Betty, and Sue and Elaine—work in two other places in the interior. I suspect they'll remain safe as long as they stay out of Brazzaville. Nevertheless, no one has reached the women by radio and we pray for them night and day.

❖ ❖ ❖

June 15, 1997
Nairobi, Kenya

Dear Maggie and Emma,

Someone received word that Betty and Liza plan to leave their place up north if the Peace Corps leaves. I'm so thankful someone has finally heard from them.

Your grandpa and I gave up sleeping under mosquito nets shortly after our orientation course because they're such a pain to use. You must tuck them in, thoroughly, under the mattress while you're lying on it—I suggest you picture yourself trying to do that—because if you don't, you'll leave gaps around the bottom and mosquitoes will fly through them and bite you. Even if you succeed in tucking it in, you can't let any part of your body touch the net because a mosquito can bite through it. And if you get up in the night, you must again perform the contortions necessary to tuck the net under your mattress. For all those reasons, and since most people believe that Nairobi's mosquitoes don't carry malaria, we decided to forego a mosquito net.

Mosquitoes! Mosquitoes are among the most irritating critters God created. They cause us serious sleep-deprivation by hovering just outside our ears at night and doing their little screamy-humming thing. I have no idea how many thousands of times your grandpa and I have whacked ourselves on the side of the head trying to smash the little beasts. And we never succeed—they always zip away before we can squash them—so I don't know why we keep doing it. I guess it's because we don't want to get out of bed and take more drastic steps.

Your grandfather knows he doesn't need to get out of bed to spray bug killer on them. It took him only a short while to figure out that if he can pretend to be asleep longer than I can pretend to be asleep, eventually I'll get so mad at those mosquitoes that I'll jump out of bed, flip on the light, grab the insect spray, and chase after them. I'm probably poisoning us with that spray but, in the short run, we can get some sleep. (In the long run—well, we'll worry about that later.) I can't tell you how much pleasure I feel each time I murder a mosquito.

I've never seen myself in a mirror while chasing mosquitoes in the middle of the night, but I'm sure fire streams from my nostrils. One night those mosquitoes and I engaged in a fierce battle. Determined to win the victory, I fought on and on, lunging and leaping around our bedroom, spraying poison into the air—when suddenly as I rounded the corner at the foot of the bed, my feet slipped out from under me and I crashed. That hard smooth terrazzo floor, drenched with insect spray, might as well have been greased.

Mad? Yes.
Bruised? Yes.
But, quaint? I ain't!

❖ ❖ ❖

Tuesday, June 17, 1997
Nairobi, Kenya

Dear Maggie and Emma,

According to *The New York Times* and CNN, the presidents of several African nations—Gabon, Chad, Mali, and Central African Republic—met in Libreville, Gabon, with representatives of Congo's warring factions to set up peace talks. The prime minister of Equatorial Guinea and Senegal's foreign minister also participated. Diplomats from France, the European Union, and the United Nations observed the talks.

While we grieve with and for our Brazzaville friends, we also must deal with trouble here in Nairobi surrounding upcoming elections. People here worry that mayhem in other African countries might give bad ideas to segments of Kenyan society. One major riot occurred here on May 31, and certain groups plan to storm Parliament next Thursday. Political rallies on Saturday, in Nairobi and other cities, will likely produce more violence.

Our office is located about two city blocks from our apartment, through a quiet residential area, so we don't expect troubles. If any arise, though, we'll simply stay home. We have a good network to alert us to such problems.

❖   ❖   ❖

June 20, 1997
Nairobi, Kenya

Dear Maggie and Emma,

Only minor violence occurred here, a sweet answer to prayer. University students rioted but stayed near the heart of town. I smiled when I saw rain start to fall. I suspect God sent it to keep the crowds small.

Officials cancelled rallies scheduled for Saturday across Kenya, another answer to prayer. Nevertheless, we know that hotheaded troublemakers could stir up problems.

Marc's wife Krissie rushed into my office today, bursting with joy, because she talked on the phone with Liza and Betty! They arrived safely in Franceville, Gabon, after a three-day drive across central Congo. Before they left, they spoke with Sue and Elaine on the radio. The four had hoped to drive together but Sue and Elaine didn't have enough fuel to join them.

Before the unrest broke out, Elaine sent her passport to the immigration office to get her long-term visa—and her passport is still there! Without her passport, she can't cross the border.

Nevertheless, we received even more good news. Alec and Marie evacuated safely to Libreville, Gabon, and then to Paris. Alec sent this summary of their departure:

> June 19, 1997
> No one could have foreseen it coming.
> And before we knew what was happening, the U.S. Embassy was calling it an obligatory evacuation. We were to pack a single suitcase, hand-carry size, and be ready to leave when called. We waited and listened to the walkie-talkie as others were escorted from their homes.... With the arrival of the French Legionnaires, the evacuations began in earnest. We shared a final meal, turned off the hot water heaters and locked the doors. Thirteen of us climbed into the group Land Cruiser and, then when the convoy arrived, we fell into line third behind the tank for the rendezvous at the cathedral. Twenty cars later, the

convoy left for temporary quarters at Orstom, a French scientific facility in a safe part of town. Eighty more cars eventually joined the group, and about seven hundred of us spent the night in fairly primitive conditions, some asleep in their vehicles, most under the stars. Soldiers who had sprayed the area for mosquitoes brought us army rations for the evening meal.

"Be ready at 7:00 AM," we were told, for the trip to the airport. And right on time the convoy set out again, depositing us at the Aeroclub from where the flight would leave. We spent the day waiting and lying low because the airport was one object of contention between the rival forces, and shooting never stopped. At about 2:00 PM, we were walked to a French military aircraft and loaded for travel to Libreville, the nearest safe city.

A two-hour flight brought us to a Gabonese military base, another temporary set of quarters for another night. Long lines of those being processed made us aware that we were few among many being evacuated. (Altogether nearly five thousand were flown out of Brazzaville.) The final flight left Libreville for Paris at 2:00 AM the next morning and brought an end for us to the rescue operation....

The evening before leaving Brazzaville, [we] sang and prayed ... affirming God's control and reminding ourselves again of God's ownership of all we saw around us....

Alec

Today Marc flew to Kinshasa to work with two of our men from Central African Republic on arranging a flight for missionaries still waiting in Impfondo. He will also work with another mission agency on evacuation plans for Sue and Elaine. If they're not successful, down on the coast, in Pointe-Noire, a man named Étienne is looking into help from commercial airlines, and our colleagues in Cameroon are arranging for their plane to assist. Help comes from many directions, and it reminds me of Hebrews 12:1 that says a great cloud of heavenly witnesses surrounds us and cheers us on. I hope Elaine, Sue, Marcus, Étienne, and the others sense that, in a similar way, we're watching, praying, and cheering them on.

At a time like this, we possess a treasure—the Bible in our own language. By reading it, meditating on it, and absorbing it, we can grab hold of God. It reassures us that He works on our behalf even if we can't see specifics at the time. The Bible gives me strength and hope when I'm troubled, and I struggle to imagine what life must be like for people with no Scriptures they can understand. How can they cope without it?

That reminds of a story about a woman who suffered severe trauma in the midst of one of Africa's war-torn places. After the worst ended, someone asked if she had prayed. She answered no and explained that since the Bible was not in her language, she assumed God didn't understand her language—so why should she pray? When I heard that, my heart broke. She must feel so alone, so cut off from God. I want her to know that God does speak her language! And He knows her and cares about her. I want her to know that God delights in her! I want her to know the warmth and security of His love! Her story renews my passion to work in support of Bible translation.

❖ ❖ ❖

Sunday, June 22, 1997
Nairobi, Kenya

Dear Maggie and Emma,

Today is day seventeen of this international crisis. Coworkers find themselves enveloped in conflict in yet another African nation: Central African Republic (CAR), north of Congo on the border with Zaire. A colleague in CAR said that unrest broke out yesterday and has hampered their evacuation plans.

And, south of there, in Congo, Étienne couldn't line up a commercial flight for Sue and Elaine so will now look for a helicopter to evacuate them.

The only relief agency remaining in Brazzaville, the Red Cross, evacuated sixty orphans to a safer locale, but they can't keep up with burying the corpses on the ground.

❖ ❖ ❖

Wednesday, June 25, 1997
Nairobi, Kenya

Dear Maggie and Emma,

People still can't contact Sue and Elaine, but—good news! Étienne found an HF radio located in a quiet spot so he will try again. More good news! He has arranged for a helicopter to fly the ladies out. Knowing that, I'll sleep better tonight.

A colleague in Bangui, CAR, said mortars and rockets flew over their heads all day. Because of the unrest there, Avions Sans Frontiere postponed their rescue flight for the thirteen missionaries in Impfondo, but our aviation department in Cameroon will continue their evacuation plans.

My coffee break is over so I'll close for now. See you soon!

Love,
Grandma

29

Lord, Hear Our Prayers!

*Give ear to my words, O Lord, consider my sighing.
Listen to my cry for help, my King and my God, for to you I pray.
Psalm 5:1-2*

June 27, 1997
Nairobi, Kenya

Dear Maggie and Emma,

    In the midst of several weeks of sheer chaos, today your grandma skidded across the half-century mark. My mother phoned to wish me happy birthday, bless her heart. Your dad and Aunt Karen called me too—she's visiting your family in California. You talked to me, too, Maggie! I couldn't understand everything you said because in your excitement, you talked too fast! However, I did understand, "I love you, Grandma Thomas!"—a perfect birthday gift.

    Every Friday our staff takes a half-hour coffee break with cookies and coffee, but today they served birthday cake. Then at noon the ladies on our staff, plus Krissie, took me out to lunch. I almost choke up when I think I'll leave them soon. (One of them whispered to me that these are not hot flashes I'm experiencing—they're power surges!)

    Celebrating at a time like this seems absurd while people in Zaire, Congo, and Central African Republic suffer unspeakable violence and two urgent rescue operations are underway. On the other hand, perhaps our hour of frivolity gave us a brief break from our worries.

Your grandpa and I worked with Darlene Jerome on our two trips to Yaoundé, Cameroon. As Director of Personnel there, and now part of the Congo Crisis Management Team, she and her colleagues have requested authorization to evacuate the thirteen people from Impfondo.

Here are their plans. First, the pilot, Paul, will fill the plane with barrels of fuel and fly to Libongo, an Italian-run forestry strip near Cameroon's border with Congo. There he will unload the fuel, notify authorities, and refuel the plane. (We met Paul on one of our trips to Cameroon and enjoyed lunch with him and his wife in their lovely home. Their monkey attacked my head, though. Quaint I ain't.)

Since the aircraft holds only six people—the pilot and five passengers—Paul will make several shuttle flights across the border between the Congo town of Ouesso and the forestry strip.

After everyone arrives safely on the Cameroon side, Paul will shuttle flights from Libongo to Yaoundé. Some evacuees might have to spend the night on the airstrip, but Darlene suspects the Italians might supply them with pizza.

She hopes they'll receive authorizations by today so Paul can fly out tomorrow. They want to transport all thirteen to Yaoundé by next Tuesday. Everyone here, and there, too, feels a little jittery because of this complicated mission.

June 29, 1997
Nairobi, Kenya

Dear Maggie and Emma,

Bernard is one of those men whose wife and children work upcountry on the *shamba* while he works in Nairobi. He is the man I told you about who sold his maize harvest but never received payment for it. He works as a driver but always looks for additional work to supplement that income. May God bless him for his willingness to work hard. Your grandpa has created small jobs for Bernard and has given him money to buy fertilizer for this year's crop.

A few days ago, we invited Bernard and his wife to eat lunch with us. While we visited around the table, Bernard's wife didn't say much and she made odd noises while she chewed. She ate rapidly and helped herself to seconds. I'm afraid Bernard noticed our curiosity because he explained she had not eaten for several days. When we heard that, we passed more food and let her eat while we visited with her husband. That experience cut me right to the heart. Paying for their lunch seemed like almost nothing to us, yet they were so poor that they hadn't eaten in days. *Oh, Lord, thank You for the opportunity to help this dear young family.*

June 30, 1997
Nairobi, Kenya

Dear Maggie and Emma,

The Red Cross has now crossed the river by boat to Kinshasa. People there report that they can hear the destruction in Brazzaville. I picture people looking across the river and wondering about their homes, offices, pets, and especially their Congolese friends.

Our colleagues in Yaoundé, Cameroon, have collected clothes and toys for the Impfondo evacuees they expect this week.

Today Krissie sent me a sweet e-mail:

> Dear Linda,
> Thank you so much for all your kindness to us and for your prayers! You've been like a sister to me!
>
> Love, Krissie

I wish I could do more to help her. I can only pray and welcome her to my office to talk, use my computer, and make phone calls. From Cameroon, Darlene Jerome e-mailed this today:

> Hello folks,
> We managed to get all the authorizations we needed to cross the border of Congo—not easy when a country is at war. Guess it went all the way to the presidency in Congo, and I believe here, too. Dennis and Bob had on nice suits for a few days there.
> The two embassies, American and Canadian, helped a lot in this effort....
> Saturday morning Dennis and Bob put on their suits again and picked up the Congolese embassy rep

who would go along to the [Italian] logging camp and monitor the flights going in and out. He turned out to be a very understanding and responsive man. His wife was at home praying for the mission. Thank you, Lord.

They got down to the logging camp in good time and started the shuttles. They got two of the three done on Saturday and then settled in for the evening. It was pretty rough—air-conditioned rooms in the middle of the rainforest and a several-course Italian meal that lasted until 11:00 PM. David put away eleven pieces of pizza after his spaghetti and veal cutlets and before finishing it all off with cake! He's a growing thirteen year old. As you can see, the logging officials were doing their best to meet the needs of the evacuees.

The next morning they completed the last shuttle out of Congo with excellent support from the Congolese aviation officials and local authorities. So, by Sunday midmorning they were starting the shuttles up to Yaoundé.

Becky and their three boys came in around 12:30 PM, and we were there to greet her and refuel the plane. We processed them for visas there at the airport....

The plane then headed back for the logging camp. About halfway into his 2.7 hours flight, Steve [another pilot, a coworker of Paul's] decided the weather was too bad to continue on to the camp, so he said he would put down in Batouri for the night. We did not have final confirmation that he was down and okay, and we were not able to confirm it through another mission (the phones would not go through) or through the *gendarmerie* or through flight control out of Yaoundé or Bangui.... But, just a bit ago, we heard Steve on the radio say he was up and on his way back down to the logging camp. So, he and Paul will trade off and keep this operation going.

It looks like we will get the rest up here to Yaoundé today if the weather holds, but it looks like a very low ceiling, so we will see....

Thanks for all your prayers. We will give you a final update when all are here.

In His Hands,
Darlene

❖   ❖   ❖

July 1, 1997
Nairobi, Kenya

Dear Maggie and Emma,

Late yesterday Darlene sent news from Cameroon that Steve and Paul completed their evacuations.

> 6/30/97 5:19 PM
> Dear Colleagues near and far,
>
> Well, the news here is that the plane is to land in about thirty minutes with the final load.... [Their arrival] will complete the operation Impfondo–Yaoundé. Everyone seems in good health and spirits. And they seem to think that this is a pretty nice place to vacation....
>
> Unfortunately, the news from Brazzaville is sad and hard to imagine for these folks. Probably not easy to absorb. Let's keep them in our prayers.

Every day, people in Kinshasa hear heavy shelling and gunfire from across the river in Brazzaville. What can be left of the city by now? Refugees continue to flee into Kinshasa despite gunfire there nightly. Those poor dear people! I marvel at Krissie's composure while Marc works from there.

July 2, 1997
Nairobi, Kenya

Dear Maggie and Emma,

Each morning after I read the Bible and pray, I look at the day's selection from one of my favorite devotional books. This morning I opened *Streams in the Desert* to July 2. Throughout the years, I underlined passages and wrote notes in the margins. One year I highlighted a sentence in green. Another year I underlined phrases in purple, and in 1993 I wrote in red ink. This morning when I saw that marked-up page, I smiled because I knew I would re-read a bit of my history.

The book's author, Mrs. Charles E. Cowman, wrote about faith and what it is not. Faith is not waiting until we see sufficient proof that everything will work out okay. As Paul said in 2 Corinthians 5:7, "We live by faith, not by sight." The author of the book of Hebrews wrote of the same thing, "Now faith is being ... certain of what we do not see" (11:1). I had always loved the story of Abraham stepping out in faith: "By faith Abraham ... obeyed and went, even though he did not know where he was going" (Hebrews 11:8). In fact, one of my favorite books is based on that verse.

Back on July 2, 1993, I envisioned both Karen and myself as stepping out in faith—we didn't really know what awaited us, and we had no proof that all would work out well. In the margin next to Mrs. Cowman's words, I wrote in red, "1993—Anticipating leaving for Africa. Perhaps today moving out of beloved home. Trusting God to meet *every* need for *Karen*."

I remember those dark days—I remember the sick dread leading up to the day I'd leave my girl all alone and remove myself to Africa with your grandpa. Those days, I felt my way through a fog. And by July 2, 1993, I had already taken my terrifying, outrageous, blind leap of faith and, mid-hurdle, I wondered what to expect when I hit the ground.

And I never knew a heart could hurt so much.

This morning I continued reading down the page. Mrs. Cowman wrote, "We sit and weep in vain. The voice of the Almighty said, 'Up and onward forevermore.'" I had underlined the next sentence in red, the 1993 color: "Let us move on and step out boldly, though it be into the night, and we can scarcely see the way." Oh, I knew what she meant! She continued, "The path will open, as we progress, like the trail through the forest.... There are guides and wayside inns along the road. We will find food, clothes, and friends at every stage of the journey...."[1] I circled "friends" in red and wrote in the margin, "1993—My prayer for me, and especially for Karen." She had just graduated from college and moved 1400 miles away to take her first teaching job—yes, she'd need new friends. And I prayed I would make new friends, too.

This morning I used turquoise ink to underline those words, draw brackets around the whole paragraph, and jot down a happy face. I wrote in the margin, "1997—Leaving Nairobi in a few days for furlough. God *has* given me wonderful friends here." And He had given Karen friends, too, in both Port Angeles and Nairobi.

July 3, 1997
Nairobi, Kenya

Dear Maggie and Emma,

Good news! Étienne reached Sue and Elaine by radio! And, more good news! Brazzaville now has ten functioning international phone lines.

Today the U.N. Security Council announced a deployment of multinational forces to Congo to help end the warring and to supervise a cease-fire. Kofi Annan's envoy to the region says the airport must be secured so that humanitarian organizations and goods can arrive.

July 4, 1997
Nairobi, Kenya

Dear Maggie and Emma,

I'm struggling to dismantle both office and home before we leave for furlough in two weeks. All of a sudden, I realize that I'm exhausted. But why? How did that happen?

Something twitches in a narrow back corner of my memory. I am in Calgary, sitting in the back seat of a car, but I can't remember where I am. Fast forward to SeaTac Airport. I hear my brother's calm voice, "Let's count how many countries you've been in recently," and when I count sixteen countries in fourteen months, he says, "No wonder you couldn't remember where you were."

Now, if I step back and look over the past year or so, maybe I'll discover another "no wonder" and figure out why I'm so tuckered out.

Not until tonight have I recognized how hard I've pushed through the past year. In fact, for more than a year—from June 3, 1996, until now—someone extra has lived with us every day except one. I think back to the teachers' accident and the attempted carjacking and I see now that they left me shaken. I recall frequent power outages and the weekends and evenings we returned to the office to catch up. I think of the blocks of time I devoted to help your grandpa when new teachers arrived.

And—only now I realize—I still have unused vacation days! I can still see Brian's sweet face during orientation when he explained the importance of using our vacation days. They're coping mechanisms—those important things that keep us healthy, well balanced, and fit for working on the mission field. Now I wish I had followed Brian's wise advice.

On top of that, it's painful to watch our colleagues in crisis in Zaire, Central African Republic, and Congo. (The final stage of the final rescue operation is taking place right now in Congo.)

Then, too, we're on edge with violence here in Nairobi, and we hope and pray that the type of unrest in Zaire, Congo, and CAR won't also develop in Kenya. Opposition parties called for pre-election rallies across Kenya next Monday but they didn't wait until then—they started last night. Crowds threw boulders into streets and bent down light poles. Just before noon today, we received an alert to avoid certain parts of the city. Your grandpa was driving through that very part of town right then but I had no way to warn him. Thank God, he got back safely. These situations take a toll—more than I realized before.

Once again, I hear my brother's gentle voice. If he were here in our living room tonight, he'd say, "No wonder you're tuckered out." Some situations were beyond my control but, in other cases, I could have made choices to lessen my stress. May God help me through each day, each moment, and each responsibility—and perhaps to do things differently in the future.

July 5, 1997
Nairobi, Kenya

Dear Maggie and Emma,

The Wilsons' newborn finally received her paperwork! I'm so pleased for them. Also I heard that when Étienne made contact with Elaine and Sue in the interior, he learned that Sue is down with malaria. My heart aches for her.

Love,
Grandma

30

Of Porridge and Cornmeal

One person is thin porridge; two or three people are a handful of stiff cooked cornmeal.
East African Proverb

July 7, 1997
Nairobi, Kenya

Dear Maggie and Emma,
 The past eleven days have ticked by *polepole*—slowly, slowly—and we've sent many prayers heavenward for Sue and Elaine, especially for Sue's health; malaria makes people so awfully sick! A precarious and highly confidential rescue mission began June 26 when two Zairian pastors set out for the women, and now we've received the news we've longed to hear: they arrived in Kinshasa last night, Sunday, July 6, and Krissie talked with them on the phone!
 Around the office, we hear snippets about that rescue. The foursome navigated a river at night in the heart of Congo, walked some thirty miles, and came upon military roadblocks—without problems! Brazzaville's turmoil started June 5 so it took one month and one day for Sue and Elaine to evacuate.

❖ ❖ ❖

July 8, 1997
Nairobi, Kenya

Dear Maggie and Emma,

We continue to monitor our own civil unrest. Our part of the city has remained calm despite disturbances associated with some fifty illegal political rallies across Kenya. Rioters sought refuge inside All Saints Cathedral, located between here and downtown, and during skirmishes with the police, the church pastors received injuries. Three of them are recovering in the hospital, one in critical condition. Disturbances in Nairobi and other towns have left numerous people injured and nine dead. This violence seems so senseless. We thank God that our Kenyan and expatriate friends are safe.

July 9, 1997
Nairobi, Kenya

Dear Maggie and Emma,

Today on CNN International, we watched reports about Nairobi's protests. Disturbances on Friday and Monday, related to the upcoming presidential election, were illegal political rallies instigated by the opposition parties. Today's riots, however, involve university students. Even though the trouble is located about a mile from here, life goes on in our neighborhood and offices. CNN said university officials cancelled classes to decrease the number of both students and confrontations.

In preparation for our departure from Kenya, today we moved out of our apartment and into the Langes' flat. Since they're out of town, they offered to let us use it for our last few days of cleaning and packing.

When your grandpa and I agreed to follow God to Africa, I thought of the man who, a couple thousand years ago, said he would follow Jesus wherever He went. Jesus cautioned him, however, saying, "Foxes have holes and birds of the air have nests, but the Son of Man has no place to lay his head" (Luke 9:58). We wondered if, like that man, we would have no place to lay our heads, but by now you know that instead of no place to lay our heads, in some ways we've had too many places.

But that's okay. God's children in the Old Testament, those great heroes of the faith, those aliens and strangers on earth, moved a lot, too. They longed for a better country, a heavenly one, prepared for them by

God, both builder and architect (see Hebrews 11:10–16). I should have recognized from the beginning that whether your grandpa and I had too few or too many "places to lay our heads," we are only pilgrims heading toward our final "place to lay our heads" and it will be grand!

    I gave Elizabeth my treadle sewing machine so she'll have an additional way to earn money. We also gave her our wringer washer. It's electric so she can't use it at home, but she can sell it and use the money. And I'm so thankful—so relieved!—she also has income from the rentals we helped her finance.

    Elizabeth and her sister Agnes live next door to each other in the slums, an inseparable team in caring for their families and making the best of their trying situations. They know the truth of the East African proverb, "One person is thin porridge; two or three people are a handful of stiff cooked cornmeal," and oh, how Kenyans love stiff cooked cornmeal! That proverb reminds me of Ecclesiastes 4:9–12, "Two are better than one.... If one falls down, his friend can help him up.... Though one may be overpowered, two can defend themselves." A friend of mine employs Agnes and recently helped her purchase a small plot of ground up north so that, if all else fails and she needs to leave Nairobi, she can farm the land. I'm sure Agnes would let Elizabeth and her girls move to the *shamba* if they needed to, and that gives me added peace about leaving her.

July 11, 1997
Nairobi, Kenya

Dear Maggie and Emma,
    Harry James, reunited with Ingrid and their children, sent this dispatch. My heart soared when I read it!

> We have arrived in my mother's house near Bristol [England]. We got here yesterday.... We found the place leafy and warm. Loretta went straight down to the garden and started picking the redcurrants and gooseberries. It is a very good time of year to be here....

    I have read Harry's words at least ten times. Each time, I imagine his relief and picture that sweet young family together in that safe, pretty spot.

Information from Brazzaville and Kinshasa continues to arrive. Some details nearly take away my breath. I thought fighting had stayed in Brazzaville, but now I've learned that Sue and Elaine's region had its own turmoil. When the Zairian pastors arrived for them, Sue was so sick with malaria that they gave her a day to rest before their return trip. By the next day, however, her health had deteriorated so, instead of walking, they hired a truck to drive them the thirty miles to the river. There they climbed into the pastors' canoe and motored down the river for several days until they reached safety in Kinshasa. Though danger surrounded the four of them, they experienced no harm. I am moved to tears at the way those Zairian pastors risked their lives and worked so hard to rescue our two ladies. Imagine the courage and stamina that eleven-day journey required. May God bless them!

Two pastors plus two missionaries equals stiff cooked cornmeal!

July 13, 1997
Nairobi, Kenya

Dear Maggie and Emma,

More protests took place here yesterday and today, but they're almost a mile away and we can't hear them. We still go out, but we choose carefully where we go.

Despite my whining a few days ago about how tired I am, I want to make it clear that this year has been one of the best of my life. Each of our houseguests was a delight and, except for an occasional situation, I don't think I recognized the stress upon me. Maybe I rushed through the year on a God-given adrenalin-high. Throughout this busy and difficult year, when I came to the end of my own energy, God's grace and strength kept me going. Like Pastor Mike said at our staff retreat, "In the midst of my poverty, I can discover God's abundance."

July 15, 1997
Nairobi, Kenya

Dear Maggie and Emma,

When I step back and review Africa's history, I realize that the current crises in Zaire, Central African Republic, and Congo, and the small-scale turmoil here in Kenya, are nothing new. Warfare has erupted across Africa throughout my lifetime. Africa is not alone in this—unrest flares up around the world. Even though wars are nothing new, and even though Jesus told us, "In this world you will have trouble" (John 16:33), these crises take us by surprise. They can turn our homes, our ministries, and our very worlds upside down. Wars' enormous ramifications can knock the air out of us.

At times like this, many people question if they can ever resume their work with and for the African people they've come to love. I think now is a good time to follow the example of our African friends who, like Abraham, against all hope, in hope believe (Romans 4:18). Yes, like those past and present role models (Pastor Mike would call them "choice saints"), we must face the facts, the grim realities. Now we see only bedlam, bloodshed, and broken dreams, and yet like Abraham and our African friends, we must not waver through unbelief in God's power to accomplish His best for them and for our colleagues' ministries among them. We cannot know God's specific answers yet, or His timeline, but against all hope, we must in hope believe.

Right now, we reel in shock because of the immediacy and scope of these crises, but even so, we must also remember that this world is not whirling out of control without purpose or meaning. Instead, there is a divinely appointed time for everything.

> There is a time for everything, and a season for every activity under heaven: a time to be born and a time to die, a time to plant and a time to uproot, a time to kill and a time to heal, a time to tear down and a time to build, a time to weep and a time to laugh, a time to mourn and a time to dance, a time to scatter stones and a time to gather them, a time to embrace and a time to refrain, a time to search and a time to give up, a time to keep and a time to throw away, a time to tear and a time to mend, a time to be silent and a time to speak, a time to love and a time to hate, a time for war and a time for peace (Ecclesiastes 3:1–8).

For millions of people this is a time of war, but a time of peace will come. This is a time of death and tearing down, but a time to heal and build will come. This is a time to weep and mourn, but a time to laugh and dance will come.

Love,
Grandma

31

Utterly Amazed

*Come and see what God has done, how awesome
his works in man's behalf!*
Psalm 66:5

July 17, 1997—Emma's first birthday!
Nairobi, Kenya

Dear Maggie and Emma,

I've been thinking about Habakkuk. A couple of weeks ago, in the midst of the chaos and injustices within these four African countries, I wondered if God could, or would, answer our prayers in ways we would not have believed possible. Would His answers leave us, like Habakkuk, utterly amazed? Now I have my answer. Yes!

When I look back on the past month and a half, I want to fall on my face before God because of the countless and specific ways He directed all these events and people.

Indeed, that African proverb is true: One person is thin porridge; two or three people are a handful of stiff cooked cornmeal. God brought together countless individuals—*really* stiff cooked cornmeal!—governments, mission agencies, soldiers from many countries, people in the private sector, and local Christians—in Congo, Zaire, Central African Republic, Cameroon, Gabon, Chad, Mali, Equatorial Guinea, Senegal, and

Kenya. God worked through the President of the United States of America, the U.S. Embassy, the U.N. Security Council, and U.N. Ambassador Bill Richardson. He used the Canadian Embassy, Italian logging officials on the Congo-Cameroon border, South African President Nelson Mandela, and diplomats from France and the European Union—God used all of them to spare the lives of every one of our colleagues and, I believe, members of other missions as well. I want to sing—no, I want to shout!—that great old hymn, "Great is Thy faithfulness, O God, my Father.... Great is Thy faithfulness! All I"—*all we*—"have needed Thy hand hath provided. Great is Thy faithfulness…!"[1]

I love you and look forward to seeing you soon,
Grandma Thomas

EPILOGUE
A Psalm of Africa

Dear Maggie and Emma,

On your Great-grandma Thomas's seventy-fifth birthday, July 19, 1997, your grandpa and I flew out of Nairobi. We deplaned at SeaTac Airport and I was home.

Yes, I was back home, but I was not the same person I was when I left for Africa four years earlier. Slowly, gently, Africa wooed me, embraced me, and changed me.

When I see throngs of tourists riding their excursion buses and checking into their opulent hotels, I'm sad to think of what they won't experience. I see them—in their pith helmets, many-pocketed vests, and leather safari boots, all of which they bought at an expensive shop where their bus stopped on the first day. I see them—with their sunglasses, binoculars, cameras, guidebooks, sunscreen, and sometimes even with their hair braided in African cornrows.

Tour guides show tourists a chic, exotic Africa and the glitz and luxury created by the tourist industry, but tourists cannot encounter the real Africa. They spend seventy-two hours in Maasai Mara, snap pictures of big game, and spend money at shops frequented by tourists, but they don't get to know the real Africa—its spirit, its people, the essence of its wildlife, its shimmering savannahs, bone-dry deserts, and steamy jungles. These cannot settle into a person who hurries into and out of Africa.

No, those tourists likely fly out of Jomo Kenyatta International Airport talking among themselves, "Africa is so rugged, so wild, so free!"

"Magical! Full of exotic wonders!"

"So foreign, so charming!"

"Stunning! And, so romantic!"

Africa is all that, but so much more. I want to call out to them, "Stay longer! Don't miss the most important parts!"

Now, back home, I close my eyes and see Africa. I see blue skies that go on forever. I see the harsh beauty of open land—wide, parched landscapes dotted with flat-topped acacias and arched umbrella thorn trees. I smell again the spicy-sweet aroma of sun-baked grasses. I see steamy tropical cities, sun-bleached sub-Saharan towns, sprawling untamed jungle, and immense open stretches of lean, simmering desert.

When I close my eyes, I see animals the way God created them—perfect, wild, and innocent. I picture grazing zebras and hear their strange high-pitched bark. I see lion prides, graceful giraffes, and ill-tempered Cape buffaloes. I hear the fish eagles' shrill cries at Lake Naivasha, the doves' gentle coo, the ibis's raucous calls. I hear the hippos' bellows and snorts, and a mother elephant's trumpet, protecting her baby.

I see God's sense of beauty in the African moon-glow and star-shine. I think of my stroll along powdery white beaches on the Indian Ocean and a hike up cracked red clay paths in the highlands. I feel the African sun cooking my skin. I recall the hot, heavy stillness of the air, and I hear the faint rustle of grass.

Etched in my mind's eye is lush vegetation in all its brilliant colors, always in a hurry to grow taller and thicker. I see a mosaic of vegetables and fruit on display: green peppers and red apples, cauliflower and eggplant, papayas and avocados, grapefruit and broccoli, tomatoes and oranges—a kaleidoscope of colors.

—All of it a celebration of God's handiwork.

But Africa is more than the land and its wildlife.

Only when I laughed with our African friends, sang with them, cried with them, and worshipped with them—only then did I begin to hear Africa's song. Only then did I dance to its rhythm. And only when God used me to answer their prayers when they needed food or medicine or a job—and only when God used them when I needed their smiles, their prayers, their grace—only then did I hear Africa's heartbeat, feel its textures, inhale its fragrance, and taste its salty tears—tears of joy and tears of sorrow. Only then did Africa become a part of me. And, I like to think I became a part of Africa.

I can still see my African friends' quick smiles, bright eyes, and velvet-brown skin. I hear their rich laughter and their pulsing, full African harmonies. I see beautiful African b'donk- b'donk hips.

I hear the echo of our Maasai guard's prayer for us when we visited his home, and I hear Mundara's words of blessing to send me on my way to help Karen. I remember Elizabeth's loyalty—working for us when we moved across town even though her long commute and extra-long workdays left her exhausted, and I hear her voice saying she'd pray for me when I faced surgery. I think of the Mwakodis who bought food for us that they couldn't afford and would never have bought for themselves—and tears sting my eyes. From those lovely people I received the love, mercy, and grace of God, who surely noticed that they did those things as unto one of the least of His brothers, and that they did it for Him.

If I had come to Africa as only a tourist, I couldn't have known how honorable and dignified Africans are. I think of their hard labor, their suffering, their tenacity in hopeless situations. There's something gallant about them.

And if I'd come as only a tourist, I couldn't have known the heroic faith of the desperate ones—the Mwakodis, Elizabeth, Japheth, Bernard, Wycliffe, and Hellen. They showed me what God wants in each of us: a trusting, seeking, humble heart. In them, I witnessed what it looks like and feels like to lay down one's life for another, to make costly personal sacrifices. I'm certain God looks down from heaven and says to each, "Well done, good and faithful servant." Truly, they possess greatness according to God's measure of greatness. I am humbled and changed because God let me know and work alongside such people.

With a grateful heart,
Grandma Thomas

POSTSCRIPT

Dear Maggie and Emma,

Back in the States on furlough, I drove down the right side of the road, satin-smooth, and sat on the left side of the car. I enjoyed Burger King Whoppers,° corn chips, supermarkets, and a wide array of television stations—and all the programs started on time. I dried our laundry in a clothes dryer. No longer did I worry about bird poop or mud splatters.

We had both electricity and water—all day and all night—and hot water all the time. One day on television, I watched a woman walk to her kitchen sink, turn on the tap, fill a drinking glass, and drink the water! I gasped. Then I remembered both she and I live in the States and we can drink water right from the tap.

When your grandpa and I drove through the country, I scanned open fields for zebras or gazelles or Cape buffalos, and spotted them sometimes—only to discover they were cows or horses.

One of my most embarrassing situations happened at a beauty salon when I got a haircut and perm. In Kenya, we paid separately for the individual services we wanted—a shampoo, a cut, perm, blow-dry, and style—but I couldn't remember if we followed the same procedure in the States.

Since I lived on a tight missionary budget, I asked the beautician, "Does the price include the shampoo?" She assured me it did.

Later, while she cut my hair, I asked, "Does the price include a blow-dry and style?"

She started to answer, then stopped, dropped her hands to her sides, and stared at me. She stuttered and sputtered and then asked, "Is this your first time in a beauty shop?" Her face revealed a mixture of bewilderment and panic. What she really wanted to ask is, "Did you just crawl out from under a rock? Are you some kind of freak?" I hurried to explain I'd just returned from Africa and that they charge separately there. Oh, well. Quaint I ain't.

By that time, I'd lived without a phone at home for several years and had grown accustomed to e-mailing friends and relatives. In the States, I continued to e-mail until one day our dear friends, Dave and Liz Randles, poked fun at me for e-mailing them. They couldn't understand why I didn't pick up the phone and call. Or, for that matter, they lived only three miles away—not on the other side of the world any more—and I could have driven over for a visit.

On August 7, 1998, your grandpa and I helped your Aunt Karen move to California for her new teaching position at Calvary Christian School in Pacific Palisades. Grandpa drove a U-Haul truck and I drove behind in our car. Along the way, I turned on the radio and learned that Al Qaeda had bombed the U.S. Embassy in Nairobi—the one with the American-type restroom that I enjoyed so much—and I grieved for innocent Kenyans hurt or killed in the attack. That incident was the first of more and worse Al Qaeda attacks against American interests.

One day Karen wrote in an e-mail, "I have a date this weekend. I'll let you know if anything comes of it." Well, something did come of it: your three cousins, Chase, Finn, and Kade, all because your Aunt Karen and Brian Kelly fell in love and got married.

Now I have one more granddaughter, your sister, Miss Claire Sophia Grace Thomas, and I tell people, "My son has three daughters and my daughter has three sons." Each is a special gift from God and every morning I pray for them.

By now you know that all I ever wanted was to live in a little white house with a picket fence and a rose garden, but I married a man who, well—let me explain him this way. Making its rounds on the Internet is something your grandfather could have written:

> Life should not be a journey to the grave with the intention of arriving safely in an attractive and well preserved body, but rather to skid in sideways, champagne in one hand, chocolate covered strawberries in the other, body thoroughly used up, totally worn out and screaming "WOO HOOOO!!! What a ride!" (author unknown)

I'm a homebody, but your grandpa invited me to join him on great adventures. Back in 1993, though, an African adventure meant pain to me. I remember the raw ache in my heart when I moved far away from my family, and I recall the times I cried and asked God to show me how I could be a good mother, grandmother, daughter, wife, and missionary—all at the same time. I recall Chuck Swindoll's words on the radio, "God does not waste our suffering," and I remember writing in my journal in capital letters, "I'm counting on God not to waste our suffering. I'm counting on that to be true for Karen, Matt, my mom, Dave's parents, and me." And He didn't waste our heartache. Oh, no, He didn't. He gave my loved ones and me joys that outweighed the pain.

I think back to the poster in our room in England on our way to Africa. There in that dark World War II barracks, I stood before that poster and dared God to show me He could change my tears to joy—and He did! Oh, yes, He did, over and over again. I've written those stories for you to read, but I want to tell you one more story.

Shortly before we left Nairobi, a language group in an African country held a celebration to dedicate the New Testament and part of the Old Testament in their own language. (Civil war, drought, floods, corruption, and famine have ripped this country apart and because Christians there endure unspeakable persecution, I won't tell you the country's name.) Some people walked four days to get to the celebration, knowing that when they arrived they'd find no food there because of the famine. Others traveled five days on a barge, despite the food crisis and malaria mosquitoes, all because they were so eager to have Scriptures in the language of their hearts.

Stories like that astound me. I am grateful that God let me play a minuscule role in the Scriptures they celebrated that day. We'll spend eternity singing praises to God with thousands of Africans who are there because God sent missionaries to help them translate His Word into their own languages. I would have missed this and countless other joys if I hadn't followed God and your grandpa to Africa.

A few years ago, your grandpa and I bought a little white house with a white fence and a rose garden. After all those years, we found it—small and old-fashioned, but we loved it. Margaret and Edwin Jeske lived here for over sixty years before they moved to a nursing home. Locals tell us the Jeskes filled that house with love. I could feel it.

And, if we drove about forty miles down a country road, we could visit Potholes State Park. Potholes! We can't get away from them! I'm an old woman now and to paraphrase a timeworn Will Rogers quote, some people try to turn back their odometers, but not me. I want people to know why I look this way. I've traveled a long way and many of the roads were full of potholes.

Recently we moved out of the little white house with a white fence and a rose garden, and now we live across the street from you, Maggie and Emma, and your parents and Claire! The wise teacher said in Ecclesiastes, "There is a time for everything, and a season for every activity under heaven…" (3:1). There was a time for me to move to Africa, a time to live in my little white house with a white fence and a rose garden, and now there is a time to live near family.

And so, Maggie and Emma—and Chase, Finn, Kade, and Claire—I'm sure you agree with me: the dreadful truth is that quaint I ain't. And, although I left for Africa with fierce reluctance, I'm so glad I went. The adventuresome spirits of both God and your grandpa have shown me a far richer life and faith than I could ever have imagined.

I have more tales to tell you about our return to Africa, more yarns to spin about our final years there, and one of these days—or years—I'll share them with you.

Love you, always and forever,
Grandma Thomas
August 2009

About the Author

Linda Thomas and her husband, Dave, worked with Wycliffe Bible Translators for three years in South America and eight years in Africa. She is a former Teaching Leader with Bible Study Fellowship International. Currently she teaches memoir classes based on Deuteronomy 4:9 (paraphrased), "Always remember, and never forget, what you've seen God do for you, and be sure to tell your children and grandchildren!"

Proud natives of Washington State, Linda and Dave recently moved out of their little white house with a white fence and a rose garden and now live in Missouri—across the street from their son Matt, daughter-in-law Jill, and granddaughters Maggie, Emma, and Claire. As often as possible, Linda and Dave visit their daughter Karen, son-in-law Brian, and grandsons Chase, Finn, and Kade in Malibu, California. As the wise teacher said in Ecclesiastes, "There is a time for everything, and a season for every activity under heaven…" (3:1). There was a time for Linda to move to Africa, and now there is a time to live near family.

To see photos from Linda's scrapbook, read behind-the-scenes stories, and dialogue with her, please visit Linda's blog at www.grandmaslettersfromafrica.blogspot.com.

NOTES

Chapter 2

1. Isaac Watts and Lowell Mason, "When I Survey the Wondrous Cross," in *Baptist Hymnal*, ed. Walter Hines Sims (Nashville: Convention Press, 1956), 99.

2. Mrs. Charles E. Cowman, *Streams in the Desert* (Grand Rapids, MI: Zondervan Publishing House, 1965).

Chapter 4

1. Amy Carmichael, *Edges of His Ways* (Fort Washington, PA: Christian Literature Crusade, 1975), 20.

Chapter 5

1. Isak Dinesen, *Out of Africa* and *Shadows on the Grass* (New York: Vintage Books, 1985), 311.

Chapter 13

1. Isak Dinesen, *Out of Africa* and *Shadows on the Grass* (New York: Vintage Books, 1985), 3.

2. Ibid., 4–5.

3. Ibid., 247.

Chapter 20

1. Barbara Thomas, *Through the Outhouse Floor* (New York: iUniverse, Inc., 2007), 232–235.

> We sensed that our time left in Zaire was short. The government was increasingly unstable....
>
> We were close to finishing the first draft of the Komo New Testament. The translation was going forward with three Komo teams from three denominations. An interdenominational committee met each Friday to review and check material. Literacy classes were being held up and down the Komo road....
>
> Paul and I had a special two-week trip scheduled to Mulita, 60 miles south of our home, to work with a translation team there as soon as we arrived back from our annual conference in Kenya. We were staging camping equipment we would need for our visit to Mulita and packing for our flight north. Paul went into town and visited with a business acquaintance. He expressed his thanks to us. If I were to have guessed what anyone would thank us for, I would have guessed: for facilitating the translation of a major portion of the New Testament, for holding literacy classes, for encouraging worship and singing in their own language, for having them write down their folktales. This man said, "Thank-you for coming to live with us. It used to be that our children would run from white people. Because you have lived with us, they are not afraid of white people anymore. Because our children have seen you, they know that there are other parts of the world. We know that where you go, you will tell others about us, so we have a place on the map." It was a potent reminder that "being" was more important than "doing"—a difficult lesson I constantly had to reinforce by living with the Komo people.
>
> In October we went to Rethy [Academy, in Zaire] for Parent's Weekend, then on to Kenya for our annual conference. While there, violence erupted in Bukavu.... The Komo church radioed us a message to be relayed to us in Kenya. We were a couple of days from our return

flight to Zaire and received the message, "Don't come to Lubutu or Mulita...." [A group of men] burned the old church office that held the stock of Komo [Scripture book of] Matthew as well as other Komo literature for sale. We could understand why our presence in Lubutu could be dangerous for us and make matters worse for the church leaders. But [our sons] Robert and Joel were still in Zaire at Rethy Academy.

We returned to Zaire immediately after conference, as scheduled, going to Rethy Academy instead of Lubutu, to stay with the boys until we knew how the situation was developing. The church again radioed us, frantic to know if we had received their first message to not return to Lubutu. We assured them that we had, that we were with the boys until we saw how everything developed....

The church informed us that they had broken the locks on our house in order to hide goods from [looters]. Now remembering my lesson from the first evacuation, I prayed with open palms that everything in our house would be distributed to where it would serve the most good.

MAF [Missionary Aviation Fellowship] began evacuating missionaries from both Nyankunde and Bunia. There were now 100 extra people at Rethy Academy. A businessman from the nearby town was kidnapped. Word got to us that [militants] were now asking directions to Rethy with plans to loot the hospital and school.

It was standard for every mission station to have contingency plans.... The MAF planes had all been moved to Rethy and to the Diguna mission station nearby. But the only legal way out of the country was through Bunia airport, now occupied.... We were sitting ducks. I thought, *This time we might not get out alive.*

I was not O.K. with this.... We had gone through so much, and this was how it was going to end? Being hacked into pieces by a machete? Our task, as we saw it, wasn't finished. We had two more books [of the New Testament] to translate. And we had begun to love the Komo people with all their foibles, even as they had made allowances for us through all our years with them.

Had that, after all, been God's primary task for us?

The missionary community at Rethy met regularly for prayer, news updates, and planning. A proposed order had been drawn up of whom to fly out first as flights became available. Single women were evacuated first, then a man with a heart condition. Our family was listed as borderline non-essential personnel as far as the running of Rethy Academy and Rethy Hospital, but now the airport was unsafe for further flights.

After several days, an agreement was reached in Bunia to fly a large plane of soldiers to their homes in Kinshasa. This opened the airport.

Paul radioed the church in Lubutu and told them, "Our hearts are full for you. Have strength."

Katinga and Pastor Unabwako radioed back, "Go well."

"Stay well."

"Koko!"

"Oye!"

Chapter 21

1. Mrs. Charles E. Cowman, *Streams in the Desert* (Grand Rapids, MI: Zondervan Publishing House, 1965), 1.
2. Theodore Roosevelt, "Wild Man and Wild Beast in Africa," *National Geographic*, January, 1911, 13.
3. Ibid., 19.

Chapter 22

1. Thomas Ken and Louis Bourgeois, "Old Hundredth," in *Hymns of the Centuries*, ed. Benjamin Shepherd (New York: The A. S. Barnes Company, 1914), 48.

Chapter 28

1. The following names are fictitious but their stories are true: Alec, Marie, Liza, Betty, Sue, Elaine, Étienne, and members of the following families: Wilson, James, Smith, and Miller.

Chapter 29

1. Mrs. Charles E. Cowman, *Streams in the Desert* (Grand Rapids, MI: Zondervan Publishing House, 1965), 197.

Chapter 31

1. Thomas O. Chisholm and William M. Runyan, "Great is Thy Faithfulness," in *Baptist Hymnal,* ed. Walter Hines Sims (Nashville: Convention Press, 1956), 47.

RESOURCES

Wycliffe Bible Translators, www.wycliffe.org

> Wycliffe is committed to seeing God's Word become available to all people in the language they understand best, the language of their hearts. All kinds of people with all kinds of gifts do their part to help with this task. Some Wycliffe workers carry out language-related roles and others fill important support roles.

The Finishers Project, www.finishers.org

> The Finishers Project helps match mid-life adults with mission assignments in the U.S. and abroad—either short-term or long-term as a second career—by filling out a personal profile which searches for matches in more than 16,000 opportunities.

Teachers In Service (TIS), www.teachers-in-service.org

> In pursuit of its vision, the mission of Teachers In Service is to address professional needs of teachers and schools of missionary children, to contribute to recruitment and preparation of new teachers of missionary children, and to participate in activities related to teachers and schools of missionary children—that is, to do those things that address the vision.

LaVergne, TN USA
19 May 2010
183147LV00004B/257/P